MOTORMOUTH

The Complete Canadian Car-Buying Guide 2010 Edition

Zack Spencer
Host of Driving Television

John Wiley & Sons Canada, Ltd.

Library and Archives Canada Cataloguing in Publication

Spencer, Zack
    Motormouth: the complete Canadian car-buying guide /Zack Spencer. — 2010 ed.

ISBN 978-0-470-16026-8

    1. Automobiles—Purchasing—Canada. I. Title.

TL162.S64 2009   629.222029   C2009-904491-9

Production Credits
Cover design: Ian Koo
Interior design and typesetting: Pat Loi
Printer: Tri-Graphic Printing Ltd.

John Wiley & Sons Canada, Ltd.
6045 Freemont Blvd.
Mississauga, Ontario
L5R 4J3

Printed in Canada

1 2 3 4 5 TRI 13 12 11 10 09

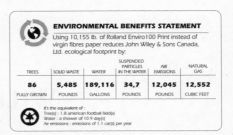

Dedicated to Andrea, Jack and Charlie

Table of Contents

Part**One**
The Basics

1 Choices abound—How to find the best vehicle for you

I am a car buff, and always have been from a very early age. As I write this book, out of the corner of my eye I can see a model car my father gave me in 1974 sitting on my desk. In fact, I still have all of the toy cars he gave me over the years, dating back to the 1960s. My early passion for cars has never faded; it grew into a career as an auto reviewer on television, on radio and in newspapers. For a car guy, this is not a job, it's a wonderful pastime.

Over the years, I've had the opportunity to drive almost every modern car on the road and I've also had the pleasure to own some very special vehicles. In fact, my very first car was called a Special. Do you remember the movie *Rainman* with Dustin Hoffman? Well, the car featured in that movie was a 1949 Buick Roadmaster convertible and my very first car was a 1949 Buick Special, the sedan version of that car. Once again my father was involved. I was 17 and we purchased the car together as part of a restoration project. The grand plan was to bring the big green beast back to its glory. Well, we had the Special for more than 20 years and I can fondly remember driving it to high school and picking up my friends along the way, it was so big. We never did restore the car, but it is still running today and in the hands of an owner who loves it as much as we did.

Along the way I have had so many cars. I have bought, sold, leased cars of all shapes and sizes, and often the hunt for my next prized possession began as soon as I signed the paperwork for my current vehicle. It is a bit of a sickness, being so car crazy, but it has also given me plenty of knowledge that I hope to pass on to you.

Choosing the right vehicle for your needs can be a tough and sometimes very frustrating decision. For example, cars offer better handling and performance than a sport utility vehicle (SUV) but they don't provide the same high seating position that so many drivers like. An SUV has plenty of space inside for a family, towing capacity and large powerful engines but they can be hard on fuel. A crossover tries to give the best of both worlds. But does it do either very well?

Buying a vehicle is always a compromise. There is no perfect vehicle out there for every person and situation; all you can do is decide which one is the best possible fit—including your budget—for you at the time you go car shopping. For every one attribute you add, you can take another away. For example, to get power and performance, you may sacrifice fuel economy and cost savings. To get the best gas mileage, you will have to go with a 4-cylinder engine and sacrifice the power of a V6 or V8. To acquire space and functionality, you will need a taller and longer vehicle, in which case you may lose a degree of handling. To get an inexpensive car, you have to give up the kinds of appointments that luxury vehicles offer—leather, heated seats and so on. It is very much like a yin and yang situation—you need to find the right balance.

There is a lot to think about before going shopping and spending tens of thousands of dollars, so let's look at the different types of vehicles available in the market today. Hopefully, it will help narrow the kind of car you're looking for.

THE MODERN CAR

What a lot of people don't realize is that the grandfather of many of today's most popular vehicles is the tried and true, but sometimes boring, four-door family sedan. Auto makers don't invent a brand-new vehicle every time they put out a new model; in fact, they re-purpose many of the same components and platforms used from one vehicle to another. A perfect example of this is the very popular Honda CR-V. It is a compact SUV but it is based on the Honda Civic car platform and powered by the Honda Accord car engine. Carmakers cut and paste just like you do on your computer, but they do it with components, engines and vehicle chassis. The reason I bring this up is to point out that a typical car might not look very appealing to some people, but in fact it can be transformed into a capable and more rugged SUV.

Sedans and coupes have the advantage of being the best-handling vehicles on the road. The taller design of SUVs and crossovers allows more headroom and overall space, but the higher centre of gravity leads to body roll and incidents of rollover. Much has been done to mitigate the chances of such accidents, ever since Ford was criticized for problems with its Explorer SUV in the 1990s. But if you're a driver who puts an emphasis on handling characteristics, then a car may be your best choice.

Vehicles come in all sizes—from subcompact models to high-end luxury cars and trucks—so let's start with smaller cars and work up to crossovers, vans and SUVs so you can decide which might suit you best. Don't worry too much if your short list includes cars, crossovers and SUVs; if you follow the process through this book, you will narrow your choices to the right vehicle for you.

SUBCOMPACTS AND COMPACTS

Three of the best-selling cars in Canada are compact models: the Honda Civic, Toyota Corolla and Mazda3. In fact, the majority of vehicles sold in Canada fall into the compact class. Out of the top 10 cars sold in Canada for 2008, all but one, the Toyota Camry, was a compact. Unlike Americans, we prefer efficient, compact, inexpensive cars that do a majority of things well. For consumers in the United States, until their recent financial hardship, compact cars were looked on as vehicles for students, or a second or third car, but here in Canada it is common for a compact to be the only car in a family.

To capitalize on this massive segment of the market, the major auto manufacturers have increasingly introduced features only found in much more expensive cars just a few years ago. Today, you can buy a compact car with heated seats, tilt and telescopic steering, height adjustable driver's seat, iPod jacks, high-powered stereos, leather seats, navigation systems, Bluetooth connectivity, voice commands, panoramic sunroofs and a whole host of safety features such as traction and stability control, a full complement of air bags, ABS and even all-wheel-drive.

Compact cars typically start around the $15,000 range, and fully loaded top out around $27,000. Having sat through endless PowerPoint presentations from manufacturers on this topic, I can tell you that most Canadians typically opt for the middle-of-the-road versions, with some of the available goodies, but not all, with the total cost (not including freight ands taxes) totalling about $20,000. Some compact models are offered with more than one size of 4-cylinder engine, giving buyers the option of the most fuel-efficient version or a more powerful engine. There are only two hybrids offered in this segment—the Honda Civic Hybrid and Honda Insight hybrid (the Toyota Prius is considered a mid-size car due to the larger interior space). The only diesel offered in this class is the VW Jetta.

Just as inexpensive compact cars are growing in popularity, so too are premium compact models. The Audi A3 and A4, along with BMW's 1 Series and 3 Series, the Mercedes C Class, Lexus IS and Volvo S40, fall into this expanding class but are targeted at a totally different market than the Corolla and Civic. Premium buyers are attracted to brand appeal, handling and power. These compact models get buyers into the luxury market without having to fork over the big money that some of these brands command.

Premium compact cars usually come in rear-wheel and all-wheel-drive configurations for better handling, whereas entry-level compacts are mostly front-wheel drive, while only a few all-wheel drive cars are offered, such as the Suzuki SX4 and Dodge Caliber. Premium compacts usually start in the low to mid-$30,000 range, but you can expect to pay plenty more than the starting price to get a nicely equipped version. In the premium compact market, 4-cylinder motors do exist, some with turbo, but most are sold with 6-cylinder engines. Expensive premium gasoline is the fuel of choice for these cars. There are no hybrids offered, but Audi and BMW do make diesel versions.

As the price of fuel shot up over the past few years, not only did sales of compact cars shoot through the roof, but sales of the emerging subcompact class spiked as well. Best-sellers in this class include the Toyota Yaris, Honda Fit, Nissan Versa, Hyundai Accents and Pontiac Wave. Most of these cars have small yet lively 4-cylinder engines in the 1.5- to 1.8-litre range that offer exellent fuel economy. Some models, such as the Hyundai Accent, have been on sale recently for less than $10,000. These are a wonderful option for consumers looking to get into a brand-new car for the same price as a used car, for buyers who want similar efficiency as a hybrid without having to spend the extra money, and most importantly, for those who have limited funds to spend. Just as the compact class has seen the expansion of convenience and entertainment features, the subcompact category is enjoying many of the same improvements.

Prices for subcompacts start around the $10,000 mark, but most are sold in the $13,000 to $18,000 range, depending on the desired trim.

Subcompact cars have the closest resemblance to the small cars that are common in Europe and Asia, and just like those vehicles, they have a fun-to-drive attitude and a surprising amount of interior space. Even though they're small, they don't feel tiny.

When Toyota first introduced the Yaris as a replacement for the Echo, I had a base two-door hatchback version as a test vehicle for a week, the same week my brother visited and wanted to go skiing. We packed our gear and headed for the mountains. Even though the Yaris is one of the smallest cars on the road, it offered a comfortable ride with plenty of room, and it handled surprisingly well through the twisty turns and even had enough power to keep up to bigger, more powerful cars on the highway. After that trip, I had a new appreciation for just how versatile these small cars are.

Canadians love their small cars, and it shows how sensible we are about our vehicle choices.

If I were in the market for a small run-around car that sips fuel like a hybrid, I wouldn't hesitate to buy a subcompact or compact. There are no diesel subcompacts on the road, but these models typically deliver some of the best mileage in the market.

MID-SIZE CARS

Some drivers require more room and refinement than compacts or subcompacts, and that is why the mid-size range is so competitive.

In a comparison show for *Driving Television*, we tested the best-selling mid-size sedans in the country to determine our favourite. I came to realize just how close all the products have become in terms of standard appointments, engine options, fuel economy and fit and finish. The mid-size sedan market might just be the most competitive, with all manufacturers delivering very good product. One car that gave us a pleasant surprise was the Chevy Malibu; in fact, it came in second place in our test, just behind the Honda Accord and well ahead of the best-selling car in this class, the Toyota Camry. The Malibu is an example of what the auto makers from Detroit are doing well. These domestic manufacturers get a rough ride in the minds of many Canadians; GM, Ford and Chrysler are paying for their sins of the past with falling market share and a perception of poor quality, but in reality they are making some very good cars.

If you are in the market for a mid-size car, there comes a point when it all comes down to personal taste because so much has been copied, including the design and interior finish. The offerings in this class all tend to be very similar in size, features and price. Of all the vehicles in the market, this is the most homogenous of the bunch. That said, there seems to be a trend to either soft, smooth and luxurious or engaged, spirited and performance in this group. Cars such as the Toyota Camry, Hyundai Sonata, Chevy Malibu and Ford Fusion tend to appeal to passive drivers, whereas the Honda Accord, Nissan Altima, Subaru Legacy and Mazda6 are favoured by more spirited drivers. Even though the entire group is very similar on paper, they do have unique driving styles, and once again it comes down to personal choice.

With advancements in engine technology, engineers have been able to get more and more power and torque out of smaller engines. I always mention to consumers that they should try the 4-cylinder versions of these cars, and if they are happy with the performance, then there is no need to pay more for a V6 engine. A 4-cylinder mid-size car has more power than a V6 did just a decade ago. Today's cars offer great efficiency and reasonable power, a compromise many can live with. Also in this class, there are a number of hybrids, including the Toyota Camry, Nissan Altima and Toyota Prius and Ford Fusion. Diesel is offered only on premium mid-size cars like Mercedes.

At the higher end of the mid-size class are the import sedans—featuring powerful engines, inspired handling and equally inspired prices. Buyers of cars such as the BMW 5 series, Mercedes E Class, Audi A6, Lexus ES, Infiniti M and Volvo S80 are looking for a capable, big, safe and prestigious car, with the respect their price tag brings. This high-end segment was once dominated by European auto makers, but the Japanese luxury brands have come on with force since they were introduced in the late 1990s, stealing market share from the European makers by injecting a higher level of quality into their product. For example, Lexus has been on top of the JD Power and Associates dependability study for more than 14 years. This is a remarkable achievement and it is no wonder this brand has captured such a solid chunk of the luxury sedan market.

As baby boomers mature, so does the market for performance. Coupes and convertibles such as the Mustang, Challengers and Camaros of the 60s and 70s used to be the hot, sought-after models, but today sedans are offered with the kind of power and handling pure sports cars had just a decade ago. Even sedans that would not be regarded as prestige models, the Honda Accord or Nissan Altima, for example, have engines producing 270 horsepower or more, and premium sedans such as the Mercedes E63 can deliver more than

500 horsepower. Baby boomers have changed the way car makers look at mid-size sedans; they offer basic transportation but also a very spirited driving experience, and in some cases you don't have to break the bank.

Mid-size sedans are wonderful choices for people who want handling and are not looking for a bigger or taller utility vehicle, but want something more substantial than a compact car. The mid-size sedans are bought by all kinds of consumers: people in sales positions, families needing a second vehicle to augment their SUV, and buyers looking for luxury or performance.

Premium sedans typically come with 6-cylinder and V8 engines, some even have V10 engines, and all require expensive premium gasoline. There is only one premium mid-size hybrid on the market, the Lexus GS. There is a growing demand for powerful, yet clean diesel technology that is offered in mostly German manufacturers; as of this writing you can buy only the Mercedes E Class diesel.

FULL-SIZE MODELS

When I first got my driver's licence, I learned to drive on my dad's 1972 Buick LeSabre. I loved that car, the big powerful engine, roomy interior and AM radio. Okay, I kid about the radio, but one thing has remained—my love for big cars. Sure, I like small, fun-to-drive vehicles and sports cars, but every now and again I get back in a full-size sedan and it feels like home again. People who like big sedans, like me, will (I think) always be attracted to them.

The full-size market is not a large one, and it is crowded with mostly luxury brands filling the needs of big car buyers. There are a few basic full-size models such as the Chrysler 300, Ford Crown Victoria, Ford Taurus and the Chevy Impala, but on the whole, luxury rules.

When you hear names such as Cadillac, Lincoln, Lexus, BMW and Mercedes, I'm sure large luxury sedans come to mind.

The domestic luxury brands have tried to keep pace with the imports when it comes to handling and performance, but if you like the pure luxury feel of space, quiet, comfortable seats and plenty of electronic toys, Cadillac and Lincoln do it better than most. Lexus has also built a reputation for very comfortable, luxurious cars and this brand has the advantage of a strong following for quality, as do most Japanese manufacturers, which helps sell their cars. Earlier, I mentioned that Lexus has been number one on the JD Power and

Associates reliability report for years, but Cadillac and Lincoln are routinely near the top of the list.

European manufacturers, in contrast to North American car makers emphasize power and handling along with all the luxury one could imagine. In the eyes of many, nothing says you have arrived like arriving in an expensive German car.

If you're in the market for a new or used premium sedan, keep in mind they are some of the most technologically advanced vehicles on the road; in fact, many of the latest advancements in automotive comfort, entertainment, safety and luxury are first built into premium sedans and eventually trickle down to less expensive cars. But buyer beware: while a large sedan loaded with a long list of toys can be rewarding when new, they can be a repair waiting to happen once out of warranty. If you're shopping for a used full-size sedan loaded with options, be prepared to spend money keeping the cutting-edge technology working. And before you buy one, it is imperative that you have the vehicle fully inspected to establish if any work needs to be done.

In the full-size class of cars, there is only one hybrid—the Lexus LS. No diesel models are available yet.

WAGONS, CROSSOVERS AND SUVS

The Tall Wagon Segment

I mentioned that several of the most popular vehicles are based on the platform of the modest family sedan. They include tall wagons, crossovers and SUVs. These vehicles try to match the handling of a car to the utility families are demanding; since there are so many different types of utility vehicles, let's start with the small and work our way up.

The average age of a Corolla buyer has been in the mid- to high 50s for many years, so Toyota decided that, to attract younger buyers, it needed to come up with a vehicle based on the Corolla, but a little hipper. The Matrix is that car, a tall hatchback version of the Corolla with the same solid reputation but with more space for cargo, a more rugged appearance and not nearly as conservative. Compact, tall wagons and hatchbacks such as the Matrix have grown in popularity, just as compact cars have, and in many instances are more popular. The Subaru Impreza 5-door hatch is more popular than the sedan version, and the Mazda3 sport hatchback is more popular than the sedan in some parts of the country. Oddly, Ford dropped the wagon and hatchback version of its fun-to-drive Focus. As I mentioned, many Canadians would buy a compact vehicle to fill the needs of a whole family, so these more practical versions of the most popular models makes sense.

Europeans have not adapted to SUVs to the same extent as North Americans because they pay so much more for fuel, drive shorter distances on smaller roads, and have space restrictions on city streets. The most popular cars in Europe are station wagons. Europeans call them "estate" or "touring" cars; either way, Europeans know what very few people in North America do—station wagons offer just as much space and utility as an SUV yet retain the same handling and performance characteristics of a sedan. I've stated that when you buy a vehicle you have to sacrifice certain features in order to gain others. In the case of a wagon, you get the handling of a car along with the utility of a bigger vehicle; what you have to give up is the cool image.

To get over this dilemma, companies such as Volvo, Subaru and Audi have decided to dress up their wagons. The more rugged-looking Subaru Outback is, in essence, a Legacy station wagon with body mouldings and aggressive tires to give the impression of an SUV. The same goes for the Audi A6 wagon called the Allroad, or the Volvo V70 wagon called the XC70. Styling counts for a lot, so I can understand consumers wanting a more rugged-looking wagon. However, you might be able to save a few dollars if you opt for the regular wagon, which in many instances provides better handling and road manners than the dolled-up version. There are no hybrids or diesel cars available as mid-size wagons yet, but VW offers the Jetta in a diesel wagon and could soon offer a diesel power plant in the Passat wagon.

The Crossover Segment—The Refinement of the SUV

When the SUV craze took off in the early 1990s with the huge success of the Ford Explorer, Jeep Cherokee, Toyota 4Runner and Nissan Pathfinder, auto makers realized the public was attracted to the rugged attitude of these vehicles. When producing their hot sellers, most car companies built them on pickup truck platforms. Not only did these units look rugged but they also they had off-road capability and basically drove like a fancy pickup truck. As time went on, auto makers realized that buyers really didn't want rugged-driving vehicles, but rather rugged-looking vehicles that gave a softer ride and better handling. As the SUV craze continued into the new millennium, the handling of many SUVs improved, the ride became more car-like and, instead of utilitarian interiors, these vehicles became as luxurious as many sedans. Even the way SUVs were produced changed; no longer did manufacturers take a truck and turn it into a family SUV, but went the other way around—they took a car and turned it into a rugged-looking crossover.

Crossovers are not limited to small vehicles. There are plenty of mid to large crossovers, and many of them offer an excellent option for buyers who need a lot of room for their family but don't want to drive a van or truck-based SUV.

The term "crossover" has been one of the most overused in the auto industry. As I mentioned, car companies cut and paste components, engines and, most importantly, vehicle platforms. When a new product straddles two categories, manufacturers will sometimes market that product as a crossover. A perfect example is the new Toyota Venza, introduced in 2009. It is based on a car platform and is taller than a conventional wagon, but is not as big as an SUV, so it crosses over many categories. The Mazda5 is another crossover vehicle; based on the Mazda3 sedan, it is taller than a wagon but smaller than a van. It's getting very confusing for consumers to determine what a crossover is, so they should do some research online and ask a salesperson about platforms and components.

The "cute utility" phenomenon started when Toyota and Honda first introduced the RAV4 and CR-V in the 1990s. These are small crossovers offering high utility and are based on compact car platforms. Just like compact cars, they have shot up in popularity. The Ford Escape is the best-selling small crossover in Canada along with the RAV4 and CR-V. Just like compact cars, the efficient, less expensive utility vehicles are popular with people who need more space than a car or hatchback, but don't want to break the bank. This segment of the market is one of the fastest growing because it offers an alternative to a company car or wagon, with a bit more curb appeal, all-weather capability and a price tag that doesn't exceed the family budget.

If you are considering purchasing a compact utility vehicle over a car, there are a few things to be aware of. Unlike a compact car, a compact utility vehicle is bigger, heavier and often offered in all-wheel drive and in many instances comes with slightly bigger engines. All that extra mass needs energy to push it through the air and move down the road. If fuel consumption is a concern for you, then be aware that more fuel will be consumed than with a sensible car or hatchback. But many people are willing to pay a little more to buy and run these vehicles because they fulfill many basic needs in one vehicle.

At the other end of the spectrum, the premium compact utility vehicle is one of the fastest-growing markets. As fuel prices and sticker shock keep people from getting a mid-size SUV, there are now smaller options with all the luxury and badge appeal that comes with larger vehicles. It seems that all the premium brands now have compact SUVs including the BMW X3, Audi Q5, Volvo XC60, Acura RDX, Infiniti EX and Mercedes GLK. What this group of vehicles brings to the table is a superior level of finish, above-average handling and a taste of luxury. These, too, are for the most part based on premium compact cars with similar handling and performance but in a slightly bigger package. The only compact SUV sold as a hybrid is the Ford Escape and no diesels are offered.

Compact cars and compact SUVs, whether economical or premium, are where the majority of the market is headed. Smaller means more affordable to buy, cheaper to run and less of an impact on the environment.

The truck-based Ford Explorer, Toyota 4Runners and GMC Jimmy have had their day in the sun; the new hot vehicles in the mid-size SUV segment are crossovers, based on car platforms such as the Toyota Highlander, based on the Camry; the Nissan Murano, mirroring the Altima; and the Ford Edge, built on the Ford Fusion. These are just a few examples of the direction the market is headed in. This is not to say that rugged off-road-capable SUVs don't have a place, it's just that the market has shifted. With car-like handling and quiet, luxurious interiors, these types of vehicles offer buyers the best of a sedan or wagon in a much more appealing design, attractive to a large number of people.

Many mid-size crossovers are redesigned with more emphasis on luxury and re-branded under luxury names such as Lexus, Infiniti and Lincoln. If you want to buy the cheaper version of essentially the same vehicle, then find out what platform a particular luxury crossover is built on and then buy the mainstream model. One example is the Lincoln MKX, which is the luxury version of the Ford Edge.

The Ford has the same platform, engine, transmission and interior layout but lacks some of the luxury touches of the Lincoln. For thousands less a buyer can essentially get the same vehicle.

The premium market for mid-size SUVs had dropped in the past few years due to their higher gas consumption rates, and in most cases, use of premium fuel. To overcome this issue, BMW, Mercedes and Audi have introduced diesel versions of their SUVs, and Lexus has a hybrid RX. Since BMW and Mercedes started offering their ML and GL SUVs as diesels, their sales have shot up, so the market for bigger, premium SUVs might still have legs.

"Minivan killer" is what I called the GMC Acadia when I reviewed it, and I used the same line when reviewing the Ford Flex. Some buyers of minivans want to escape the "soccer mom" image of a van by moving to large crossovers that add a little "cool" on the way to school. These large crossovers have the utility of a van with SUV appeal. Full-size crossovers don't have sliding side doors like a van, but conventional rear doors. They have three rows of seats and big lift gates at the back, plenty of room on the inside and they're very easy to drive and manoeuvre. In the past, if a family wanted a big SUV with three rows of seats, they would have to buy a V8-powered Chevy Suburban or Ford Excursion or something similar, based on pickup platforms. Now these large car-like V6 crossovers make the jump from a van, and are not so daunting and less expensive to operate. V6 engines power the majority of full-size crossovers, and there are no hybrids or diesels offered.

As gas prices have continued to trend higher—along with growing awareness of environmental issues—sales of big SUVs and full-size pickups have continued to fall. These vehicles have a place for people who have large families and need the extra power and towing capacity of a pickup-based SUV. Full-size pickup trucks such as the Ford F150, Chevy Silverado and Dodge Ram will always have a place for those who need them for work and recreation, but there has been a movement toward mid-size pickup trucks and even a resurgence in compact pickups. These large vehicles get a bad rap from people who think their owners are overindulgent, but they are purchased by those who need them for work or need the towing capacity that a big vehicle offers.

The Minivan Is Not Deceased

One of the biggest perks of being an automotive reviewer is getting to test drive new vehicles introduced to the marketplace. Over the years, I have put full-size pickup trucks to the test while landscaping my back yard, taking garbage to the dump and towing. One of my favourite vehicles to test while on vacation is a minivan. There is no better vehicle for a road trip with the family than a minivan with a rear DVD entertainment system to keep kids quiet on a long trip. During the 1990s, minivan sales exploded along with SUV sales as families went shopping for vehicles that would help them move around in space and comfort. In the last 10 years, minivans sales have waned but the ubiquitous minivan remains one of the best options for a family.

Around 1998, some good friends of mine wanted to trade in their VW Jetta for a bigger family vehicle. They had one child and a second on the way. Among the features they were looking for in a new vehicle were more space to stow a stroller, larger back seats for the kids, a high seating position for better road visibility and more versatility. "You just described a minivan," I told them, but that's not what they wanted to hear. The couple both scrunched up their faces in disgust; what they wanted was for me to agree with their choice to buy a Jeep Cherokee, and went out and bought one, regardless of my opinion.

A minivan does everything well for a family; it offers more room than almost all SUVs, it is less expensive to buy and can cost less to run. Even though there are only 6-cylinder minivans on the market, they tend to be just as or more efficient than many truck-based SUVs.

Minivans have an image problem. They tend to be vehicles people *have* to buy instead of *want* to buy. I'm sure you've heard that certain vehicles get the nickname "chick car." Well, drivers of minivans have been given the handle "soccer mom." Consequently, many people won't even try a van because of the image they portray, and that's too bad.

After about six months of owning their Jeep Cherokee, I asked my friends how they were enjoying it, and their answer didn't surprise me. They had hoped that buying an SUV would solve their space problems, but they found that it didn't offer much more room than their old Jetta. They still wouldn't buy a minivan, but did admit that an SUV isn't always the answer.

If you have a family with more than two children, a minivan is very hard to beat for ease of use, space and overall practicality. Give one a try—it might just surprise you, and I bet if you ask friends and family who do drive a minivan they will probably rave about how much they like having one and driving it isn't the end of the world. As mentioned, there are no 4-cylinder minivans, only V6 gasoline versions with no hybrid or diesel options available.

THE MARKET TRENDS

This is a snapshot of what is going on in the marketplace right now. The trend is to smaller, lighter, more efficient vehicles, even in the SUV segment. As more and more features are available in less expensive vehicles, it is a good time to buy. Inexpensive no longer means cheap—and premium small vehicles have an increasing large following.

Buying a very small car for a large family will not work, but in general it is a good practice to buy the most efficient vehicle that meets your needs. For some buyers, that will be a subcompact car, but for others a big vehicle might be the only answer. As I mentioned, buying a vehicle is a compromise, and you have to do what is best for your situation and your pocketbook.

2 Vroooom vrooom

WHAT POWERS YOUR VEHICLE?

You're probably like me—for your entire life, the cars you have owned or hitched a ride in have run on gasoline. A few short years ago, a time when cars would be powered by electricity or an alternative fuel that emitted only water from the tailpipe instead of ozone-producing exhaust seemed like a fantasy from a future world. Well, it's all about to become reality as the major auto manufacturers are racing to be the first to build the "next" big advancement in vehicle technology. Since high-tech cars such as plug-in hybrids and others powered by fuel cells are still a year or two away, the majority of choices for your next vehicle will probably be gasoline, hybrid or diesel. Each has its own advantages and limitations, but the fact that we have options to reduce gas consumption—and emissions—is encouraging.

Just prior to the oil crash, I had a memorable dinner with Beth Lowery from General Motors. She has a challenging role as GM's chief environmental officer, responsible for the company's environmental, energy and safety policies worldwide. In essence, she is the top person for the new direction in which GM is headed as auto makers bring the new generation of power plants online.

The dinner took place as oil prices had just hit record highs, and there was a lot of talk about the fact the planet is heading into an era of more scarce and expensive oil. Along with that, there is immense pressure from governments and the public on auto companies to build cleaner, more efficient vehicles. I asked Beth if a company such as GM is developing new products like the Volt plug-in electric car as a way to "wash" the company in green, giving the impression of taking a leadership role, or does GM believe it is moving in new directions? Her answer was very candid, especially coming from a person in such a high position. She agreed that producing green technology is a good public relations move. But she went on to say that GM had just celebrated its 100th anniversary, and if it wanted to be in business in another 100 years, it would have to move away from gas- and fossil fuel–powered vehicles. Building smaller and more efficient gasoline cars along with hybrids, flex-fuel and ultimately electric and hydrogen-powered cars is the transition that has to take place for the industry to survive.

You see, we will still be driving cars in decades to come; they will just be different from those we're used to. Much of the technology is not yet available for the average buyer, so all we can do is make the best car-buying decision based on what's currently on the market.

The Gasoline Engine

Here is some techie talk: variable valve timing, direct injection, fuel management and cylinder management. If you don't know what these terms mean, don't worry. Most people don't know or care how their car works, they just want it to start in the morning and help them get on with their day. The technology inside your car is marvellous and seamless, and you don't need to know a thing about it except that newer vehicles are much more environmentally friendly and efficient.

The gasoline engine has come a long way from the cars we drove just 20 years ago. Efficiency and emissions have improved a great deal over the past few decades, but manufacturers have not taken that added efficiency and translated it into better mileage; they have put it toward increased horsepower. The Honda Civic is a perfect example. It is the best-selling car in Canada and has been for a decade. The 2005 model has a 4-cylinder engine that puts out just over 100 horsepower. Today, the Civic pushes 140 horsepower but the mileage has not improved dramatically. The benefit is that today we have vehicles that are wonderful to drive and have plenty of power yet still produce fewer emissions. The public wasn't demanding better mileage when gasoline was relatively cheap—drivers preferred power—but that's changing. Over the next few years, you will see auto makers put more emphasis on mileage as US lawmakers have enacted a law that will require all manufacturers to have an average fuel mileage of 35 mpg (US gallon) or 42 mpg (Imperial) (55 km/g) over their entire fleet by 2016.

There are some benefits to gasoline-powered cars; the public is comfortable with the product, they're less expensive than alternative power plants, the distribution of fuel is established and these vehicles have a known resale value.

On *Driving Television,* we conducted a test of six of the best-selling cars in the country to see if drivers could get close to the posted fuel consumption numbers that Transport Canada publishes. Four were gasoline-powered 4-cylinders: the Toyota Yaris, Honda Civic, Honda Accord and Ford Escape. All were chosen because they represent different sizes, classes and price points. The driver of each car was asked to drive it for two weeks. The first week they could drive as they normally would, and the second week they were to drive as smoothly and conservatively as possible. At the end of the two weeks, we compared the vehicles' fuel consumption.

What the tests showed is that today, you can get a subcompact, compact, mid-size car or even an SUV that has an efficient engine, and if you drive it with an eye on fuel consumption, you can save money. The lesson is that the mileage you get is set not only by the car design, but also the habits of the driver.

If you've ever been to Europe or Asia, you know the cars we drive here in North America are huge compared to the small, efficient and fun-to-drive cars that are the norm there. But things are changing in our domestic market; the companies that sell small, efficient cars are being rewarded with huge jumps in sales. Toyota makes the popular Corolla here in Canada, as does Honda with the Civic. Both models are in the compact class and are best-sellers in Canada because Canadians who are trying to save on fuel are snapping them up.

There is an even smaller class of cars called the subcompact class that features vehicles with strong European and Asian roots. For example, the Honda Fit, which is now sold around the world, was first introduced to consumers in Asia and Europe to much acclaim. The Toyota Yaris was developed in Japan and Europe with an eye to those markets, but it has become a favourite here in Canada too.

The wonderful thing about these small, efficient gasoline-powered cars is that while they are inexpensive to purchase, they don't feel cheap. I'm sure somewhere in your past you remember owning a basic 4-cylinder car. The interior was vinyl and cheap plastic. The floor was uncarpeted. The only air conditioning available was rolling down the windows. The sound system was a tinny AM radio. And it was gutless. (All hail the Pinto, Chevette and Horizon!) Today, in the subcompact class, you can buy a car with power windows and doors, air conditioning, all the safety features, a host of in-car entertainment including iPod and Bluetooth connectivity, plus a responsive and efficient engine. The amount of fuel used by this class rivals many hybrid and diesel options, so you can have your cake and eat it too—inexpensive to buy and operate.

Gas-powered cars still make up the bulk of sales in Canada, and that trend isn't going to change any time soon. Yes, there will be more alternatives to the traditional power plant, but they will never reach the same level of acceptance as the gas engine. If you're in the market for a gas-powered car, know that the technology developed to power the engine is helping to keep the engine running as efficiently as possible, and if you're retiring an older gasoline car, the benefit to the environment is great.

The Hybrid

By 2008, Toyota had achieved sales of one million Prius hybrid cars worldwide in a 10-year period. One million sounds like a big number, but in reality, it's a drop in the bucket for typical passenger cars. Historically, more than one million cars are sold every month in the United States. But the Prius is not your typical passenger car; it is a marvel of technology that has helped revolutionize the auto industry. Hybrids are here to stay, and the public has warmed to them nicely. In fact, most of the one million Prius sales have occurred over the last few years.

It must have been 1996 or 1997 when I first drove the Prius. Toyota Canada decided to bring a few right-hand-drive hybrids from Japan for auto journalists to drive in advance of the Prius coming to North America. I clearly remember pulling out from a fancy downtown Vancouver hotel and wondering if the Prius was running. It was, but under just electric power; there was no engine noise, just a muted electric motor whine. I looked at the public relations person from Toyota and then at the digital readout on the dash explaining how the hybrid system was working, and thought to myself that this is just too complex for people to adapt to, and it must be a time bomb of repairs waiting to go off. I was wrong on both counts. Today, Canadians have to put their names on waiting lists to get a Prius and they have proven to be one of the most reliable cars Toyota makes. It was one of the first hybrids sold in Canada and continues to be the sales champ. So much has changed over the last 10 years, the market for hybrids has grown and the types being offered have also expanded.

For instance, Toyota has developed what it calls a full hybrid that is used in all Toyota and Lexus products, and initially licensed by Ford for the Escape SUV and Nissan for its Altima. A full hybrid means the vehicles have the ability to start under full electric power and can switch to a combination of gas and electric power or just gasoline. The benefit of electric-only power is that the car can drive in stop-and-go traffic without ever using a drop of gasoline. But keep in mind this is limited to low-speed driving—once the car reaches speeds over 30 km/h, the gasoline engine engages. All the vehicles that use this type of system deploy the power through a continuously variable transmission (essentially a one-gear transmission that varies the ratio depending on speed), which gives a very smooth drive, but for some drivers takes a little getting used to.

Other manufacturers have adopted a different form called the mild hybrid. Unlike a full hybrid, in this mild form the gasoline engine operates when the car is in motion and the electric system is designed to assist the gasoline engine. The benefit to this design is that the driver can't really tell that he is driving a hybrid. While mild hybrids don't always deliver the same kind of mileage that a full hybrid can because the gas engine is almost always operating, they are cheaper to build and hence less expensive to buy. Honda uses a mild hybrid in the Civic and Insight. That said, I have been able to achieve fantastic mileage with the Honda Insight, getting close to or even better mileage than the Transport Canada ratings. One thing both the full and mild hybrids have in common is that the gasoline engine is switched off when the vehicle comes to a stop; the radio, heat and air conditioning continue to run off the battery. Once the driver lifts off the brake and presses the gas, the gasoline engine is restarted, similar to a gas-powered golf cart.

There is another hybrid system called the two-mode hybrid, co-developed by GM, BMW, Mercedes and Chrysler. It is a full hybrid at low speeds, able to operate with electric-assist at higher speeds. When the gasoline engine kicks in, electric-assist is provided for those higher speeds, thus two modes. At higher speeds, the gas engine has the ability to shut down half the cylinders and the electric motor makes up for the loss in power, allowing the vehicle to run on fewer cylinders longer. For example, when used in a V8, half of the cylinders switch off, allowing the vehicle to run on four cylinders and electric power. This two-mode configuration has been introduced on full-size SUVs such as the Chevy Tahoe, Cadillac Escalade, BMW X6, Chrysler Aspen and Mercedes ML, along with pickup trucks for GM and Chrysler. These auto makers claim this system can achieve a 25% improvement in combined city and highway mileage. Not only does the two-mode deliver exceptional mileage, it also provides full towing capacity. Look for this system to be rolled out in smaller vehicles in the coming years.

When hybrids were first introduced, the premium price was not a good economic decision for many buyers. Hybrids' prices have come down as more models are available, allowing more Canadians to take advantage of the fuel savings. One important thing to remember is that to fully utilize the efficiencies of a full or mild hybrid, you should be driving in mostly stop-and-go traffic. It's only when the two-mode system is widely adopted that using a hybrid on the highway will be beneficial.

Hybrid sales will continue to grow as the price of fuel trends higher and auto manufacturers have to meet new, tougher efficiency standards. The technology has proven to be very reliable and consumers who have been early adopters are some of the most vocal advocates.

The Diesel Power Plant

I recently took my family to Scotland to visit relatives so my young sons could meet their Highland cousins. I booked a rental car online; a station wagon seemed like a good choice for a family of four with car seats and a stroller. You know how it is when you book a rental car—you're never quite sure you will get what you asked for. Well, I was pleasantly surprised that I got exactly what I wanted. It wasn't the station wagon so much as a diesel that got me excited. After running around the city of Edinburgh (okay, which isn't quite in the Highlands), visiting family and with short trips on the "motorway," we used a grand total of a half tank of fuel over a two-week period. That's it! Not only did the diesel use very little fuel, it had a lot of power (especially torque), which is best for driving in the city and scooting down the highway.

Europeans have adopted diesel in force, and more than 50% of all cars sold on that continent are diesel powered, and in some countries the percentage exceeds 70%. Diesel power plants achieve 20% to 30% better fuel consumption than a similar gas vehicle, and the fuel advantage is attainable at all speeds. Not only will a diesel get good mileage in stop-and-go city driving, but also cruising down the highway; the percentage advantage from driving a diesel is the same. The diesel engine is also a durable design, giving years of service and hundreds of thousands of kilometres of driving.

The fuel comparison episode we did for *Driving Television* included a new 2009 VW Jetta clean-burning diesel, and the mileage from that car was absolutely amazing. The young man who drove the vehicles for that segment is a TV editor named Adrian who has a passion for diesel cars. In fact, he drives a vintage diesel VW Rabbit from the era of bell-bottoms and shag rugs. Wait a second—that's all back! Regardless, his old car is what most people remember about diesel cars: slow, smelly, loud and not very appealing. Forget those diesels of old. For the model year 2009, all the manufacturers which sell diesel-powered cars in North America have to achieve the same tailpipe emissions as a gasoline model. This isn't a problem with respect to CO_2 emissions; diesel is a richer fuel than gasoline and it has more stored energy, allowing an engine the capability to drive farther on the same amount of fuel, and in turn producing less CO_2. The soot and nitrous oxide have always been the issue with diesel power plants.

The good news is that the challenge has been met, and today's new breed of clean diesels has some of the lowest tailpipe emissions on the planet (and some manufacturers claim they are cleaner than hybrids). In addition, the new diesels are only slightly more expensive than a regular gasoline car, and there's no battery pack to recycle like there is in a hybrid car. I have to admit I am a big fan of diesel because it offers so much. So just how well did the Jetta perform in our fuel test? Young Adrian was able to achieve 5.8L/100km when driving the way he normally would day to day. This works out to 48 mpg in mixed city and highway driving. Amazingly, when he drove as conservatively as possible, the fuel rating improved even further to 5.2L/100km, or 54 mpg in mixed city and highway driving. With numbers like that, the Jetta is almost as efficient as a Prius hybrid, but remember that diesel engines produce less CO_2, so the impact on the environment is even less. In addition, the diesel Jetta has more power than the Prius and much more driver-friendly torque.

Here is another real-world example. Imagine a car that delivers the power of a V8 from a 6-cylinder engine and with the efficiency of a 4-cylinder. It's true! I had a chance to drive the Mercedes E Class diesel that throws off almost 400 ft lbs of torque, and the engine consumed only 7L/100km in mixed city and highway driving. That works out to 40 mpg from a big heavy luxury car. The mileage these diesels can achieve and the power they deliver is incredible.

All of the German manufacturers are testing the market with diesel product. Mercedes has the largest number of models available, and its sales have been some of the strongest in years—more than 60% of its sales being diesel. With that kind of success, I can only imagine the reception these clean and powerful engines will enjoy once the public at large gets a chance to drive them.

There are a few things to be aware of. Diesel fuel is not widely sold in Canada, so owners have to find service stations that they can use on a regular basis and pre-plan fuelling on longer trips. The other concern is maintenance. Regular service on a diesel can be more expensive than a gasoline car (oil changes, for example), so it's a good idea to ask the service person in the dealership for the cost of regular maintenance on a diesel car before you buy.

We are just at the beginning of a huge wave of diesel vehicles finally about to arrive in Canada. If the number of calls to my radio show is any indication, Canadians trying to improve the impact on their wallet and the environment will greet them very favourably.

Just What is Flex-Fuel?

The next time you're sitting at a traffic light, have a look at the car in front of you. Other than an undecipherable vanity plate, it might have a badge on the back saying "Flex Fuel." That means the vehicle has a special fuel delivery system that will allow the car to run on both regular gasoline or a fuel that is a mixture of 85% ethanol and 15% gas; it doesn't matter which is put in the car, it will run on both. Conventional gas engines cannot run on more than a 10% ethanol to 90% gasoline ratio.

This 85% ethanol fuel is called E85 and is produced from grain and corn, and is mostly produced in the US midwest where the crops are grown. But making ethanol has an impact on the food chain. Many farmers have switched from growing grain and corn to feed humans and animals to providing a fuel source for automobiles. This has lessened the supply of grains and related food products, which has caused increases in food prices. When it comes to cars competing with humans for fuel, humans will always prevail. Car makers are trying to find ways to make ethanol without affecting the food chain by using bio-waste from garbage, sewage and wood fibre. If we can get to a place where ethanol does not affect our food supply, then E85 will be a sensible alternative.

Brazil has the largest ethanol fleet of cars in the world, with the majority running on either 100% ethanol or a mandatory 25% ethanol-gasoline mix. By using the by-products of farmed sugar cane to make ethanol, Brazil has been able to reduce the amount of oil its fleet burns and has converted a significant number of vehicles to this cleaner-burning fuel.

In Canada, as in the United States, the flex-fuel infrastructure is in its infancy. The majority of E85 being sold in North America is close to the production centres in the American midwest; there are more than over 700 stations in the US. In Canada, we have no E85 infrastructure at all, but we do have 10% ethanol blended gasoline (E10) in some provinces provided by Husky/Mohawk, Sunoco and others. This E10 blend of ethanol doesn't require the vehicle to be modified at all, but read your owner's manual to make sure it won't harm your engine. Ethanol is not as rich a fuel as gasoline; it has less available energy so it's not as efficient as gasoline or diesel. The hope is that a blended fuel will be cheaper to buy and the loss in efficiency will be offset by the lower cost. The other factor is a reduced dependency on oil. This works well in theory, but the truth is the E10 being sold right now is no cheaper; the only benefit is that it burns slightly cleaner and isn't using as much fossil fuel.

If you're shopping for a vehicle and it is E85 capable, buying one gives you the option of being able to use that fuel, should it become available in the future. I wouldn't go out of my way to find an E85 car, but having one does provide options.

Plug-In Hybrids

In all my years covering the auto market, I have never experienced the kind of anticipation surrounding the Chevy Volt plug-in hybrid due out at the end of 2010. Sure, there is always a buzz around a hot new sports car like the Audi R8, but to get calls to my radio show, e-mails and general questions from passersby about such an environmental advance indicates that the public is hungry for this type of technology. General Motors and other auto makers are racing to be the first to market with a new technology that will revolutionize the way we look at cars.

How does a plug-in hybrid differ from a typical hybrid? A typical hybrid combines a gasoline engine with an electric system to power the car. The electric motor can propel the vehicle on its own for a limited amount of time at low speeds. A plug-in hybrid extends the distance and increases the speed the vehicle can travel on pure electric power and, unlike a conventional hybrid, the gasoline engine is a support system.

Picture this . . . getting up in the morning and walking out to your new Chevy Volt, unplugging the extension cord from the side of the car, getting in and driving to work and home without using a drop of gasoline. The Volt uses electric power from a battery pack to propel the car for roughly 65 km without the gas engine ever switching on. The small three-cylinder gas engine under the hood doesn't drive the car but acts as a generator to create electricity to extend the range of the Volt from 65 km all the way to 300 km.

The majority of Canadians drive less than 65 km a day, so having a vehicle like this would reduce their fuel consumption to zero. In fact, the engineers at General Motors claim the Volt costs less to charge than it does to run a refrigerator for one day. In places such as Canada where we generate a lot of electricity from clean hydro or nuclear power, the impact on the environment could be greatly reduced.

The problem down the road could be that if this technology was fully adopted and we all plugged in our cars at night, what would this do to the price of electricity? How many more coal- and natural gas-powered electricity plants would have to be built to feed the demand?

The Chevy Volt and cars like it will be small players initially but will grow in acceptance as the public becomes comfortable with the technology, as they did with hybrids. I have yet to drive the Volt but can't wait to try it and experience the thrill of being in such an important car.

THE RETURN OF THE ELECTRIC CAR

Who killed the electric car? It never really went away; it just wasn't ready for its big debut. The EV1 electric car featured in the movie *Who Killed the Electric Car?* was introduced as part of California's mandate to have 2% of new car sales with zero emissions by 1998 and 10% by 2003. Even though there was a loyal base of supporters for the EV1, it was never profitable for General Motors; in fact, the company lost money on every one delivered. Remember that in the late 1990s, gasoline was still a relatively cheap form of fuel, and the trend was to bigger, more powerful cars and SUVs; only a very small percentage of the public was ready to adopt an all-electric vehicle. Fast-forward to today: with high gasoline prices and an elevated awareness of pollution surrounding the automobile, there is a much bigger appetite for these cars. The mandate for zero emission cars was delayed, but stricter emissions standards for regular gasoline cars have continued to evolve in California (in fact, the state has the strictest standards in the world).

I was lucky enough to be one of the few Canadians to drive an EV1, which had the working name "Impact." Ouch! Not a good name for a car. I clearly remember the slippery shape of the body, the futuristic dash and eerie lack of noise when driving the car. The range on a single charge was limited and I wonder how well that car would have handled a cold Canadian winter; with the headlights, windshield wipers, heat and radio all running, the battery would have a hard time keeping up. For fans of the original EV1, it's comforting to know that some of the technology invented for the EV1 is being integrated into the new Chevy Volt.

In 2008, a small California-based company called Tesla Motors began producing a full electric sports car with lightning-quick acceleration and almost 400 km of driving range on a single charge. The firm is also building a mass-appeal sedan.

This type of performance electric car differs from many of the low-speed electric cars currently being produced for use in urban areas at speeds less than 50 km/h. The ZENN Motor Company, a Canadian brand based in Quebec, produces cute hatchback cars for city driving. However, many of the provinces and municipalities have not opened up their regulations for these cars to be sold and licensed across the country. ZENN, which stands for Zero Emissions, No Noise, is trying to get around this hurdle by also developing a car capable of higher speeds along with new battery technology.

Chrysler too has announced it will be introducing a full electric car by 2010. Hmmm, sounds like the same year as GM's Volt . . . I like this competition. Initially, Chrysler will have a Dodge full electric sports car, a Jeep plug-in hybrid and Chrysler minivan plug-in for testing purposes. Chrysler hopes that by using the latest lithium-ion battery technology developed by General Electric, the pure electric sports car will be able to travel more than 300 km on a single eight-hour charge from a standard wall socket. The plug-in hybrids featured in the Jeep and Chrysler minivan will be able to drive on pure electric power for up to 65 km and with a gasoline generator on board be able to extend the range to beyond 600 km. Unfortunately, only one of the three prototype vehicles will be produced and sold by 2010.

With GM putting so much effort into the Volt plug-in hybrid, a competitive company such as Chrysler would probably opt for a plug-in hybrid too, and the pure electric sports car might take a back seat.

Regardless of whether it's a high-performance vehicle or a compact car, the appetite for electric cars is growing and the public will demand these vehicles be developed and introduced onto our roads. There are announcements from car makers stating their plans to build electric coming out almost on a weekly basis. The race is on to see which mass-appeal electric vehicle can be sold in large enough volumes that it makes sense for the manufacturers to market and produce them at a profit.

THE FUTURE OF FUEL CELLS

I recently asked an automotive engineer about the delay in getting a fuel cell car to market. Ten years ago, companies promised fuel cell cars would be available within 10 to 15 years, yet it hasn't happened. And why are we still waiting? The answer really is simple: cost. Making the fuel cell small enough to fit into a passenger car with the ability to produce sufficient electricity is expensive.

Fuel cell technology is already being used in many applications worldwide, including generating stations for large buildings and even for forklifts in warehouses. But making that same technology work in hot and cold conditions, and packaging it in a reliable and inexpensive car, will take time.

In 2007, Ford brought an Edge HySeries vehicle to Canada to let automotive journalists drive its latest hydrogen prototype at the Ballard fuel cell facility in Vancouver. We had a chance to tour the facility that made the components for the Edge, and Ford engineers explained just how the vehicle is powered. In simple terms, the Edge HySeries is a plug-in hybrid with a battery pack to provide power to the electric motors. When the batteries' charge drops below a certain level, the hydrogen (in a tank) sends fuel to the Ballard fuel cell, creating electricity to top up the battery. The hydrogen doesn't power the vehicle directly, but it does create the electricity to keep the vehicle running, just like the gasoline engine does on the Chevy Volt.

The styling on the Edge was terrific, the way it drove was very smooth and quiet, just like driving a full electric car, plus it had lots of room for four adults. Here's the problem: I asked the engineer how much it would cost to buy an Edge HySeries. His answer: $2 million. Now keep in mind this was a one-of-a-kind prototype, so if and when hydrogen cars do come to market, the biggest challenge will be making them at a cost that the public is willing to pay. Ford believes a combination of plug-in hybrid technology along with smaller and cheaper fuel cells will eventually make hydrogen cars cheaper to produce, compared to using larger more expensive fuel cells on their own. Taking the electricity from your home and extending the range of a vehicle through hydrogen technology will make it easier for the auto makers to produce fuel cell cars in larger numbers.

There are already test fleets of hydrogen cars on the road all over the world, made by manufacturers studying the advantages and struggles they will face to bring this technology to market. One major hurdle is that there are only a handful of hydrogen filling stations in Canada with a promise from government to deliver more as part of the Hydrogen Highway from California to British Columbia. Just in time for the 2010 Olympic games, BC is planning for this demonstration highway from Whistler to Vancouver and over to Victoria to be up and running, able to fill hydrogen cars as a showcase for sustainable living. General Motors is the major automotive sponsor for the Games, so we will just see six Chevy Equinox fuel cell SUVs as part of a demonstration on Whistler's Sea to Sky highway. Each of these vehicles is hand assembled and worth over one million dollars but the testing in real-world conditions will ultimately provide the kind of knowledge the car makers need to produce cost-effective fuel cell vehicles.

In California, Honda has fuel cell cars for lease as part of a test program, promising to make them commercially available in the next 10 years. Filling these cars will be done at designated stations, but Honda has developed the capability that gives owners the convenience of fuelling their cars with a home hydrogen converter. This unit takes natural gas and produces electricity for the home at the same time as producing and filling a car with hydrogen. Unfortunately, the initial production run will not have this capability, but Honda is committed to eventually making this technology available.

For now, the limited number of fuel cell cars will have to fill up at the very small number of stations. There is a commitment from government, industry and other stakeholders to eventually make more hydrogen stations available, but it will take time.

I have a wait-and-see attitude with hydrogen fuel cell vehicles. The technology has been successful in larger vehicles such as transit buses, but making it affordable for the car-buying masses will be hard to achieve.

As Ballard Power engineer Sabina Russel said, "If you look in hindsight at how long it took to develop the combustion engine compared to the fuel cell, we've actually made very rapid technology progress in the last 15 years." She went on to say, "I have two little girls, a four-year-old and a two-year-old, and their first car will be a fuel cell car." A bold statement and one I hope comes true.

THE DRIVETRAIN

After deciding what type of fuel you would like to your next vehicle to run on, it's a good idea to review the different kinds of power delivery systems available.

When I was a kid growing up in Ontario in the 1970s, most of the cars on the road were rear-wheel-drive sedans. SUVs hadn't really been invented yet; with the exception of a few large vehicles such as Suburbans and Jeeps, most Canadians drove a car or a station wagon. When winter arrived, these rear-wheel-drive cars had serious drawbacks.

On the street I grew up on, there was a stop sign just a few doors down from our house. Beyond the stop sign was a major thoroughfare. When winter arrived, the cars that stopped at the sign had an almost impossible job of entering the main road without spinning their wheels. The slight grade of the road, along with the rear-wheel design of most of the vehicles, left many of them requiring a push from the neighbourhood kids. Thankfully, so much has changed in the decades since. Yes, there are still rear-wheel-drive cars, but there are also many other options and technology available to today's buyers.

As fuel consumption standards began to rise in the late 1970s and early 1980s, along with the emergence of Japanese imports in the North American market, the trend changed from big rear-wheel-drive

(RWD) cars to lighter front-wheel-drive (FWD) cars. The advantage is that FWD cars are easier and cheaper to make, and the engine sits overtop the front wheels, providing weight to assist in winter traction. Even today, the vast majority of vehicles are FWD; some of the small SUVs on the market that have all-wheel-drive capability still put most of the power to the ground through the front wheels. Not only did the move toward FWD provide better traction, in many instances it also provides better handling and, by eliminating the components for RWD, allows automotive designers to increase the space inside the cabin and trunk of today's cars.

Many Canadians opt to spend extra money for an all-wheel-drive vehicle, but with the advancement of electronic safety features such as traction and stability control, a front-wheel-drive car is going to fill most drivers' needs.

My neighbour recently asked my opinion on what type of new vehicle he should buy. The first thing I asked was what type he wanted. An SUV, he said. Why? He likes to go skiing once or twice a year and wants all-wheel-drive for winter traction. I mentioned he might be able to buy a cheaper FWD vehicle and equip it with good winter tires for those occasional trips to the ski hill. It was like a light bulb went off—he hadn't even thought of that option. In his mind, it was all-wheel-drive or nothing. If you're in the market for a new car and thinking you must have AWD, you might be able to achieve the same results with a less expensive vehicle, plus you'll have the added safety of good winter tires.

All-wheel- and four-wheel-drive cars do have their place, and many manufacturers take the best characteristics of FWD and RWD technology and improve on it. With a four-wheel-drive system, all four wheels are fully engaged at all times; with part-time four-wheel-drive, the driver can choose either drivetrain, depending on conditions. Four-wheel-drive vehicles sometimes have a low setting, allowing them to crawl along, which is especially useful for driving off road. Vehicles equipped with four-wheel-drive are typically pickup trucks, Jeeps and some SUVs used for work and recreational purposes. Some 4WD systems have the engine power locked so the same amount of power goes to all wheels. This can be a problem on dry roads when the system can bind up, meaning the locked driveline cannot rotate the inside tire less than the outside tire when turning, causing the tires to skid. These types of systems are wonderful on snow and loose dirt, but should be disengaged on dry roads. Other four-wheel systems, such as on the Toyota Highlander, allow the driver to use the vehicle as they normally would in all conditions, because the system is locked, simultaneously providing 50% of the power to the front wheels and 50% to the back, allowing the vehicle to drive without binding up. This offers the best of both worlds.

All-wheel-drive differs from four-wheel-drive because it provides power to all four wheels but only when required, plus it is done automatically. When a car is designed, it usually has either an FWD or RWD bias. For example, the base model of the Ford Escape compact SUV offers FWD only; on the higher trim levels, all-wheel drive is available. Even if a buyer chooses all-wheel drive, the system provides power to the front wheels for the majority of the time and will send a percentage of power to the rear wheels only if extra traction is needed. An example of a RWD bias is the BMW X3. This vehicle is based on the 3 Series RWD, so in the all-wheel-drive variant it sends most of the power to the rear wheels and will send extra power to the front wheels when needed. The difference in front or rear bias all-wheel-drive systems is the handling they provide. Rear-wheel bias vehicles are usually higher end performance models, while front-wheel bias systems tend to be offered on less expensive vehicles.

Some car companies, such as Audi and Subaru, have built their whole brand around all-wheel-drive. The advanced all-wheel-drive systems offered by such companies deliver instant power to any of the four wheels for better traction, but on dry roads also provide better handling. All-wheel-drive is much more popular than four-wheel-drive because it realizes better fuel economy, since all four wheels are powered only when necessary.

Keep in mind that four-wheel-drive and all-wheel-drive provide better traction in slippery conditions, but they don't offer better braking and turning ability. The same laws of physics apply to all vehicles, but with better traction and electronic stability programs, many drivers of these vehicles can feel invincible, which can lead to more accidents.

One winter in British Columbia, the RCMP asked drivers of SUVs and trucks to slow down on icy roads because they had to pull too many of these vehicles out of the ditch. It seems these drivers drove much faster than others, thinking they had a superior vehicle in the snow. If you buy an all-wheel or four-wheel-drive vehicle, be aware that they offer only a slight advantage over those with front-wheel-drive.

Rear-wheel-drive cars are the preferred choice for driving enthusiasts looking for the best balance and road manners from a car. Expensive import cars such as BMW, Mercedes, Porsche and others tend to have RWD power trains, but more and more models are offered in all-wheel-drive configurations. The rear bias of these types of cars lets the rear wheels drive the car while the front wheels steer, instead of the front wheels doing both. The road feel of a rear-wheel-drive car cannot be replicated, and for many enthusiasts it's the only way to go. In fact, in recent years, there has been a resurgence of RWD cars, such as the Chrysler 300, Hyundai Genesis, Cadillac CTS and old favourites like the Ford Mustang, Chevy Camaro and Dodge Challenger. There will always be a market for RWD cars, but it is shrinking.

WRAPPING UP

Before you choose which vehicle to buy, really think about what you're going to use it for, what type of engine you want, and whether you need front-, rear- or all-wheel-drive. The good news is that many manufacturers offer the same model of vehicle with different configurations to appeal to as many buyers as possible, so take the time to research which one you want, and ask a lot of questions when shopping.

Part Two

Consider This . . .

3 Going green and saving money: Myth and reality

THE HYBRID: THE GREEN OPTION?

"Drive Smart to Save Green" was a clever ad campaign initiated in 2008 by the Insurance Corporation of British Columbia to get drivers to change their habits in order to save money and reduce pollution. I was asked to play the moderator in the TV commercials, which you can view on my web site www.motormouth.ca. The basis of the campaign was to feature "dirty drivers" who have come to their senses, changed their habits and reduced the amount of fuel they use and the pollution they create. Funny characters were used to get the message across, including a coffee-drinking student who decided to spend the money he saved on expensive coffee beans, a jilted fiancé who almost ran over her ex-boyfriend, a soccer mom who hit her son's school bus, and several others. The characters—who sat together and confessed their dirty habits— came to realize that by changing the way they drove, they were able to drive smart and save green. The campaign was a lot of fun to do and had a simple message: reducing the amount of fuel you use benefits your pocketbook and the environment. Taking control of your actions has an impact, so driving conservatively, the type of vehicle you drive and keeping it operating properly will save fuel.

This book is about researching and buying cars, but there might also be an opportunity to think about your existing vehicle and the way you drive in order to effect change. I am often asked, "What kind of car should I buy?" and in return I always ask the person why they want to buy a new car. Lately, the most common answer has been "to save money on gas." This is a very legitimate reason for wanting to make a change, but in some instances it can have a dramatic impact on your wallet. I'll often respond with "Buying a new car is an expensive way to save a few bucks on gas." The cost of fuel is the one expense we see regularly when we fill up; the numbers are right there on the pump in front of our face. For more and more Canadians, that number is getting harder to swallow. What you don't see is the cost to buy and insure the car, as well as the depreciation. These costs, in many instances, are withdrawn right from your bank account so you don't even notice, and depreciation is only a factor when you go to sell your vehicle, which means the cost is deferred.

If saving money is the main reason for car shopping, then you must look at the overall cost of ownership. For example, a five-year-old car that has been paid off will cost less to own and operate than buying a new fuel-efficient model. The fuel going into the car is a fraction of the cost to borrow the money to buy a new vehicle. You also need to consider the initial depreciation, extra taxes and possible increased insurance costs. It's very important to add up all of the costs and then calculate how long it will take you to make up that extra money in fuel savings. In many cases, it can take years.

A good friend of my family lives in Winnipeg and uses his vehicle to visit clients for his sales job. Over the last few years, he has purchased a new car every two to three years, always looking for a more efficient model. His main focus is the cost of fuel, but he fails to realize how much money he spends buying a new car. If he had kept one vehicle for the past six years, instead of owning three cars, he might have been able to pay for all the fuel he used with the extra expenses of changing vehicles. Keep this phrase in mind: "Buying a new car is an expensive way to save a few bucks on gas."

Another thing a lot of people don't realize is the amount of energy it takes to produce a car, from mining ore to making steel, shipping parts, assembling the car and shipping it to market. The environmental impact of a vehicle is not just the fuel you burn when you drive it, but the total amount of energy it takes to produce, drive and recycle it. If you have a vehicle that isn't to the point where it's falling apart and includes modern emissions equipment (ideally a catalytic converter), then you might want to consider keeping it until you have no choice but to buy.

This is one reason I say hybrids are guilt-free driving. But just because a car has a hybrid badge on it doesn't mean that it has less of an impact on the environment. Sure, it might burn less gasoline, but what about the energy to make the batteries, along with a separate electrical system from the regular engine? Once again, it's the in-your-face costs and perceived impact on the environment that attracts buyers to hybrids, but if you read further about what I call the European model, there are other options for buyers who want to reduce fuel consumption and become greener.

At a dinner party we had with neighbours a few years ago, the topic of going green came up, and one guest asked me about buying a hybrid car. I asked the same question I always do: Why? As it turns out, the school that her two children attend had been teaching the kids about the environment; this in turn led to some uncomfortable questions about their ownership of a Toyota 4Runner, a mid-size SUV. Their son wanted to know why they had an SUV and why his parents weren't driving a vehicle that had less of an environmental impact. Our guests were ready to go out and spend a bunch of money on a hybrid, when I pointed out that the issue could be solved much less painfully. Yes, they own a big 4Runner, but they also own a compact VW Jetta that the dad drives to work. I suggested a solution that they hadn't even thought of. They had always taken the larger SUV when they went out as a family. It made sense, since it was the "family vehicle," and they never even considered taking the smaller car. I suggested they use the big 4X4 when they go skiing or times when they really do need the extra space, and leave it parked the rest of the time. Instead, they should take the smaller vehicle for the short trips such as to the grocery store, movies and visiting. Sure enough, the next day our family was out in front of our house raking leaves, and who should pull up in their efficient 4-cylinder VW Jetta but our neighbours, all four of them comfortably running errands. Sometimes making a change doesn't have to be dramatic; it can just be a shift in thinking and behaviour.

SOME TRUTHS ABOUT FUEL ECONOMY

If you're at a point in your life that you want to make a change and buy a new or used car, it's important to look at the fuel consumption ratings of a prospective vehicle. Calculating what it might cost you to run a vehicle for a year and what the approximate carbon impact might be is great, but there's a problem. A common complaint is that the fuel numbers posted by the manufacturers are misleading. I've had callers saying the manufacturers lie about the fuel ratings, and that they're trying to scam buyers into thinking a vehicle is fuel-efficient when it doesn't achieve the published ratings. In reality, it isn't the manufacturer's fault; the fuel ratings you see advertised and placed on the vehicle window sticker are not provided by the auto maker but by Transport Canada in a laboratory. Each vehicle model is tested exactly the same way—driven on a machine and tested once to simulate city driving and a second time simulate highway driving. The testing is constant from one vehicle to the next.

As you can imagine, testing a car on a machine is very different than driving it in real life. So I invited Stephen Akehurst from Natural Resources Canada to be a guest on my radio show to explain why many Canadians, including me, have never been able to get even close to the posted fuel ratings. He claims that it all comes down to driving style, road conditions and the weather. The posted ratings can be achieved if the driver adapts to a very conservative driving style, and Natural Resources Canada has had feedback from average Canadians claiming they've been able to achieve the posted ratings.

This got me thinking. After the interview, we decided to try for ourselves on *Driving Television* to get as close as we could to the posted ratings, and the results were interesting. We asked six staff member to drive some of the best-selling vehicles in Canada as conservatively as possible for one whole week and see how they did. Here are some of the highlights from that TV special:

- The 2009 Toyota Prius has an official fuel rating of 4L/100km in the city and 4.2L/100km on the highway. Our test vehicle achieved 4.72L/100km in mostly city driving, not far off the posted numbers.

- The Honda Accord 4-cylinder has a posted fuel rating of 9.9L/100km in the city and 6.5L/100km on the highway. Our test vehicle landed very close to the posted city numbers at 9.7L/100km.

- The vehicle that was closest to the official numbers was the VW Jetta clean diesel. It has a posted rating of 6.8L/100km in the city and 4.9L/100km on the highway, and we achieved 5.1L/100km in mixed driving.

It's true you can get very close to the posted ratings if you drive conservatively, but—and there is a but—all of our drivers found it extremely hard to maintain the driving style necessary to get good results. One driver said he would rather take the bus than have to drive so slowly because cars around our test vehicles became irate as we delayed faster-moving traffic. It can be done, but it isn't easy.

I would prefer a testing procedure that's more realistic. As I mentioned, Natural Resources Canada does one test each for city and highway driving. The city drive is 12 kilometres, simulating stop-and-go city traffic and lower speeds. The highway simulation is done over 16 kilometres at higher speeds, but the vehicle's speed never exceeds 97km/h. I don't know about you, but I think two tests done over a grand total of 28 kilometres is not a very realistic measure of a vehicle's efficiency. Since 2008, the testing process in the United States has gone from a similar one-cycle test for city and highway driving and added three new simulations of different conditions. This is a much more accurate reflection of real-world driving and closer to what the public will actually achieve after buying a car. Unlike the Canadian test, the Environmental Protection Agency in the US tests vehicles under hard acceleration, cold weather starts, air conditioning usage and higher highway speeds trying to mimic real-world driving. What the new testing procedure found is that the results for many larger, already inefficient cars didn't change too much, but hybrid cars that did well with the previous less aggressive testing had their fuel ratings drop by up to 20%. Under the new testing criteria, the 2009 Toyota Prius had a 20% drop in city mileage from 60 mpg to 48 mpg. The Honda Civic Hybrid dropped 18.4% from 49 mpg in the city to 40 mpg. Yes, these two hybrids represented some of the biggest changes in the new fuel ratings, but they are still some of the most fuel-efficient vehicles overall.

Not only does the US government post fuel ratings from its own test facilities, but it also posts results from consumers who report to the site. On average, consumers who post their own ratings get similar mileage to the new and improved 5-cycle test implemented in the US in 2008. In Canada, the rating for a 4-cylinder (1.8 litre) automatic Toyota Corolla is 31 mpg (per US gallon); in the US the car is rated at 27 mpg, and the average posted by individuals on the US government web site is 28 mpg. The difference between the Canadian and US numbers might not seem like a large discrepancy, but when you add up the increased fuel consumption over thousands of miles or kilometres, the extra cost is considerable.

If you're concerned about fuel consumption and want to do some research before buying a new or used vehicle, it's worth visiting the Natural Resources Canada web site. The address is very long and hard to remember so the easiest way to look up Canadian ratings is to type "fuel ratings Canada" into your search engine. In the US, the web page is much easier to remember—www.fueleconomy.gov.

Both sites have wonderful tips on how to use the posted information, driving tips and easy-to-use search functions for finding fuel ratings for new and used vehicles. Keep in mind if you use either site as a comparison, you will have to convert from metric to US gallons and vice versa. There are many online calculators that will do this easily.

Regardless of which ratings you follow, every person will have different mileage outcomes due to unique driving styles and road conditions. These "official" ratings are really a guideline and a basis for comparison from one vehicle to the next, but remember the best mileage for a particular vehicle is dictated by driving style.

If you've lived or travelled in Europe, you know the vehicles Europeans drive are generally smaller and more efficient than ours. Even the larger ones have smaller engines than the same vehicles sold in North America. I like to call this "the European model," and for the most part Canadians are moving in this direction.

There are a variety of reasons Europeans drive so many small cars. First, gasoline is taxed at a much higher rate than in Canada; this was done intentionally to push buyers toward smaller engines. The second is that vehicles with large engines face higher taxes. Many of the best-selling cars in Europe are offered with 1.0-litre engines or 1.3-litre engines, compared to 1.8 litre or larger versions found here. Diesel engines have become 50% of the European market due to their 20% to 30% advantage in efficiency, plus many European countries subsidize the price of diesel fuel to move buyers in this direction.

In Canada, by comparison, more than 60% of all vehicles sold are compact or subcompact models, and now consumers have even more diesel options. In contrast to the United States, we have a smaller and more efficient fleet of vehicles on our roads, so in some ways we are somewhere between Europe and the US in our driving habits. This too is due to the higher taxes we pay in Canada for fuel. As the price of fuel increases, Canadians buy smaller vehicles, and now that we have a larger selection of diesel vehicles, sales of these efficient vehicles is rising. For example, Mercedes-Benz has the largest fleet of diesel product on the market and already more than 50% of its sales are diesel. As the long-term trend toward higher gas prices continues and more and more diesel is available, Canadians will continue to move toward the European model.

SIZE MATTERS

This brings me back to my point about looking at the overall cost of ownership. It's a good idea to buy the most efficient vehicle you can because the price of the vehicle, along with depreciation, interest rates, taxes and the cost of fuel all increase with more powerful vehicles. For example, the price of a V6 sedan is thousands more than the same car equipped with a 4-cylinder, and buying a car with the less expensive, smaller engine is often not a compromise.

In 2002, I started a newspaper car review column designed to give a male and female point of view. Obviously, for a male and female review we needed a woman to drive the cars to give her impressions, so we asked one of the women I worked with in television to co-write the column. The basic idea was a he said/she said type of review, by reviewing the same product but with a different outlook. My co-worker knew nothing about cars other than she had been driving for 20 years. This was a perfect contrast to my background. I clearly remember one of the first cars we test-drove, a Honda Accord. I drove it for a few days and then handed it off to her, and afterwards we met up to compare notes. I asked her how she liked the engine in the Accord, and she commented how powerful and smooth it was. When I revealed that we were driving a 4-cylinder, she almost drove off the road; her mouth opened, and she exclaimed, "I don't believe it." Sure enough, we had the 4-cylinder version and she had no idea; she thought it was the more powerful V6 version.

I say it time and again when reviewing cars—test drive the vehicle with the smaller engine first; if it meets your needs, don't even bother trying the same car with a bigger engine because it will be more expensive, it will cost more in taxes and interest and unless you need the extra power for towing, it will be lost on the average driver.

Here's a quick story about just how far engine development has come over the last 20 years. I remember going shopping with my dad for a new car back in 1989, around the time the Japanese were introducing their luxury brands. Toyota had Lexus, Nissan had introduced Infiniti and Honda developed Acura. I clearly remember when we went to the Acura dealer to pick up his new Legend 4-door sedan for a hard-to-believe price of $29,000. It seems like a bargain today, but it was a good chunk of money back then. My dad loved that car, it was the top-of-the-line, most powerful car in the Acura fleet and he drove it for more than a decade until he gave it to my brother, who drove it daily until it was retired in 2008, almost 20 years later. When new, we marvelled at the powerful, sophisticated V6 engine of the Legend. The 151-hp engine was so smooth and accelerated so well, it really was a great engine.

The reason I relate this story is that today, a base model Honda Accord has a 4-cylinder engine that provides more power than my father's top-of-the-line Acura sedan did just a short time ago. The latest Accord squeezes 177 hp from a 4-cylinder engine and the original Acura Legend offered 151 hp. So if you haven't driven one of today's wonderful crop of sophisticated cars with the latest engineering, you should give a 4-cylinder version a shot. They fulfill the requirements of almost all of today's drivers. Plus, the emission controls on these vehicles means they are cleaner, so you can save money and go a bit greener too.

Hybrids have become a good barometer of the Canadian market as fuel prices have shot up over the last few years; sales of hybrids have also increased. I claim that most buyers of hybrids decide to purchase based more on their pocketbook than impact on the environment. Now before you start to craft a clever e-mail to me saying how hybrids are going to save the planet from the evils of CO_2 emissions, let me first give you my thoughts on ways, other than buying a hybrid, that will make a small impact on your wallet and the environment.

CAR-SHARING: A GROWING POPULAR OPTION TO OWNING

What do most European countries have in common? Distance. The cities are more compact, having evolved long before the combustion engine. Due to this fact and the transportation systems that have evolved over the last 100 years, many Europeans can leave the car at home and take transit quite easily. In North America, our cities have grown in lock step with the automobile; only the oldest parts of our cities were designed when horse and carriage ruled the road. What does this comparison show us? In Europe, transit is looked upon as transportation for the masses, but in North America we tend to view it as transportation for people who can't afford a car. In actual fact, you can blend transit and the automobile nicely to save costs and reduce your carbon footprint.

If you live in an area where transit is an option, you might want to consider taking the bus, subway or streetcar once or twice a week to see if you can live with the perceived inconvenience. By taking transit, you will reduce your costs for gas and parking, as well as tailpipe emissions. In conjunction with transit, you might want to have a compact or subcompact car to use, as an inexpensive run-around vehicle to take on the days that transit isn't an option. Buying a good used car and supplementing with transit can keep your overall ownership costs low.

There are other options as well. Have you ever heard of car-sharing? Over the last 10 years, the idea of people sharing a car and its costs has really taken off. One of the most successful car-sharing groups is based in Vancouver, called the Co-Operative Auto Network. Here is how it works. For a small refundable fee, a person becomes a member of the co-op, so they are part owner of the hundreds of cars available to drive. Whenever a member needs a car, van or pickup truck, they call a central number and book a car in for a set amount of time from one hour to a whole day. Cars are scattered all around the city core and members have a special key to get into them. Prior to driving the vehicle, the member fills out a log. The cost of gasoline, insurance and maintenance is included. There is a fee for every hour driven and kilometre travelled, but it is a fraction of the cost of running your own car. Currently, the costs are $2.50 an hour. Their average user spends $117 a month in total costs for using a car, when they need it, compared to hundreds of dollars to finance, insure and maintain their own personal vehicle.

The co-op buys solid used vehicles, with the emphasis on practicality and reliability, such as the Toyota Yaris and Corolla, Mazda3 and 5, Mini, Ford Ranger and VW Beetle. Car co-ops are popping up all over the country. Another company, Zip Car, operates in Toronto, Montreal and Vancouver. Zip Car's costs are higher because it is a for-profit enterprise versus a not-for-profit co-op, but its fleet of cars are newer, with a wider range of appeal. A new outfit called CityFlitz operates car-sharing programs in several Canadian cities where they charge only $1 a day. The trade-off is that the car is wrapped in advertising. For driving a mobile bill-board, the person behind the wheel is charged only $1. Sounds like a great trade-off to me.

How can car-sharing work into your desire to save money and go green? For a person who has access to transit and feels comfort-able using it, the ability to augment transit with a car on-demand can be liberating. Car-sharing gives you access to a car when you need it, but you don't have to carry the costs associated with owner-ship all the time. It's also wonderful for families who have a primary vehicle but only need a second car once in a while. Using car-sharing is not as easy as walking out your front door and driving away; there is extra effort in booking the car and walking the few blocks to pick it up and drop it off. But for many, it's worth the free-dom this service provides.

Car-sharing has indeed taken off. The Co-Operative Auto Network in Vancouver has grown year after year, and more people sign up to become members—every time the price of fuel jumps. Just for fun, I did a search of this co-op and Zip Car, and found two cars within two blocks of my house. Pretty easy! If you're in the market for a car for occasional use, or maybe you need a second car only once in a while, car-sharing might be an option.

THINK ABOUT HOW MUCH TIME YOU'RE ON THE ROAD

Another and perhaps more drastic way to reduce your carbon foot-print is to move closer to where you work. There's a new trend in Canada toward more density in downtown city cores, to have people living closer to work, transit and entertainment. This too is similar to the old cities of Europe which grew along with hous-ing stock, so people have the choice to live downtown.

Just like buying a car, living in the city is a compromise. You lose space and the prices are higher than in the suburbs, with big-ger houses, larger lots and longer commutes. For example, I live very close to the city core and my wife stays home with our two boys. We have a family car and she uses it most days to run errands and take kids to events. But because of our proximity to every-thing, she drives only 6,000 to 7,000 kilometres a year. In contrast, a colleague of mine in the newspaper business lives in an outlying suburb and it takes him more than an hour to get to work in the morning and almost two hours to get home at night due to traffic congestion. The mileage he puts on his car, along with the expense of gas, parking and maintenance, had him rethink his travels and now on most work days he takes the train. Another person in the same office decided to sell his home in the suburbs and move into the city core. His new house is smaller but he gets to spend more time at home, less in the car and he saves time and money. He says he misses his old home, friends and familiarity, but his new life is much less stressful. City living is not for everyone; I totally understand the need to want space and openness. But for those who are open to the idea, living closer to work and transit will reduce the amount of fuel you burn.

For people who aren't in a position to move closer to work and who put tens of thousands of kilometres on their vehicles, it's even more important they choose a vehicle that is as efficient as possible—and manufacturers are doing their part to make this happen.

One way is the use of smaller engines with turbo and superchargers, to give the same power as a larger engine yet with better fuel ratings. Ford will introduce a large number of 2010 models with engines that feature a combination of turbo chargers and direct injection technology to achieve a 20% improvement in fuel efficiency, yet provide the power drivers are used to. Ford calls this EcoBoost, and the company believes these technologies provide savings. Ford claims that in contrast to spending extra money to buy a hybrid or diesel engine and the time it takes to recoup the added expense with fuel savings, EcoBoost technology will be a fraction of the cost. For example, the Ford F-150 pickup truck has been the best-selling vehicle in North America for decades, and the majority are sold with V8 engines. Ford claims the EcoBoost turbo-charged V6 engine will deliver a similar driving experience to pickup owners who are accustomed to a V8. Another offering could be a Ford Fusion sedan equipped with an EcoBoost 4-cylinder in place of a V6 engine.

Ford isn't the first manufacturer to utilize turbo technology in order to achieve fuel savings; many European auto makers have been doing it for years, such as Saab, VW, Audi and Volvo. One example is the 2.0L turbo direct injection 4-cylinder found in many Audi and VW products. It is a potent engine with ample horsepower, and it even has more torque than the V6 engine offered in many of the same vehicles. Since VW/Audi introduced this engine, it has been a runaway success; the majority of buyers opt for this cheaper, lighter, more fuel-efficient option, and they sacrifice nothing in performance. One thing that I should warn you about: turbo engines usually need to run on premium fuel so the amount of savings is diminished by associated higher costs.

Just like turbo-charged gasoline engines, the latest trend is diesel engines with the same turbo-charged, direct injection layout but with even better results. Diesels produce less CO_2 than gasoline engines and provide 20% to 30% greater efficiency with all the power any driver would require.

To prove the ability of diesel engines, Audi entered the famous 24-hour race at Le Mans with a diesel car and the test has proven very successful—Audi has won the event many times. Le Mans was a great way to promote the advancements the company made in diesel technology and to prove that a diesel car doesn't have to be slow. The diesel you might buy today is nothing like a Le Mans car, but the slow, smelly and noisy diesel engines you might have experienced in the past are history.

As I mentioned at the beginning of chapter 1, buying a vehicle is a compromise. As you add more and more factors into the equation—from vehicle size to the type of engine to what you're going to use the car for—you'll be better able to narrow your selection. You might have had an idea of the type of vehicle you wanted to buy, but hopefully you're considering other choices, options that will be able to fill your needs at the same time as conserve fuel and reduce emissions. There's a lot of new technology available today that we didn't have just a few short years ago, so consider vehicles and technology that you might not have in the past and try them out. You might realize that something new fits just as well as the tried and true. Drive smart to save green!

4 Buying a safe vehicle

I'm sure many drivers can remember, as a child, driving in the family car with no child safety seats, standing up in the back seat or riding in the front seat without a seatbelt. I can remember the thinking of the day: if children were in the back seat, they were okay. Little did our parents or we know the huge risks we exposed ourselves to.

When you are shopping for a new or used car, it is always a good idea to consider crash worthiness and the added safety features available in today's vehicles. What safety features should you consider essential? Here is an explanation of many of the elements that go into making a vehicle safe and the cutting-edge advancements that might soon be available in all cars.

THE VEHICLE'S DESIGN AND TECHNOLOGY ARE MAJOR FACTORS

The type of vehicle and the way it is designed is crucial to how well it survives a severe crash and you should take this into serious consideration when shopping.

When a vehicle is designed, it is intended to have certain sections crumple like a piece of paper to absorb the shock of an impact and protect the occupants. If you have ever driven past a crash on the road and seen the whole front end of a vehicle pushed in, or the trunk squished up against the rear window, this is intended to happen. The energy of the impact is absorbed as the vehicle is crumpled so the speed at which the occupants are slowing down is reduced relative to the speed of the car. The crumple zones are sacrificed and take most of the impact—not the people inside. In contrast, the centre of the vehicle, where the occupants sit, is called the safety cell, and is designed not to crumple but stay as strong as possible to protect the passengers from the impact.

Cars have different crumple zones than SUVs, vans or trucks. Cars typically score higher in crash tests but more of these techniques are being implemented into other vehicle designs; in fact, over the years, manufacturers have improved their products with safety in mind. Today's vehicles are designed from the ground up to protect the occupants from a severe crash. In Canada, crash tests are conducted to ensure vehicles to comply with Canadian requirements, but the industry benchmark is the US crash tests performed by the National Highway Traffic Safety Administration (NHTSA). They do tests to determine a vehicle's safety in front and side crashes but not rear crashes. The vehicles are then rated from one to five stars based on crash performance. You might have noticed some auto makers highlight a vehicle's 5-star crash rating in advertising. Manufacturers have been so successful in achieving the highest rating that the NHTSA is considering making the tests more stringent and the 5-star rating harder to achieve. If you are considering buying a new vehicle, it is a good idea to check the NHTSA's web site for the results on each vehicle: www.safecar.gov.

Just as the design of a car helps save the occupants in a crash, the handling of a vehicle can help avoid a collision in the first place. Vehicles with independent suspension are more stable in emergency situations than those without. Also, pickup trucks and SUVs based on pickups are not as agile as they tend to be top heavy, leading to more rollover accidents. Buying a vehicle with an independent suspension, which is lower to the ground, will result in better handling than a top-heavy truck. Cars, vans and crossover vehicles tend to have the best handling.

Air bags have been another huge advance in vehicle safety, and in Canada front air bags for the driver and passenger have been mandatory for years. Air bags are a controlled explosion meant to inflate the bag for a very short period of time. The initial air bags introduced in the early 80s were primitive compared to today's versions. The latest air bags have a different rate of expansion (explosion) depending on the speed of the collision. At lower speeds, the air bag deploys with less force. This is designed to offset injuries from the air bag deployment in low-speed fender benders. (At a low speed, the rapid inflation of older air bags could cause more injuries than the accident itself.) These new "two-stage" or "logical" air bags have helped to correct the problem—but keep in mind an air bag is there to save your life, and in doing so might cause minor injuries.

Only front air bags are mandatory, but even on some of the least expensive models side curtain and side air bags have become standard equipment. Side curtain air bags are designed to protect the head in the event of a side collision. The air bag runs along the roof of the vehicle from the front window, just above the doors to the back window and falls down and inflates. When they hang down they look like a curtain; this is how they got the name. Since there is only a piece of glass separating your head from the vehicle hitting the side of your car, these curtain air bags provide a vital cushion and, I believe, they should be included on any person's new car shopping list. These air bags can also stay inflated for a longer period of time to mitigate head injuries in the event of a rollover.

Many buyers are confused about the differences between side air bags and side curtain air bags. As mentioned, the curtain provides protection for your head; the side air bag protects your body. Some manufacturers install the side air bags in the door, and they inflate to provide a cushion in the event of a side collision. Other manufacturers install them in the side of the seat so the bag moves forward and backward with the seat adjustment, always keeping them in the proper position. The bags in the door tend to be a little bigger to provide a wider area of protection and the ones in the seat are a bit smaller but pinpoint the protection.

The very latest development in air bag technology is rear curtain and knee air bags. The rear curtain bag drops down from the rear, mostly on minivans, to provide extra protection to the occupants sitting in the third row of seats, just in front of the back hatch. Knee air bags are becoming more popular on expensive luxury cars and are meant to keep the knees of the front passengers from hitting the lower part of the dash in a frontal collision. Dashboards are meant to absorb some of the impact from the body in a crash, but these new air bags lessen the number of lower body injuries sustained from severe collisions.

I would recommend that anyone looking at a new or used vehicle buy one with front, side and curtain air bags. The good news is that these are being offered in most new cars as standard equipment, but some manufacturers of less expensive models are omitting them to keep prices down. To me, the extra money involved is worth it for the peace of mind. Knee and rear air bags are on the cutting edge, but look for more and more cars to be equipped with these too.

Do you know the most powerful system in your vehicle? No, it isn't the engine, but the brakes. Imagine the force it takes to stop a vehicle weighing thousands of pounds or going down a hill at high speed; plus, brakes must be reliable over and over. The forces at work are remarkable and are vitally important for your safety. When you examine any potential new vehicle, check to see what type of brakes it has. It is best to have disc brakes on all four wheels. These are common on most of today's cars, but some less expensive or older models still use drum brakes on the rear wheels. Not to say that drum brakes are unsafe; it is just that disc brakes have more braking force and have a greater ability to stay cool when used in extreme conditions.

Most of today's vehicles have anti-lock brakes (ABS), but many buyers are not aware just how much ABS technology has changed and how it has revolutionized the safety systems in modern cars. You might have heard of traction and stability control or intelligent all-wheel drive. Well, none of those advancements would have been possible without the invention of ABS. ABS was first widely introduced in the 1980s, initially on high-end cars and later on entry-level cars. The technology works by way of sensors on each wheel which talk to each other through a computer, and the program can tell if one wheel is spinning slower than the others when braking. The braking system then releases the brake of the wheel that has stopped turning just enough to keep the wheel rolling in order to keep control and steer the car. This is done repeatedly, in fractions of a second, so that the driver doesn't lock the brakes and can continue steering the vehicle while braking. It also prevents sliding down the road. Over the years, the electronics companies that supply the car manufacturers with ABS have improved the technology immensely. You might have even experienced a vehicle with an early generation of ABS. The first versions sent pulsating sensations through the brake pedal and loud noises from the car that could sometimes startle the driver. Today these systems have been refined to the point that they don't intrude too much. They also help to eliminate the driver's first reaction—to take their foot off the brakes—when in fact they should keep pressure on for the best possible outcome.

Most new vehicles have ABS as standard equipment, but on some less expensive models the manufacturer will omit ABS to keep the price down. I urge any buyer of a new car to spend the small additional amount to get ABS. The ability to stay in control on slippery or wet roads in an emergency is worth the extra cost. If you're shopping for a used vehicle, look for one equipped with ABS; there are plenty on the market.

I am reluctant to include four-wheel drive and all-wheel drive as a safety consideration when buying a vehicle. Although these systems do help provide better traction in adverse conditions, they also leave the driver with a false sense of security. There is an old saying, "All-wheel drive will only get you to the ditch faster." You might have experienced this too. Driving in winter takes patience, finesse and traction to get around. How often have you been driving in snowy conditions and witnessed an SUV driver whiz past in their 4X4 or AWD only to see them a few minutes later in the ditch down the road? I've seen it over and over, and so has the RCMP. I remember a news story from a few years ago: the RCMP asked drivers of SUVs and pickup trucks to slow down and take more care when driving over snow-covered roads. That particular winter the RCMP had to attend to countless single-vehicle accidents because 4X4 owners had been driving beyond their ability and ended up in the ditch. Car drivers traversed the same roads more sensibly, without incident. The way you drive, the attitude you have, along with proper winter tires, will get most vehicles through our Canadian winter conditions. Yes, 4X4 or AWD vehicles do have better traction, but keep in mind the ability to stop and steer is the same for all vehicles. I would rather see potential buyers spend their money on good winter tires instead of AWD. That said, investing in both is a good idea, and for those who travel in off-road conditions, AWD and 4X4 is advisable.

As I mentioned, ABS has been a significant breakthrough in vehicle safety and has facilitated the advent of traction and stability control, rollover protection and intelligent AWD. The same sensors that detect if a wheel has stopped turning in the ABS are used to determine if the wheels are spinning. In the case of traction control, if a wheel is spinning, the sensor will send a signal that will activate brake force to that wheel, and at the same time cut power to the engine until the spinning tire regains traction. Traction control has become widespread throughout the industry on new cars and provides much-needed safety. Imagine driving through a snow-covered intersection and seeing a truck—unable to stop—sliding toward you? To get out of the way, your first instinct would be to hit the gas. But if the road is slippery, all the gas will do is spin the wheels and you would be left a sitting duck. If, however, the same car was equipped with traction control the wheels would slip, then the system would apply brake force and cut engine power for a fraction of a second so the wheels could regain control. This happens over and over again in split seconds, allowing the vehicle to keep moving forward and out of harm's way.

As for stability control, take that same principle and apply it to all four wheels, regardless of whether they have power. The sensors have the ability to sense changes in wheel speed and in the case of a slide or skid, a vehicle with stability control can apply braking force to certain wheels and simultaneously cut power to the drive wheels to keep the vehicle going in the right direction.

I had a chance to attend a safety course with Porsche at its driving school in Alabama several years ago. The vehicles we drove were Porsche Cayenne SUVs that had the ability to drive with or without stability control. We did several runs through a set of pylons to simulate a sudden lane change at 50km/h. Imagine a very quick, sudden jerk of the steering wheel from one side to the other. The first run was without traction control and the Cayenne was easily able to turn quickly from one lane to the next. But when I straightened the wheel to continue down the new lane, the vehicle kept rotating until we slid 180 degrees and ended up facing in the opposite direction. The second pass was done with the stability control on. Just as before, the Cayenne made the lane change without any trouble, but when straightening the wheel, instead of sliding completely around, the vehicle was able to complete the manoeuvre and continue down the road. The computer sensed that certain wheels were sliding and the vehicle automatically reduced throttle and applied braking forces to certain wheels to keep it from sliding. These systems are so seamless that the driver has relatively little idea that they are at work; it is only when they are switched off that the power of stability control becomes evident.

You might be thinking, "That's nice for Porsche owners!" Not to worry, the systems used in most vehicles equipped with stability controls work in the same way as the one developed for Porsche. And keep in mind that the manufacturers don't make these systems all on their own; they are developed by outside suppliers that in turn sell them to auto makers. So you never know—the system you buy just might be related to the Porsche technology.

These advanced electronic aids have also helped to minimize the risk of a rollover in vehicles with a higher centre of gravity, such as SUVs. In many instances, the parameters of the stability control systems have been adapted to include the angle at which the vehicle is relative to the road. The computer can tell if a rollover is about to occur, and the same braking and throttle reaction is orchestrated to mitigate the risk.

You may be aware of advertising slogans from AWD manufacturers stating that their vehicles have the ability to sense road conditions and direct power to the wheels that have traction. What is really going on is the same traction control sensors talk to the AWD computer, and in addition to applying the brakes to wheels that have lost traction, the AWD system shifts traction away from the wheel that is slipping to the wheels that still have traction. So not only can the driver continue down the road with the ability to provide power, but at the same time the vehicle regains traction to the wheel that is spinning.

This is all wonderful stuff and it can be attributed to the advent of ABS way back in the 1980s. The good news is that more and more manufacturers are including these advanced safety systems as standard equipment on most of today's more expensive cars and optional equipment on most others. The additional expense of upgrading to these features is an investment in the safety of your family.

One of the best investments is a proper set of tires. We've all heard the phrase "where the rubber hits the road," but it is absolutely true that the only thing keeping your vehicle on the ground are four small patches of rubber, and those contact points are vital to the stability and safety of your car. Keeping your tires in good condition includes inflating them to the proper pressure, ensuring the alignment of the suspension isn't wearing them prematurely, and that they are not worn to the point of being ineffective. The proper type of tire is also crucial to its longevity, and it ensures your safety in different driving conditions.

This brings me to the term all-season tire. There really isn't an all-season tire; I like to call them three-season tires because they are a compromise. They work well enough in the summer, they're pretty good in the rain—but when the temperature turns cold the rubber hardens and loses traction. When you add in ice and snow, the ability of an all-season tire is limited. I'm a firm believer in using summer or all-season tires in the spring, summer and fall and switching to winter tires for cold weather.

The province of Quebec recently implemented a law requiring that all vehicles be equipped with winter tires from November 15 until April 15, or face severe fines and loss of insurance coverage.

Such laws are common in northern European countries, and for Canada, it makes sense to use winter tires even though it isn't the law in most provinces. Many people resist buying winter tires due to the expense; but when you take the additional cost, and average it out over the four to five winters these tires will last, it's a small price to pay for additional safety. When shopping for winter tires, it is vital that you get a set that has the approval of the Rubber Association of Canada. Every product that qualifies as a winter tire has a small symbol on the side depicting a mountain with a snowflake inside. Make sure to ask the technician if the tire you're purchasing qualifies as a true winter tire, and ask to see the mountain/snowflake symbol. In the past, winter tires had "M+S" stamped on the side, which referred to "mud and snow." Today, M+S is used on all-season tires. I would hate for anyone to buy a tire thinking they're protected in winter and find out that their M+S tire is really only an all-season model.

This mountain/snowflake symbol was developed because a young woman was killed on the snowy highway between Vancouver and Whistler. On a drive soon after her parents installed what they thought were winter tires, the woman's vehicle spun into oncoming traffic. Her parents had been told that the tires were true snow tires, when in fact they were only all-season tires. Think of the heartache they must have endured; they were only trying to do the best they could for their daughter, and it cost her life.

That crash happened in 1994, followed by an inquiry from the RCMP, the local coroner and the Insurance Corporation of British Columbia. The coroner's report recommended that Transport Canada implement performance specifications for winter tires to clear up the confusion surrounding winter tires and all-season tires. Transport Canada worked with the Rubber Association of Canada, and the Rubber Manufacturers Association in the US decided to implement a new test procedure for winter tires. It took until 1999 for the tire manufacturers to adopt the new test and that same year they implemented the new winter symbol. The good news is that there is no longer any confusion, and anyone buying winter tires can do so knowing that they meet the very latest standards.

I encourage anyone purchasing a new car to get the dealership to order you a separate set of inexpensive steel wheels and winter tires so you will have them when the cold weather arrives. When you're negotiating the price of the car, tell the sales person and manager that you would like them to order you winter wheels and tires at their wholesale cost! Remember, you are still going to buy a vehicle from the dealer; but you might be able to take advantage of their buying power and get the winter equipment for wholesale. If the dealer doesn't want to do this for you, there are plenty of shops that can order inexpensive steel wheels and equip your vehicle with winter tires for a lot less than dealers sell their winter packages for. Keep in mind, the dealership wants to sell you a car, and if that means making no extra money on a set of spare wheels and tires, then at least they have made money on the sale of the car, and you will be a much happier client.

In a perfect world, I would love it if dealerships offered a winter wheel package the same way they offer rust proofing, paint sealer and extended warranties when it is time to close the deal. This would make it easier for new car buyers to get properly equipped for winter with little hassle.

The reason a spare set of winter wheels and tires is preferable is to avoid mounting and unmounting the tires on the same rims each season. Plus, the more expensive alloy wheels found on some cars can be saved from the harsh salt and winter conditions. A painted steel wheel with a hubcap or second set of inexpensive alloy wheels will keep your more expensive summer wheels looking good for a longer period of time.

You might be asking yourself about the need for two sets of wheels and tires—and whether there is anything on the market that will work all year around and not cost any more money. Over the last few years, "all-weather tires" have become increasingly popular, but these should not be confused with all-season tires. All-weather tires have passed the new test for winter conditions and have the mountain/snowflake symbol, but they can also be driven year-round. This saves the need for two sets of tires. The all-weather tires have a unique compound that allows them to stay soft and stick to the road in cold weather yet not wear out too quickly on dry roads or in hot weather. They work for most applications, especially city driving when the roads are cleared quickly. But for areas where the roads are regularly covered with snow, the best way to get winter traction is a pure winter tire.

Be it with a winter tire or a very capable all-weather tire, the safety advantages are so great that all Canadians should be driving on them, even if it isn't the law.

Just as ABS has led to so many other safety advancements, the advent of automatic cruise control has developed into the next big movement in vehicle safety. How can cruise control help save lives? Automatic cruise control is different from the cruise control that you may have used in the past. Instead of just monitoring the speed of the vehicle, today's systems have laser, sonar or camera systems that also detect objects around the car.

Unlike conventional cruise control, these new systems actually slow the vehicle as it approaches a slower-moving car without driver involvement. When the vehicle in front speeds up again, the active system adjusts the speed accordingly, helping to maintain a safe distance from the vehicle in front. Currently, it is only expensive, high-end vehicles that have these types of systems, but as the years pass this technology will be as common as ABS.

One application already being implemented is crash avoidance. Even when the cruise control is not being used, the sensors can tell the computer that the vehicle in front has slowed quickly and if action is not taken a crash might take place. The car will then give off an audible warning to the driver; in some cases there is a flashing light projected onto the windscreen and the vehicle pre-loads the brakes for maximum effectiveness. In addition, some vehicles then adjust the active suspension to make the vehicle more manoeuvrable for emergency steering.

I've had a chance to drive many cars with these systems and on one occasion it actually saved me. I was looking down at the radio as I approached stopped traffic. The warning alarm sounded and I looked up and saw nothing but brake lights, and I jammed on the brakes just in time to stop. I wasn't travelling at high speed but it did prevent a fender bender.

There is an even more advanced version of this system that will actually brake for the driver if no action at all is taken. In my example, if I had done nothing, the car would automatically slow down for me, even coming to a complete stop. This advanced crash avoidance system is currently available on only very few vehicles, but it's not hard to imagine a day when it is used widely. Crashes could be reduced drastically as the car would take over when drivers are inattentive or otherwise not prepared.

The active cruise control can be used for busy highway driving as well. The car automatically keeps a safe distance from the vehicle in front; it adjusts speed to the flow of traffic and provides an extra level of safety. There is even an application for bumper-to-bumper traffic that lets the driver relax while the car automatically creeps along in busy traffic with little input from the driver. Amazing!

Just as these systems monitor the speed of the vehicle in front, they can also monitor the lines on the road. If the driver starts to wander out of the lane, a warning beep and vibration through the steering wheel alert the driver to take action. This lane departure technology is being included in many of the same vehicles that have active cruise control. Just think, we might some day let the car do all the steering and braking for us.

The electronic goodies don't stop there. Many of today's vehicles have blind spot warning systems that alert the driver to another vehicle travelling in the blind spot. We have all done it—attempted to change lanes, looked to see if there is a vehicle next to us, moved the steering wheel only to have the vehicle next to us honk their horn. It's an innocent error that happens daily, but with the help of sensors and cameras the blind spot is eliminated. Most of these systems have a light that is located either on the side mirror or inside the car, very close to the side mirror. When the turn signal is activated, the system will alert the driver to a vehicle in the blind spot by flashing a light. If the driver sees the light, they don't change lanes; if the light does not come on, then it is all clear and safe to make the lane change. Some of these systems are always on regardless of the driver's use of the turn signal. All the driver has to do is look, and if the light is off, it's safe to change lanes. This is particularly helpful when an emergency lane change is required without time to signal or look.

One convenience that I could not live without is also a safety feature—park assist. Most vehicles today have an option that helps the driver manoeuvre into tight parking spaces through the use of sonar sensors, a camera or both. When the vehicle is put into reverse gear the system activates, and in the case of sonar sensors, a series of beeps will alert the driver. As the driver gets closer to an object the beeps become more frequent and eventually turn into a steady tone when the driver is too close to the object. Once you have had a vehicle with this system, it becomes second nature to park without having to strain your neck to look back, plus the driver can manoeuvre into very tight parking spots without fear of scratching the bumper. My last three cars had this system, helping protect all of them from ever receiving a single scratch from parking, which means they pay for themselves in saved bodywork. The camera versions have a tiny super-wide-angle lens tucked under the trunk lid. The image is then displayed on the inside of the car on the same screen as the navigation system or a small second monitor. Instead of looking back through the rear window when reversing, the driver can watch the display to see what's going on behind the car. Some vehicles use the camera and the sonar system together for maximum assistance. I prefer the sonar system because the camera's wide-angle lens can distort the view, and when it is raining, snowing or dark, the view isn't always clear. Sonar doesn't show you what's behind; it just alerts you that there is an object and that is all that really matters. Some luxury vehicles even use four cameras to display a 360-degree view of what's going on around the vehicle. There is the regular camera on the back of the car, along with small units placed under the side mirrors and one hidden inside the front grille. When the vehicle is put in reverse, all four views are placed on the screen and the driver can see exactly what is going on from all angles. This is particularly handy when parallel parking, because the driver can tell how close the curb is to those expensive alloy wheels!

So, how is a parking assist system a safety feature? There have been tragic instances where a young child has run out behind a reversing vehicle and been seriously injured or killed. If these cars had been equipped with sensors, the driver would have been alerted and applied the brakes, and in the case of a camera, the driver would have been able to see the child. Not only is a parking system a treat for the driver to use, it can help prevent tragic accidents and it also pays for itself in reduced bodywork. Sounds like a win, win, win to me.

As stated earlier, the crash tests in the US include front, side and rollover ratings for today's vehicles, but little testing is done for rear collisions. However, insurance companies and car manufacturers are working on this, what I call the last frontier of vehicle safety. Some of the biggest claims to insurance companies are soft-tissue-related injuries resulting from rear-end collisions and whiplash. When an impact occurs, an occupant's head snaps back and only stops when it comes in contact with the headrest. Today, the headrest is referred to as the head restraint since it does just that—restrains the head from snapping back in the event of a rear collision. If you're looking at a new vehicle, try to find one with active head restraints. When the vehicle is involved in a rear collision, the weight of the body pushing back into the seat activates the head restraint, pushing it forward closer to the head, so the distance travelled by the head is lessened, helping to reduce whiplash. If you're interested in a car without active head restraints, or an older vehicle, it is always a good idea to sit in the seats and see if the head restraint is close to the head. Some vehicles have the head restraints several inches from the back of the head; it is best to have the seat back as erect as is comfortable, with the head restraint as close to the head as possible.

I'm sure you've heard of some of these safety features and some might be new to you, but it's important to know that we have become more protected than ever in the event of an accident. Buying a car is a compromise, but one area I stress you don't scrimp on is safety. Not all of these features are available on all cars, but if you can afford to buy a vehicle with as many of these systems as possible, your likelihood of surviving or avoiding a collision is greatly enhanced.

5 Cool runnings

The idea behind this book is to help demystify many of the terms used to describe vehicles and identify what items you might want to include in your next purchase. Hopefully, through each chapter you have been able to narrow the type of vehicle you require, from a car to crossover to SUV. You might have been able to decide if a regular gasoline, diesel or hybrid is in your future and which safety features you desire. The next step is to figure out which of the latest cool options you want and which ones you can go without. Many potential buyers are misled when they go shopping for a vehicle, because the prices advertised are typically for a base model, and to get the vehicle just the way they like is much more expensive. Features such as bigger alloy wheels, metallic paint, leather seats and upgraded engine choices are all factors to take into consideration, but the latest creature comforts and electronics are what really drive up the price. I can remember a friend looking to buy a car and she turned a $16,000 compact into a $23,000 model just by adding more and more features. The numbers get much bigger with the more options available and can also depend on the type of vehicle you're buying. Some import manufacturers charge much more for similar features only because their brand is more prestigious. ("More prestigious" must be code for "charge more for the same thing.") So here are some of the latest and most popular "cool" features that might be tempting to include in your next vehicle and my thoughts on whether they are worth the added expense.

KEYLESS ENTRY AND START

Over the last five years, the ability to enter a car and start it without even holding a key has blossomed from just luxury manufacturers into more mainstream vehicles. For example, the very first time I experienced a system like this was on a Mercedes–Benz worth more than $100,000. Now the base model Nissan Altima has a keyless ignition as standard equipment. So what is keyless entry and start? The key still needs to be carried to open the doors and start the engine, but it can stay in your pocket or purse and need never be removed. The vehicle can detect that the key is close to the car and when the driver touches the door handle the power doors unlock automatically within a fraction of a second. Once inside the car, the key is still recognized and the driver only needs to push a button on the dash to start and turn off the car. This is all wonderful stuff, but it does take a while to get used to, it's easy to forget the key since you don't have to handle it and some of these systems can be finicky to operate. I must admit that once you adapt to the keyless way of life, it can become liberating. But, in my opinion, if it's not standard equipment on the vehicle you're considering, it might be worth a pass. Put it this way: your entire driving life you have had to handle a key to enter a car and start it, so it's not like you're missing anything. But if it comes included, then enjoy never having to hold keys again.

HEATED AND COOLED SEATS

Can you remember the very first time you sat in a car with heated seats? Bliss! If you have never experienced the sensation of heat radiating over your backside on a cold morning, there is nothing better. Heated seats were developed to keep the driver and passengers warm even though the engine had not heated up enough to change the ambient air temperature inside the car. A warm bum takes your mind off the cold air, it's that simple. I would even suspect there are fewer marital spats when your bum is cozy. I would never order a new car without seat warmers; they take the sting out of a cold day. Plus, for anyone with a bad back, they keep your muscles happy, like a good hot water bottle. I remember discussing this feature during a TV broadcast, and I received an e-mail from a viewer who purchased a car with seat warmers, based on my suggestion. They later wrote to tell me they too had a happy bum, and will never look back!

Most cars have a heating element inside the seat, like a heating pad, but the new trend is toward perforated seats with the ability to heat and cool your nether regions. Rather than an element, the heat is blown up through the perforations with limited effect. They do get warm, it just takes longer and the cooling side of the equation is downright odd. Imagine taking your sweaty self and blowing cold air on your tush. Sure, it would cool you down, but the sensation is very strange. I love heated seats, but I'm no fan of having a fan on my fanny. It could just be me, so for sheer fun give them a try.

The next level of decadence is heated rear seats and a heated steering wheel. Heated rear seats are uncommon, but if they're offered and are not too expensive, I say go for it. In one car I owned, we had heated rear seats. On a long road trip with friends we used the seats to amuse ourselves. When a rear passenger fell asleep we would turn on the rear seat warmers and sure enough, in about five minutes, the person in the back woke with the same sensation of having their hand in a warm cup of water. Oh, the fun.

A heated steering wheel is a true luxury item that is fantastic on a cold morning. But if including this in your new vehicle would throw the budget out of whack, take a pass. If it's within your price, there's nothing better than a warm bum and warm hands.

LEATHER SEATS

I've noticed through the years that drivers who have never had leather seats in a car really desire the perceived luxury that comes with this option. Let's go through the pros and cons.

Pros

Leather can look and smell wonderful, it's easy to wipe down and can often bring added value to a car upon resale. It is perceived to be the premium-seating surface for most buyers, so image is important.

Cons

Leather seats are rarely fully covered in leather. The seat surface is often the only part that is actually leather; the side bolsters and the back are mostly of vinyl. The quality of leather on some cars is very poor—to the point that they look more like vinyl than leather. Leather seats can be cold in the winter and very hot in the summer. Also, the driver can sometimes slide around on leather seats, and if you own your vehicle for a long time, the leather can crack and fade. Leather seats are also typically more expensive.

Cloth seats don't have the same appeal but they are warmer in the winter, cooler in the summer, you don't slide around as much, plus many new fabrics clean up very well. Many of the man-made leather seats look just as good as real leather, plus they don't crack or fade and will look like new for the life of the vehicle.

I totally understand the attraction to leather seats, but they are a luxury feature and if you can live with the perception of cloth seats, you will save money and be just as, if not more, comfortable.

OF SOUND AND SATELLITES

So much has changed so quickly with stereo and entertainment features in today's vehicles. It was only a few years ago that I test-drove a car that still had a cassette player, and this was a $100,000 luxury model!

If you have not had a chance to drive in a new vehicle with the latest electronic gadgets, it can be somewhat overwhelming. Satellite radio, iPod interface, Bluetooth playback, internal hard drives, voice activation, rear DVD players and MP3-capable units are the latest features available. What items are worth the money and which ones can you live without?

Many of us have an iPod or MP3 player, and the ability to play these units through the car stereo has been limited in the past. You might have even attempted playing your player through the old cassette deck or used a small FM transmitter to do the job. Most of today's new cars have an auxiliary jack as standard equipment; even inexpensive compact cars come with them. This allows the iPod to be played by choosing the auxiliary function on the stereo. It won't display the song being played or allow you to choose a song or artist from the radio. All song selection still has to be done directly from the iPod. This means that the iPod needs to be within reach of the driver or passenger.

The latest way to access an iPod or other MP3 player is through an interface that allows the music selection to be displayed and changed on the radio display. The beauty of these systems is that the iPod can be stored out of the way, usually in the centre armrest, for convenience and so potential thieves don't see it. Other advantages include charging the player as it is being used, and not having to look down farther than the radio to change music. The standard auxiliary jack idea works well enough, although it isn't as seamless as the latest interfaces, but if cost is a factor, it still does the job. When choosing a trim level of a potential vehicle, an MP3 adapter is worth a look. If you're buying a used car made before the days of MP3 players, there are very inexpensive radios that can be installed that have iPod interfaces included. It is always a good idea to keep the factory radio after installation because some potential buyers like to purchase cars as original as possible. Regardless of the choice between auxiliary jack, interface or aftermarket unit, these MP3 players have essentially replaced the CD player and changer. They are the future, so they are worth the investment.

Most new car manufacturers through either Sirius or XM providers have adopted satellite radio integration. In the US, these two companies have merged but in Canada they are still separate entities. In a new car, the manufacturer usually includes the satellite service for a trial period ranging from three months to a year. After the trial, you are required to pay a monthly fee to retain access to the satellite stations. Is it worth the cost? Satellite channels range from any kind of music you can imagine plus comedy channels, sports, politics, business, talk, religious and international channels. So the answer is yes and no. If you drive a lot and spend hours in your vehicle, it might be worthwhile. In all the vehicles I drive, satellite is usually included and I can tell you from experience being stuck in traffic for hours, the wide array of possible channels really helps pass the time.

In 2007, I was driving the new Buick Enclave crossover. (You know, the one that Tiger Woods drove.) It was a hot summer day and I was approaching a bridge on the Trans Canada Highway when all of a sudden the traffic came to a complete stop. There was a tractor trailer on fire in the middle of the bridge and I had no way of getting off the road. So, I had to sit and wait, and wait and wait for the fire to be put out and the truck removed. It took more than four hours! First, I was glad I had a full tank of gas. Second, I was glad I hadn't had three cups of coffee before I left. And third, I was very happy that I had satellite radio on board. I think I listened to every channel to pass the time, from comedy to politics, even the BBC news. It was a lifesaver.

Not only is satellite radio advantageous for four-hour truck fires, it also offers uninterrupted service across the entire continent. If you happen to be driving from Toronto to Florida for spring break, for example, you could keep the kids entertained with the same channel all the way.

One thing to keep in mind is that installing satellite radio into a factory radio after the fact can be complex, so even if you don't activate the service it might be worthwhile getting a radio that is compatible, because if you ever change your mind and want the service, it can be switched on very easily.

I personally like having satellite radio in a car. It isn't all I listen to; I prefer the local radio for news and traffic, but it is nice to have the option. Consider the cost of the service and truly ask yourself if you want to pay for the radio every month? If not, the regular AM/FM stations are still accessible and free.

Blue and Black Technology

What used to be the radio has now become the central command centre for all the communications and navigation for today's vehicles. In addition to regular CD, radio and satellite radio, some of these powerful units have the capability to include cell phone activation, text messaging, Blackberry or iPhone integration and hard drives like a home computer.

Bluetooth connectivity is the ability for any device that is Bluetooth-enabled to connect to the car. In the case of a cell phone, the driver is able to receive calls without having to lift and hold the cell phone. When a call comes in, the radio is muted and the ring of the phone is heard through the speakers. By pushing a button, usually on the steering wheel, the driver can hear the caller through the stereo and can be heard through a hidden microphone. This is a wonderful advancement in communications but more importantly safety. Many countries and even Canadian provinces are adopting laws that ban the use of hand-held cell phones in the car, so buying a vehicle with this technology included goes a long way to reducing distractions—and avoiding possible fines. If you're in the market for a used car, only vehicles made in the last few years will have Bluetooth connectivity, but that doesn't mean you can't have it installed. There are plenty of aftermarket Bluetooth kits that can be wired into an existing stereo, and the use of a wireless earpiece eliminates the need to hold the cell phone. Just beware that you don't get out of the car with the wireless earpiece still in place, because nothing screams *Star Trek* like the people you see wearing this thing when walking around. Unless you like *Star Trek*—then beam me up!

Bluetooth also means that a driver can call from the car without holding the cell phone, and if it is equipped with voice commands, then the driver needs only to ask for a certain number, and the phone will dial it automatically. ("ET, phone home" might come to mind.)

The next level of cool is the integration of a smart phone, like the revolutionary Canadian invention, the BlackBerry. BMW was the very first auto maker to include access to the BlackBerry functions on the navigation screen. Drivers have the ability to look through address books and select phone numbers by scrolling through the menu on the screen. There are now vehicles that can access the same type of information for the Apple iPhone. Many of the functions that smart phones have are not yet accessible through the vehicle's interface, but that might be a good thing. Can you imagine the accidents caused by drivers surfing the Internet while they drive? Not a good idea.

The next level of integration is the ability to play back music and even search for music from a handheld device without touching a thing. Ford has the Sync system (developed with Microsoft) that allows the driver to play back music stored in a Bluetooth-enabled smart phone without ever having to plug it in. When the smart phone or MP3-capable device is plugged in, the driver has even more control. The driver can use voice commands like the name of a song, artist, play lists, category of music or even saying "next song" into the microphone, and the Sync system will do all the work.

I had a chance to drive the Ford Focus, which was the first to utilize Sync, and was amazed by the ability of the car to perform many advanced functions. When driving, all I had to do was say a command and Sync would find the song I was looking for. If I wanted to fast forward, I said "Next song." It was that simple. Sync also has the ability to read out text messages through the car stereo. If the driver receives a text that says "Can you pick up bread on your way home?" a computer-generated voice will read it out through the stereo. This eliminates the dangerous practice of trying to read text messages or operate the phone while driving and there are even standard text replies that the driver can use in response. The amazing thing about the Sync system is that it is standard on many Ford and Lincoln vehicles and an option for less than $500 on cars without it.

Other manufacturers have similar systems and more are being developed with every new model, so how do you know what to look for and spend your money on? One key feature is the ability to place and receive calls through the radio without holding a phone. More and more provinces are banning cell phone use when driving, so you might as well be ahead of the curve. Plus, once you have driven without holding the phone, you will wonder how you ever lived without this convenience. The level of integration all comes down to price and what you feel comfortable paying for. If a vehicle you're interested in buying has advanced smart phone integration or playback capability and it is within your price range, go for it. If, however, this new technology is going to stretch you past your budget, you can live without it. You can go hands-free by purchasing a separate earpiece for less than $100—just don't look like a "Trekkie" and wear it while you walk around!

One of the latest trends in car entertainment is an on-board hard drive that enables the vehicle to be filled with music from a home computer by inserting a memory card into the dash. Once the music is installed, there's no need for an MP3 player or iPod interface, the music is already downloaded into the stereo. There are some vehicles with 30 or 40 gigabyte hard drives, so the capacity for music, podcasts, play lists and even talking books is vast.

Map? Who Needs a Map?

One of the biggest selling features for many buyers is a navigation system. These factory-installed units typically cost thousands of dollars and are often part of a package or bundle of options that send the price of a vehicle through the roof. The question you need to ask before you splurge big money on built-in navigation is: how much will you use it? The line I always use is, "I know how to get back and forth to work." The truth is, we mostly use our vehicles over and over for the same routes, so a navigation system is really useful only on occasion. Is once in a while worth the cost? If, however, you work in a field such as real estate, sales or shipping, then a navigation system might be worth it.

There are many navigation options today that will help you keep the price reasonable if you think a device is required. Portable units have come way down in price; I regularly see navigation modules from TomTom, Garmin and Magellan on sale in most electronics stores for just a few hundred dollars. The beauty of these units is you can program your destinations in the comfort of your own home before you leave on a trip. These systems can be taken with you when you rent a car, they can be shared between different vehicles in a household and they can usually be updated just by plugging them into your home computer. One word of caution: do not leave a portable unit in the car, as they can be stolen very easily. In contrast, built-in units are limited to one vehicle, they're expensive, and to update the maps you need to buy expensive DVDs from the dealer.

In addition, many smart phones such as BlackBerry and iPhone have navigation programs that can be used instead of a built-in unit and they are always updated because they pull the data from the phone supplier on a need-to-know basis. They are not preloaded.

I don't use navigation often and one of my cars is more than 10 years old, so when I need to find a location, I use my BlackBerry or print the directions out beforehand from a navigation and map website such as MapQuest. When using my BlackBerry, once the address is put into the phone, it acts like any other portable unit with maps, directions and even a friendly voice to guide the way. The drawback to a phone-based system is the cost for airtime.

General Motors has been very successful in promoting its OnStar communications system that is available on most of its new products. This subscription-based service can be used as a hands-free phone, emergency response tool and even navigation device. At the touch of a button on the rear-view mirror, drivers with vehicles equipped with OnStar can connect to the OnStar call centre. For navigation information, the driver relays the address to the operator who in turn sends a small package of information wirelessly to the vehicle. The driver then starts the navigation and the voice guides the driver to the destination through commands. There is no navigation screen, and the driver doesn't have to pay extra for a navigation unit; all they have to do is pay a subscription fee to OnStar. Another important feature included in the service is collision notification. In the event of an accident in which the air bags deploy, the vehicle automatically sends a signal to the OnStar centre. An OnStar representative communicates with the vehicle and checks to see if anyone has been injured and even sends emergency personnel if there is no response. OnStar and its navigation capabilities is one development that, I believe, is worth the service fee. There are several packages offered to GM owners, so price out what you believe is a tolerable level of service—and paying for navigation as you need it is a clever idea.

Pass the Popcorn

Ask any parent of small children who have a rear DVD entertainment system in their vehicle and they will tell you that it can be a lifesaver on a long journey. As mentioned earlier, I often get a minivan for family vacations for room and comfort, but also because most are equipped with a rear entertainment centre. In most systems, there is a centre-mounted drop-down screen, which can be viewed from the rear seats. Other systems include small screens mounted on the back of the front head restraints so each rear passenger can watch their own screen. The drawback of the centre-mounted system is that the drop-down screen can limit the driver's view out the back of the vehicle from the rear-view mirror. The smaller, personal screens get around this problem, plus each child can be watching their own selection.

Most car manufacturers offer rear entertainment systems as an option, and they are often fully integrated into the vehicle's sound system, which allows all passengers to hear. Or, for more privacy, the rear passengers can listen via wireless headphones. Some systems are even compatible with video game players. The beauty of separate screens is that one child can be playing a game and the other watching a video. It's pure bliss on a long trip.

There are also many aftermarket options available for buyers who have purchased a vehicle without rear entertainment. Just like built-in navigation systems, these factory units can be very expensive and for less money they can be installed after purchase. (Keep in mind that if you lease a vehicle and install a rear entertainment unit, any damage to the roof might need to be paid for when the lease expires.) On the other hand, if you own a vehicle and sell it without the rear entertainment system, it can be transferred to the new car, so the cost can be averaged out over more than one vehicle. Having a built-in unit is best for people who drive long distances on a regular basis, such as back and forth to the cottage or weekend skiing trips. If you want a system like this for occasional use, another option is to buy a portable video player for a couple of hundred dollars, or a handheld video game player. These can be used in the car but also at home and when flying. I do like it when I get a car with rear entertainment but I have also driven for longer periods without one and a portable video player is just as effective.

Deciding which options to spend money on is a personal choice. On less expensive cars, many of the features I have described are offered only on the most expensive trim levels or not at all. Higher-priced models tend to include more standard features, so spending more for a vehicle with more features can sometimes be cheaper than adding them to a cheaper car. It's a good idea when shopping to get an apples-to-apples comparison. Look for vehicles that are similarly equipped or do the math on what it will take to make them similarly equipped. As I mentioned, the base price is often misleading; figure out which features you must have and which ones you can live without.

6 Now I'm comfy

We recently had a long-term big blue Hyundai Entourage mini-van to use as a production vehicle for driving while we film cars, haul camera gear and transport our technical staff. It worked flaw-lessly; in fact, the Entourage is great value and we have had several as long-term vehicles. The problem wasn't the way it drove or any mechanical defect—it was the driver's armrest. Every time our director got into the van he had to lift the armrest to access the seatbelt buckle, but in doing so placed the armrest in a position that wasn't comfortable. To return the armrest to the proper posi-tion, he had to raise it fully and then adjust it accordingly. I know what you are thinking . . .so what? This might not seem like a big deal if you only have to do it once, but repeating the same thing every single time became a nuisance. In fact, we did a segment on one of our shows about this point—and lo and behold—Hyundai fixed the problem the very next model year. Ah, the power of TV. (I wish—I think it was just coincidence.)

When something about a vehicle bothers you, it won't go away. In fact, I have found the opposite. The position of the armrest, the angle of the seat or the reach to change the radio dial are all things that will annoy you, not only initially, but over time, and might even cause you to rethink your purchase. The time you spend shopping for a new vehicle will help eliminate many of these frustrations down the road. By being diligent in not only driving but also evaluating the vehicle, just like an auto reviewer, you will weed out vehicles that don't meet your needs and you'll also be able to pinpoint items that could frustrate you over years of ownership.

Not only do you have to review each vehicle for problems the driver might face, but for passengers as well. For example, if you are older or have an elderly person in your vehicle on a regular basis, then buying a vehicle that is easy to get in and out of is paramount. You wouldn't want Grandma to have to climb into a big truck; she needs to be able to get in easily and be comfortable. Take into consideration the application of the vehicle. As I mentioned in the beginning of chapter 1, buying a vehicle is a compromise, so look for one that can offer the best appointments and the least sacrifices.

My father has had bouts with back pain for as long as I can remember, and on one visit he was having a particularly difficult time. The car I was reviewing that week was a very fancy but low-riding Porsche 911 Turbo. I decided to take my dad out for dinner but the thought of getting into the low-slung Porsche was daunting. Luckily, the car was also a convertible, so with the roof down, my dad was able to open the door, walk into the car and slide down into the seat. Without being able to take off the roof, we would have had to come up with another plan, probably a taxi. If I was responsible for my father's transportation needs, a Porsche would be out of the question. Something more sensible and with easy access would be on the list.

The design and shape of a potential vehicle has to work for most applications. A single person won't buy a sedan on the off-chance that Grandma will ride in the back seat, but drivers who use their vehicles on a regular basis for more than personal transportation should keep this in mind.

A test drive should be just that. Does a potential vehicle pass the test? Don't get caught up in the shiny paintwork and new car smell. Get down to work and check to see if a vehicle meets your requirements. Be critical: this is your hard-earned money at stake, and not spending it wisely might lead to buyer's remorse after the initial buzz of owning a new car wears off.

SEATING

The first thing to do is sit in the driver's seat and take a moment to look and feel around. Does the seat adjust to a comfortable position that allows you to see outside easily but at the same time read and reach all the gauges? All vehicles have adjustments to move the seat forward and back and tilt the seatback, but the ability to adjust the seat beyond that is often determined by the price. Inexpensive cars usually have basic back and forth adjustments, but more and more models also have the ability to raise the seat. This height adjustment allows for much better positioning relative to the steering wheel and pedals and is essential for shorter drivers who need to see over the steering wheel and down the road. Some vehicles can't accommodate a taller driver's need to adjust the seat low enough, resulting in a horrendous condition called head rub where the driver's head literally contacts the inside roof, creating an unattractive flat hairdo. And for bald drivers, the resulting rub can cause redness. All kidding aside, a seat that doesn't adjust low enough is just as uncomfortable as one that doesn't go high enough. Take the time to try a few vehicles with different seat adjustments to get a feel for what appeals to you.

I'm sure you have shopped for shoes and spotted the perfect pair, only to find one size is too small and the next size is too big and no half sizes are available. The same can be true for manual seats. There is nothing worse than driving a car where your legs are either scrunched up or too far from the pedals because the manual seat has pre-set lengths. This is also often true for the seatback. To eliminate this problem, it is best to go with power adjustable seats, which are easy to use and allow for small adjustments unavailable with manual seats. In addition, adjusting a manual seat while driving is difficult and sometimes dangerous, whereas power seats can be adjusted with the touch of a button. This is not only safer but the driver can continually adjust the seat for better comfort and leg circulation on a long trip. Power seats often come with memory positions for more than one driver. When inside the car or activated by the remote control, the seat automatically adjusts for a particular driver. If you share a car with other family members, this feature is very convenient.

Is the seat hard or too soft? The type of foam a manufacturer uses is very important, just like the different materials used in a mattress. I'm sure you've had a great night's sleep in a hotel—or conversely a miserable one—depending on the bed. The same is true for the different types of foam used in seat construction.

I always remark on just how comfortable and supportive the base Toyota products are; they use great foam. In fact, when I attended the Yaris launch, I asked a Toyota representative about this and he mentioned that a lot of the materials and seat design used in their Lexus luxury division filters down to the Toyota products. The next time you sit in a car, any car, pay attention to the comfort of the seat and the firmness of the foam.

When testing a vehicle, the only real way to know if it will be comfortable is to take it out for a long test drive. The comfort of the seat will become apparent only after spending some time using the product.

The bottom of the seat not only has to offer support for your thighs but not dig into the back of your legs, cutting circulation. The seatback has to provide support not only through the lower back but also the shoulders, which is often overlooked by many drivers. One regular caller to my radio show asked why lumbar support is not offered on many cars. His bad back requires such support, and he was frustrated by the options on the market. If you're in the same position, make sure you test a seat for comfort and lower back support.

I have received numerous e-mails from drivers who are too tall to fit in most cars, too wide to fit in most seats or are disabled and have special requirements. The bottom line is, the seat needs to be comfortable and that includes headroom, legroom, adjustment and support. Too often buyers will buy a vehicle without really doing the proper amount of research and soon become disappointed. Make sure you take the time to determine all the differences in seats to find what best suits you. No two people have the same requirements. I prefer a firmer seat and my co-host on *Driving Television* often complains that the seats I like are too hard. It's all a compromise.

Take time to sit in the vehicle and reach for the items inside the car. Feel the height of the steering wheel and the position of the pedals and how comfortable you are doing all of the above. One of the easiest ways to get the right seating position is through tilt and telescopic steering. Many cars have the tilt feature, but the ability to move the wheel closer with a telescoping steering column is even more important. It really helps when the seat is not able to move into just the right position for you. In fact, some manufacturers include adjustable pedals to help drivers attain that perfect position. The pedals can be moved closer or farther away, which is especially helpful for shorter drivers. Still, I would take telescopic steering over adjustable pedals any day.

It is also important to spend time researching the back seat. Imagine buying a car and taking it home only to realize that your two teenaged sons won't fit in the back seat? Stranger things have happened.

One mother wrote me to ask my opinion on a certain car, and she mentioned that she has a teenaged son who plays hockey several times a week. In my reply, I asked her to not only test the car herself but also take her son along with his hockey bag and stick. If her son doesn't fit comfortably and the hockey gear won't fit, then keep on looking. In another example, a mother at my son's school asked me about a vehicle to replace her seven-passenger minivan. She wanted to get a five-seat compact SUV, even though she has three large, almost teenaged sons. When I pointed out that her three sons would be cramped in the back seat, she told me that they rarely use the vehicle together as a family. I stressed to her that being comfortable and having options (such as an SUV with an occasional third row of seats) is a better buy than squishing the entire family into a compact SUV. I don't think I convinced her; she didn't seem to care much about their comfort. There is a lesson here: be nice to your mother or she will squish you in the back seat with two other smelly teenagers!

When I was shopping for a vehicle with my wife, I spent two hours walking around the showroom floor with not only two child safety seats but also a double stroller. At the time, my oldest son was in a child seat and my youngest was in a newborn rear-facing portable seat. We got strange looks from a few salespeople as I put the car seats and stroller in and out of several vehicles, testing them all for fit. In that one trip, I was able to narrow our shopping list by eliminating most of the vehicles at that dealership.

Like that hockey mom, it's important for you to really put potential vehicles to the test, not only for your own requirements as a driver but also for passengers and cargo. Scratch any that don't fit the bill off your list. Take those strollers, child seats, golf clubs, sports equipment, camping gear, tools or whatever else you might carry around into the dealership to make sure they fit!

CONTROLS AND CONVENIENCE FEATURES

Not only do the seats have to be comfortable, but the placement of controls and convenience features is also vital to your long-term satisfaction as owner. You need to be able to easily reach things that you will use frequently, such as the radio, heat controls and cup holders. You'd be surprised how many cars I review that have poorly placed controls, from the stereo being too low to see while driving, to the turn signal lever in the wrong position to the cup holders being almost useless.

A friend of mine in the radio business purchased a car and loved everything about it, except for the cup holders. You see, he loves the Super Big Gulp from 7-Eleven, and try as he might, he couldn't get those large cups to fit into the holder. It wasn't the bottom of the cup that was the problem, it was that its height prevented it from sliding under the dash to get into holder. This might seem like a small issue, but for a guy who loves more than one litre of his favourite beverage, it was heartbreaking.

I don't know why German car makers refuse to make good cup holders, but they have some of the worst designs, in my opinion. Read this next bit in a German accent: "One should not drink za coffee vile motoring." You get the idea. To Germans, driving is separate from drinking coffee, but not to Canadians. Is there a German equivalent to Tim Hortons? I believe the American auto makers do cup holders the best, followed by Asian manufacturers. Is the cup holder big enough? Will a drink spill easily? Is the holder easy to clean out? And are there enough for everyone in the vehicle? Check it out and see to it that you can remain hydrated while driving.

As recently as the past year, I have tested a few brand new models with poorly designed interiors, and I often ask myself how they could get it so wrong. In one instance, the stereo display had a glare and was not readable in bright sunlight even when wearing sunglasses. In another example, the rear-view camera wasn't visible from the driver's position. To see the readout, I had to lean way over to the passenger side. The worst offenders are radio controls, which are integrated into a computer and are too confusing to operate.

TECHNOLOGY BEEFS

This point reinforces the previous chapter in regard to options and ease of use. Many of the options in today's complex vehicles distract the driver and make the job of operating the vehicle harder, not easier. Some of the technology has been developed just for technology's sake, in my opinion. Do the ever-more complex computer interfaces make driving any easier? No. Do you really need all the gadgets offered? No. Should you eliminate vehicles with these complex systems off your list? No. What any potential owner needs to do is to understand just how these computers work, and it is essential to have them explained by a knowledgeable person at the dealer. In many instances, fumbling around on your own, trying to figure out the intricacies of a computer system, will only frustrate you. If, however, a sales rep can navigate you through the functions and show you how easy they are to understand and operate, then advanced electronics might be a consideration. I have used a few of these systems over and over and I still can't master them, even when giving my entire attention to them. Some of them are intuitive and others are not. Some drivers will take time to learn a new system and eventually become proficient, but others won't. I prefer computer interfaces that are intuitive and quick and easy to learn and navigate. Some of the really good systems will allow the driver to operate the car without ever having to enter the computer at all; it is there for when the driver has the inclination to use it. A system that takes too long to master may be poorly designed, and if you think a vehicle you're testing is too complex, try something simpler.

Shopping for a car is like a science experiment: you have to do some research beforehand, so get out and test the ones you're interested in and come up with a final conclusion. The Internet has become an invaluable resource for car shoppers. Online, most manufacturers list their features, available trim levels and the accompanying options. This will give you a good starting point from which to narrow potential candidates. What the Internet also provides is reviews of vehicles by people like me who do this for a living.

The great thing about auto reviewers is that we get to drive anywhere from 80 to 100 vehicles a year, and with that knowledge you can get a feel for a product before you actually get into a dealership and test it for yourself. Keep in mind the vehicles you see on TV and the ones reviewed by journalists are typically fully loaded with all the gadgets, so sometimes the review doesn't exactly reflect the vehicle you might be able to afford.

When I get e-mail from readers or viewers, like the hockey mom, who want my opinion on a certain vehicle, I often provide short answers and ask them to test the vehicle for themselves and let me know what they think. Taking another person's word for something can lead to disappointment if the vehicle doesn't live up to your expectations. The very best thing you can do is get out and test a vehicle for yourself. When you do, critique the interior and design, just like an auto reviewer, and you will be able to see the vehicle's flaws and attributes, not just the shiny paint and new car smell.

PartThree

Cost, Value and Doing Your Homework

7 Buying versus leasing

When the time comes to head out and actively shop for a vehicle, the choices of financing often come down to a standard term loan or leasing for a set period of time. Let's look at the way a lease is different from a loan and the significant changes that have taken place in wake of the 2008 financial crisis.

The traditional way to buy a car for generations has been to save up and buy the vehicle with cash or go to the bank and take out a loan. Over the last few decades, manufacturers have established their own financial entities to provide loans to customers, instead of buyers having to go to a bank. This has worked well for the auto makers, as they have been able to make money on the sale of the car as well as on the interest paid over the term of the loan. The benefit of traditional financing is that once the loan has been granted and the vehicle is sold to you, it is always in your name. The bank or financial institution will have a lien on the vehicle until it is fully paid for, but it is yours to do with as you please. For example, if after a year, a young couple with a sports car decides to have a baby and they need a bigger vehicle and want to trade it in, no problem, that's their choice. Conversely, if they keep the original car and the loan is paid off, the vehicle lien is released, and the car continues to be in their name. Many people like traditional financing because it gives them the freedom to make changes whenever they want or need to.

As the price of vehicles has continued to trend higher, buyers are taking out longer-term loans to pay for them. I'm sure you've seen advertisements on TV or in the newspaper for car loans as long as six or seven years. This is done to reduce the monthly payments and to compete with lease arrangements, which tend to have even lower payments. For many people, the idea of actually owning a vehicle, rather than "renting" it over a long period, provides a certain level of comfort. Some buyers are attracted to a car loan because they don't understand leasing and believe that leases are just a fancy way to rent a car, not own one. My brother is a perfect example.

He likes to buy a car and pay it off as soon as possible and drive it as long as he can without payments before spending money on his next new car. I've had countless conversations with him about the idea of possibly leasing a car, but he has no interest—he likes the idea of having an asset, which he owns and has total control over. I totally understand the logic.

Leasing, on the other hand, appeals to the vast majority of Canadians who always seem to have a car payment. The logic for these buyers is if they are going to be paying for a car every month, then why not lease and get a new vehicle every few years under full warranty? Plus, new cars have the latest safety features and are typically more efficient. In a recent radio interview I conducted with Canada's leading automotive consultant, Dennis DesRosiers, he mentioned that even though many Canadians lease cars, at the end of the term they typically buy the vehicle using a loan, so in fact they are buying a vehicle over the same six or seven years. However, some hand the vehicle back to the dealer when the lease term expires, so they get a new car every few years.

Here is a basic explanation of how a vehicle lease works:

Have you ever taken out a traditional car loan from the bank, and then four years later tried to sell the car? What often happens is that the amount you owe is exactly what the car is worth. All you have paid for over the four years is the privilege to drive the car—you really don't have any equity in it. That is essentially what a lease is, but instead of taking out a loan for the entire purchase price, you pay a monthly fee only for the amount the vehicle is depreciating. The lease company or car manufacturer decides ahead of time what they believe the vehicle will be worth at the end of the lease. For example, a $40,000 car might be worth $20,000 after three years, so all the leaseholder is paying for is the $20,000 the vehicle has depreciated. At the end of the lease term, the person leasing has the option to buy the vehicle for the remaining $20,000 or just drop off the keys and move on to another car. This provides the person leasing with the ability to drive a new vehicle for less money than the same car with traditional financing over the same period of time. Let's take the $40,000 car with a three-year traditional loan, excluding interest. The cost to buy the vehicle is $1,111 a month, but a lease over the same period would be just $555 a month. For many people who feel they will always have a car payment, the idea of having a lower monthly commitment is easier to swallow and they get to drive a more expensive car than they might have been able to afford. There are also several financial benefits for some buyers to take into consideration when leasing, and I'll explain those later.

Over the last few decades, the trend in Canada has been to more and more leases. In fact, until the financial meltdown of 2008, roughly 50% of new cars rolling off lots were leased. When the credit crisis hit the major banks, the ability for auto manufacturers to provide leases was seriously affected. You might have heard of the phrase "asset-backed commercial paper." When a bank or financial institution lends money on an asset such as a car or house, the loan is often re-sold to another institution. What happened in the US housing market is that sub-prime mortgages that had been re-sold became worthless, as banks had to foreclose on buyers who couldn't keep up their payments. Consequently, the whole asset-backed commercial paper market was affected to the point that nobody would buy these assets anymore—the market was dead. Car makers who re-sold their lease portfolios in the asset-backed market had no buyers, so the business ground to a halt. As a result, the ability to obtain a lease has been seriously affected. Not to say that leases are not available, but the biggest impact has been on the domestic manufacturers and some imports. Foreign companies that have better balance sheets and don't re-sell their lease portfolios still offer leases, but in many instances the rates are not as good as they used to be and the monthly payments are higher.

Vehicle leasing was also affected by other factors, including the record high gas prices we experienced in 2007 and 2008. As I mentioned, the company leasing the vehicle forecasts the residual value of the vehicle at the end of the lease term. In the earlier example, the residual for the $40,000 car was $20,000. What happened in 2007 and 2008 when gas prices shot up was that vehicles that used more gas, from pickup trucks to SUV or performance cars, were not as popular so they dropped in value. The companies then had vehicles coming back from lease that were worth less than the already agreed price. Instead of buying the vehicle for the set price at the end of the term, many people just returned the gas guzzler and the lease company had to absorb the loss. Why would someone buy a vehicle for the established price of $20,000, when the actual value in the marketplace was $15,000? This example of losing $5,000 on one vehicle was multiplied by thousands, as many lease holders just walked away when the term was up. Lease companies were hit with massive losses and the resulting impact has made many of them rethink their residual prices.

Vehicle prices were not only affected by the high price of gas but also the complication of a high Canadian dollar. Canadian car prices have always been set for what Canadian buyers would bear, and the difference in currency valuations. The market always dictates the price. It might take a while, but the price of cars will usually level out with comparable US prices.

Remember when our dollar was way down in the 60-cent range? Auto manufacturers couldn't adjust prices upward to compensate for the low dollar value because Canadian buyers wouldn't accept higher prices. The real price of vehicles in Canada was very low compared to the US at that time. In fact, there were many businesses set up that started shipping cheaper Canadian cars south of the border to buyers looking for a deal. Sound familiar? The opposite occurred when our dollar hit par with the US dollar; more and more Canadians went shopping in the US and imported those cars back to Canada. Also, the same companies that were shipping cheap Canadian cars south reversed the trend and began shipping cheap US cars into Canada. The market spoke very loudly when the dollar hit par, and the onslaught of cheaper cars coming into the country opened a flood of changes in our home market. Canadian auto companies, in response, adjusted prices through promotional rebates and eventually lower retail pricing, which help to level out the market. Remember, the market always dictates the price. There were still some luxury vehicles that were cheaper to buy in the US, and those vehicles continued to flow into Canada until the financial crisis hit and our dollar dropped back down to the 80-cent range. In fact, after our dollar crashed in the fall of 2008, car prices were not adjusted and the prices paid were well below what a similar vehicle would cost in the US. As our dollar fluctuates, manufacturers can't adjust prices as quickly, so at times we pay more for new cars and other times we pay less.

Just as the fluctuation of the Canadian dollar over the last few years has affected new car prices, it has also had an impact on used vehicles. When manufacturers offer rebates on cars or if they drop the price, the residual values of cars purchased before that time also have to be adjusted in the used market. There were many vehicles purchased by individuals and dealers from the US, and the impact of lower Canadian prices and cheap US cars and trucks caused a decline in the used market. This, along with the high price of gas, was the perfect storm in the leasing business; as vehicle values dropped, people returned them instead of buying them out.

I got caught in this storm along with many other Canadians. The vehicle that my wife drove to get groceries and cart our two boys around was a leased V8-powered SUV. In 2005, we decided to lease for the first time because our plan was to buy out this higher-end vehicle at the end of the term. Well, in three years, the price of gas sky-rocketed, the value of the Canadian dollar shot up, the number of cheaper US vehicles coming into the country increased—and the resale value of our vehicle went down. When our lease ended in the fall of 2008, we had to decide whether to buy it out for the pre-determined price. Unfortunately, the amount we would have had to pay was substantially higher than the same vehicle was selling for in the used market. Even though we put money down on our SUV, it was $10,000 more than a similar vehicle was selling for, so we had to walk away after the lease and get a new vehicle, this time with a traditional loan. So, even though I am fully aware of how the car purchasing process works and I went into our lease with a different outcome in mind, we were sideswiped by the market and could never have forecast the events that took place over those three years. We ended up spending a little more than we would have to buy out our old SUV, and got into a brand new vehicle with a full warranty and more efficient V6 engine.

Even though the route we took sounds like a major blunder, the lease actually helped us save some money. The buyout amount at the end of the lease is predetermined, so even though we walked away, we weren't on the hook for a vehicle that was worth thousands of dollars less. The car company, not us, absorbed the loss. If we had purchased using traditional financing, any loss in value due to market conditions would have been our loss, not the lease company's. The upside to traditional ownership is that the depreciation is only realized when the vehicle is traded or sold. If you keep your vehicle for a long period of time, this really isn't too much of a concern. However, if you get a new car every few years, it can be quite a shock when the time comes to trade it in.

Most leases are offered through the financial services arms of auto companies, but there are also third-party leasing firms that often have different products. Most car makers offer the type of lease I have described, where you know in advance the amount it will take to buy out the vehicle. This is called a closed lease, which means the terms are closed and as a contract cannot be renegotiated. Third party companies sometimes do closed leases, but they often provide open leases or those that can change depending on market conditions at the end of the term. In my example, if I had an open lease, the company could have adjusted the buyout amount to reflect the reduced resale value of the vehicle.

Closed leases are really only best for new car purchases, because setting residual prices on new cars is much easier than on used vehicles. Imagine trying to figure out what a vehicle might be worth when it is six or seven years old. Lease companies recently got it wrong on three- and four-year leases, never mind older vehicles. Leasing a used vehicle really only makes sense on higher-end vehicles that are not very common. The rarity of a model can be a factor in keeping the residual price higher, and many people looking at getting into a higher-end car will often take open leases to keep the monthly payments low. Leasing is usually hard to get on a pre-owned car, so expect to take out a traditional loan or use your line of credit, and in some cases the auto manufacturers will finance their used products.

There are pros and cons to leasing a vehicle, so let's get into the reasons why you might consider this or traditional financing.

TAXES

When you buy a vehicle with traditional financing, the tax is due when you complete the transaction. Many people finance the tax as well as the purchase price of their vehicle, so interest is charged on both amounts. I don't know about you, but I don't like paying taxes and I sure don't like paying interest on tax! When you lease a vehicle, you pay tax only on your deposit. If you put no money down, the monthly payment includes the amount to lease the car plus the provincial tax and GST. This means you are not borrowing money to pay tax. The tax is due once a month, and in the case of a tax reduction, the payment is adjusted and you get the benefit. In my case, the GST was reduced to 5% from 7% over the three years that we had our SUV, and the monthly payments were adjusted accordingly. If I had purchased the vehicle with a traditional loan, the tax would have already been paid up front, with no way of taking advantage of the lower GST amount. On the other hand, if the GST had increased, I would have to pay more each month on my lease.

At the end of the lease term, if the person leasing the vehicle wants to buy it out, there will be tax due on the remaining amount. In our previous example, the lease buyout of $20,000 would also require GST and applicable provincial sales tax.

For people who are able to write off a portion of their vehicle payment for work purposes, a lease often has its advantages. Canada Revenue Agency has set amounts that can be written off per month and these are sometimes adjusted. It's a good idea to contact an accountant to see if leasing meets the requirements for potential tax savings in your case.

With traditional financing, there are also ways to write off the depreciation of a vehicle but the amount decreases as the value of the vehicle declines over time.

With either type of financing, it's always a good idea to seek advice from an accountant before you purchase.

INSURANCE

When you take out a lease, the company that holds the lease usually wants to protect their asset, and they typically want their vehicle insured with the highest coverage. In our case, we had to take out $5 million in liability insurance, replacement coverage and full comprehensive coverage. If we had purchased the vehicle on our own, we could have insured it as we saw fit. The insurance the lease company requires is not negotiable and can cost hundreds of dollars more over the course of the lease. Find out what the insurance requirements are before you sign on the dotted line, so you can compare real costs to other purchasing options. Unfortunately, I didn't do this, and the difference between the cost of our leased vehicle's insurance and our new crossover is about $40 a month. Over a three-year period, it cost me an additional $1,440! Now I know, and I hope you can learn and save from my mistakes. Between the hit we took on our lease and the extra insurance costs, I could have had a wonderful vacation in Hawaii. Aloha to all that cash.

ACCELERATED DEPRECIATION

When a vehicle is in an accident, it's usually worth less than a similar vehicle that hasn't been in a collision. I'm sure you've read classified ads for used cars that read "no accidents." In some provinces, the seller is required by law to disclose if a vehicle has been in an accident and how big the crash was. This new disclosure information has helped to create a market for "clean" vehicles and discount those that have been in an accident. Imagine buying a new car and within the first year getting into a crash that costs $5,000 to repair. Not only will there be depreciation because the vehicle is one year old, it will also have accelerated depreciation because of the accident.

This is where a lease can help. Remember that a closed lease has a set buyout price? Well, that price remains the same even if it has been in an accident, no accelerated depreciation. The repairs have to be done at a shop the dealer approves and to standards that the lease company requires, but if this is done, then the lease company—not you—absorbs the accelerated depreciation.

A TV anchorwoman I worked with always wanted a BMW sedan, and she eventually went out and got the car of her dreams. The dream turned into a nightmare as she watched a truck drive down the side of her new baby as it sat parked on the side of the road. Her pride and joy was only a few months old. The repair shop did a fantastic job and you never would be able to tell the car had been hit. However, because she lives in a province with disclosure laws, she would have to divulge the cost of the accident. The good news for our anchorwoman is that her fancy BMW was leased and she returned the car at the end of the term and got a new one, which meant BMW had to take the hit . . . pardon the pun.

Just as I walked away from our SUV because of market conditions when the lease expired, a bad accident—and the resulting value depreciation—might similarly cause someone to abandon a vehicle at the end of the term. A lease is like a second layer of insurance from accelerated depreciation. Remember, though, that this might not be the case in an open lease. If the value of the vehicle is lower than originally estimated at the outset because of an accident, the outstanding amount will be due at the end of the term. This is another reason that I like closed leasing.

BEWARE ADDITIONAL CHARGES

Can you imagine a taxi driver leasing a car for three years and returning it with 400,000 km on the clock, scratched bumpers, smelly interior, worn-out shock absorbers, no brakes and four worn tires? It sounds like a great deal for the taxi driver, but a lousy one for the leasing company. It would never happen. When a lease is written on a vehicle, the company predetermines allowable mileage limits and levels of acceptable "normal wear and tear."

A typical lease allows for 24,000 to 26,000 km per year, and a set charge for each additional kilometre. For example, if it's a three-year lease, the vehicle can be returned with a maximum 72,000 km driven on it. If this is exceeded, the person who took the lease is on the hook for the over-charge. The national average is in the 20,000- to 30,000-kilometre per year range, so a typical lease will cover most drivers. If you drive longer distances, then a lease might not work for you. The same is true for buyers who drive very little in a year; they won't be using their allocation of kilometres and will pay the same as a buyer who does, leaving money on the table. For high- and low-mileage buyers, traditional financing is a good idea.

There are also costs at the end of a lease for above normal wear. If the brakes or tires are worn past acceptable levels for a vehicle of a particular age, there can be additional charges to replace those components. If there are scratches and dings on the body or the wheels, missing parts or broken pieces, the leaseholder is responsible for the repair. On the inside, if there are rips, scratches, stains or wear that is out of the ordinary, you can expect to pay at the end of the lease.

When the lease is taken out, there is typically a security deposit held back by the company to help pay for any extra items that may need to be addressed when the vehicle is returned. Keep in mind that if a vehicle was purchased with traditional financing, any damage would also affect its value in the market. The person selling their own vehicle would have to repair it beforehand or be forced to discount the price. If a vehicle is abused, then the person who owns pays, regardless if it is leased or financed.

WARRANTIES

New vehicles all come with a basic bumper-to-bumper warranty for a set period of time, typically three or four years or a certain number of kilometres. Some manufacturers offer extended coverage for the main engine components, but if a buyer is looking to drive a vehicle that is fully protected, then they usually have to buy a new vehicle every few years. Keeping repair costs to a minimum is one of the main reasons Canadians like to lease a vehicle every few years. Leases also have the advantage of longer-term coverage over traditional financing.

When a three- or four-year-old used car is put out on the dealer's lot, it often has what is called a certified pre-owned (CPO) warranty, which is an extension of the original coverage. The vehicle isn't protected from bumper to bumper, but the majority of expensive components that could break down are covered. These CPO warranties are offered on used cars to compete with new vehicles and to provide a level of security that people require to buy used.

So, how does a lease help protect a potential buyer for longer? When you lease a vehicle, its ownership remains in the lease company's name and is signed over to you only if you chose to buy it out at the end of the term. What you are really buying is a three- or four-year-old used car from the manufacturer, just like the same vehicle on the used lot, except that you have knowledge of the car's history since you've been driving it. The vehicle coming off lease often qualifies for the same CPO warranty. Many companies at the end of the lease will put the vehicle through their repair shop and qualify it for the CPO program. Getting a vehicle "certified" usually costs $1,500 to $3,000, and that fee is added to the buyout cost. CPO warranties add coverage for an additional two years or a set number of kilometres, and in my opinion, are good value. Any vehicle heading into its fifth or sixth year with more than 100,000 kilometres will need some kind of repairs. Small fixes might only cost a few hundred dollars, but others can run into the thousands and the CPO can save the owner a ton of money.

My uncle purchased a used high-end German sedan with a CPO warranty, and over two years ran up more than $20,000 in repairs that would have come out of his pocket had he not had the coverage. High-end German sedan or not, a CPO warranty is a good idea and the fact that it can be transferred to another owner adds value to any vehicle at resale.

Remember that the CPO warranty is available only on a used car or when it comes off lease. If you buy a new vehicle with traditional financing, there is no opportunity to extend the warranty the way you can at the end of a lease. However, there are other options available.

The first is the chance to purchase an extended warranty when the car is brand new, usually at the time of closing the deal. The person in the business office that sets up the financing and other details of the transaction will usually offer such a package. When buying this additional protection up front, the buyer is paying for coverage well ahead of time and usually paying interest on the extra costs in their car payment. Plus, the owner might not know at the time of purchase if they plan to keep the car past the three- or four-year initial warranty. One benefit of leasing is that you have the option to have the vehicle "certified" at the time of the buyout. This gives you three or four years to decide if you want to keep the vehicle. It's like having your cake and eating it too.

Some manufacturers allow buyers to purchase an extended warranty after the fact. It's a good idea when you're in the business office going over the final details of the transaction, to ask if buying an extended warranty can be done at a future date. Be prepared to pay more; as time goes by and more mileage is put on the vehicle, the price of the warranty usually increases. The best price for an extended warranty is when the vehicle is brand new.

In my example, if I had chosen to buy out our SUV I would have asked the dealership to have the vehicle "certified" and paid the extra money to ensure I had extra warranty coverage. If I had purchased the same SUV with traditional financing and included an extended warranty when it was new, then I wouldn't have benefited from the coverage when I got rid of it three years later, plus I would have paid interest on the warranty. That said, the vehicle would have been worth more than one without a warranty.

If you're a person who likes to keep a vehicle for long periods of time, well past the three or four years of most leases, then buying an extended warranty at the time of purchase is an excellent idea. The cost will be at its cheapest and the coverage is usually the best. However, when purchasing or leasing a new vehicle, if you're unsure if you want to commit to it long-term, then delaying purchasing an extended warranty might be worthwhile.

THE NEW REALITY

Thanks to the 2008 financial crisis, compounded by dropping vehicle values, high gas prices and fewer buyers, auto makers have lost their shirts on leases. Very few car companies still offer leasing. The companies that still do have adjusted their interest costs and lowered the residual values so they don't get caught owing more money than the vehicle is worth. I don't believe this situation will last forever, because with 50% of the population relying on leasing to keep their monthly payments low, the car companies know that to keep people coming into the dealership they will once again have to offer leasing. For consumers, the cost of this convenience will likely increase as manufacturers ensure they don't get caught holding the bag again.

What many companies have done to compensate for the lack of leasing is try to move people into traditional financing by extending the terms up to seven or eight years. This can keep payments as low as leasing. In many instances, the interest on these extended loans has been very, very low and in some instances zero per cent. I suspect that after a few years of offering only traditional financing, manufacturers will miss the steady flow of lease-return customers coming into dealerships, and they will be forced to look at leasing again.

Leasing has been a wonderful tool that many Canadians have adopted to keep their monthly costs in check. Traditional financing will always have a place for people who want to own a car for a long period of time and have equity in their vehicle. Regardless of the financing tools you decide to use, it's imperative that you explore the full costs. Before you sit down and negotiate the price of a vehicle, it is important to ask the sales person or business manager the real costs of financing your purchase. Ask for the interest costs of the loan or lease, and in the case of a lease, you must ask for the residual buyout number and any extra insurance costs. Also ask if the vehicle you're interested in will be eligible for a CPO warranty, and in the case of financing, ask if the vehicle can be eligible for an extended warranty if you decide to buy coverage at a later date. This will give you a true comparison of prices ahead of closing the deal.

A perfect example of not taking the time to ask the important questions are friends of mine who leased a Honda Civic but didn't do the due diligence required before signing the lease. They didn't look at the fine print and were surprised by the high buyout amount at the end of their lease. The only number they focused on was the monthly payment and not the overall cost of ownership. In their instance, they had full intentions of purchasing the vehicle at the end of the term, but they weren't prepared for what the amount would be. Getting a great deal on a lease may only have a short-term benefit. Had they been able to take advantage of a long-term loan at a low interest rate, instead of leasing, or done a bit more homework, they would have been better off.

Not only should you research the type of vehicle you require, but also the financing you need to complete the purchase. Doing as much homework as possible on the vehicle and the financing options available will provide much more satisfaction, not only from driving, but with the peace of mind that you really have made the right decision.

8 Making your short list

Hopefully, after reading the first several chapters of this book you have begun to make a short list of potential vehicles. But before you finish, there is still some more homework to do. I know, I know, homework is no fun, but if you take the time to do a little more research, the end result will be much more satisfactory.

The reason I want you to look a little deeper is that there might be a vehicle out there that you haven't considered or even thought of. After all, we all have our preferences and prejudices when it comes to our purchases. Maybe the type of car your parents drove when you were a child has influenced what you're considering now. Perhaps the stories you heard from friends and family about their vehicles have swayed you one way or another. Like it or not, we all have preconceived ideas about what certain vehicles are like before we even try them.

In 2008, when Ford, Chrysler and General Motors were in Washington looking for financial assistance, there were some serious misrepresentations made about these companies. The mainstream media, which is not involved in the auto industry on a regular basis, and the public, who might not have driven cars from Detroit in the last several decades, were quick to jump all over the Detroit Three as poor-quality car makers. Sure, in the past, Ford, Chrysler and GM built cars and trucks that disappointed many buyers, but the truth is today many of the vehicles they build are as good as—if not better than—some of the import manufacturers.

As a person who gets to test drive all the new vehicles available in the marketplace, year after year, I have a pretty good understanding of what is out there and how things have changed. All the auto makers have improved the quality, performance, safety, finish, drivability and available features. Ford, Chrysler and General Motors needed to improve not only their financial business model but also their products, and over the last several years I have noticed a distinct upgrading in what they deliver to market. In fact, they don't just compete—some of the most impressive products I've driven are from Detroit.

In the sixth season of *Driving Television*, we conducted a comparison of mid-size sedans. The vehicle that won was the Honda Accord, but finishing in second place was the Chevrolet Malibu, and it lost by only one point. In that same comparison, we also pointed out the top vehicles in this class for quality. The winner of the JD Power and Associates initial quality report for mid-size sedans was the Chevrolet Malibu, followed by the Mitsubishi Galant and the Ford Fusion. This is a perfect example of misconceptions. The Toyota Camry and Honda Accord are not even in the top three, and these two vehicles are perceived as having some of the best quality in the business. Unless you do the research to find out what the real story is, you will never know.

Another example of improvements from domestic car manufacturers was at the 2008 Automobile Journalists Association of Canada (AJAC) annual car of the year valuation. Of the 14 different categories, General Motors won five—more than any other manufacturer—and it beat out well-established brands from Asia and Europe. For the last few years, GM has won the North American International Auto Show car of the year, for its Saturn Aura and Chevrolet Malibu. If you only read the mainstream media and listen to what people's biases are toward North American cars, you might never buy one. In reality, such results show these vehicles deserve consideration.

The reason I bring this up is because I want you to consider all the options that are available on the market today. Don't discount any vehicle just because of its brand; there are many wonderful models from every corner of the world and the quality is as good as it's ever been. You still have to do your due diligence, research and good old test drives to determine what is right for you.

WHAT TYPE OF VEHICLE ARE YOU LOOKING FOR?

Hopefully by now you're been able to at least form a list in your mind of the type of vehicle you're looking for. It might be a tall station wagon, crossover or a conventional wagon, but that shouldn't stop you from getting out and testing other vehicles in different classes just to be sure. It might be only after a test drive that you realize the model you thought you wanted isn't really what you're looking for.

Earlier in this book I mentioned friends of mine who bought a Jeep Cherokee, without even trying a minivan, and then found out it didn't quite fit their needs. If they had actually tested a minivan as part of a short list, they might have ended up with one in their driveway. Then again, it might not have been what they wanted and they could have crossed it off their list. Remember that old cereal commercial with the slogan, "Try it, you might like it"? Mikey tried Life cereal and indeed he did like it. You too might end up liking a type of vehicle that you initially didn't consider.

My co-host on *Driving Television* recently had her sister visit from out of town with her newborn baby. For their trip, she decided to borrow a minivan for a week. I recall my co-host telling me that her sister was determined to buy a compact SUV and wouldn't even consider looking at a minivan. After the visit, I asked my co-host how her sister enjoyed the minivan. She told me that, much to her sister's surprise, she fell in love with the ease of use that a minivan offers. Getting a baby in and out of the back seat, putting a stroller in the cargo area, convenient power sliding doors and overall easy access won her over. She even phoned home to tell her husband that a minivan was now on the shopping list.

Even when you develop a short list, it's still a great idea to test-drive all vehicles on that list just to make sure you're doing the right thing.

People don't just have preconceived ideas about different brands, they also form biases about the type of engines that work the best. My neighbour once said she would only buy a vehicle equipped with the V6 engine because her father, who used to be in the car business decades before, said that's the only power train to use. Well, after trying a vehicle with a smaller four-cylinder engine equipped with a turbo charger, she actually found that it would more than meet her needs, and he ended up buying it.

I often get e-mail from people who feel they need a hybrid vehicle for their short commute to and from work. When I point out the cost of a hybrid, combined with their short daily commuting distances, they realize that a small, basic and efficient four-cylinder runabout car might be all they need.

Just as your short list should include vehicles you might never have considered, you should also be open to a variety of engine choices. If you've never driven a diesel vehicle, testing one might open your eyes to a whole different driving experience. Someone who might not have considered a hybrid car might, after driving one, come to realize that the smooth quiet ride is just what they're looking for.

When assessing engine options, it's always a good idea to start with the smallest engine available and move up in power to find the choice that best suits your needs. For the vast majority of people, the current crop of powerful yet efficient four-cylinder engines will be more than adequate for a daily commute. In larger vehicles, many of today's V6s are just as powerful as V8 engines were a few years ago. Not only do you need to try different power train options, you also need to be aware that some vehicles require special types of fuel. If you live in an area with few diesel stations, then this type of engine might not be a good choice. Also, determine if a vehicle requires premium gas. It's called premium because it costs a premium. Higher octane fuel, in most areas of the country, costs 10 cents more per litre than regular gasoline. On a single fill-up of fifty litres, the premium fuel will cost an extra $5. Over the life of a vehicle, the extra fuel costs could run into thousands of dollars. Beware!

A former boss of mine who had always driven average domestic cars reached a level in his career where he wanted to make the step up to an expensive German luxury sedan. He called and asked my opinion about the vehicle, and I suggested he take it for a test drive to make sure that it would fill his needs. Sure enough, he fell in love with it and decided he wanted to take the leap. One tank of gas later, my phone rang again. This time his concern was about premium fuel. "Can't I just run regular gasoline in the car?" Since we're old friends, and I knew he wouldn't take it the wrong way, I said, "Don't be so cheap—you just bought an expensive luxury sedan and now you don't want to use the proper gas?" He sheepishly said, "Okay, okay, I get the point."

I've had dozens of similar phone calls from friends asking about premium gasoline. If an engine is designed for premium, it will run best on premium. It won't operate as if it was designed for regular fuel. The power, efficiency and overall drivability will be sacrificed with the poorer quality fuel. This is not to say that vehicles that require higher octane premium gas can't run on regular gas; it's just that they don't drive as well. In fact, all premium-loving cars can run on regular for times when premium isn't available, such as when travelling. The point of the story is that it's important for you to find out ahead of time if a prospective vehicle requires expensive premium gas so you can make an informed decision.

SAFETY AND COMFORT FEATURES

Another factor to include on your short list is safety features that are "musts" for you. Whether in new or used cars, you might not realize the sacrifices you may make in this area unless you're unfortunate enough to be in an accident. Used vehicles are not likely to have the latest safety features that a new, modern car will have, and there should be a minimum requirements to meet.

Safety features that I would consider essential on a new car include anti-lock brakes, front, side and curtain airbags, as well as traction and stability control. High-tech features such as automatic cruise control, lane departure warning systems, crash avoidance systems and others found in only the most expensive vehicles, in my opinion, are not crucial. These latest additions are the direction the industry is headed, but if you use common sense when driving, the basic features will keep you and your family safe.

When searching for a used car, I would insist on ABS and as many air bags as were available at the time the vehicle was produced. Traction and stability control are other features that I would include on my list. If the vehicle you're interested in didn't have these systems available when it was made, then cross them off your list.

The great news about buying a used vehicle is that the cost difference between the high-end, pricey version and a less expensive model diminishes with time. Shopping for a higher trim option car will often get you more safety features as standard equipment, but for a lot less cost than when it was brand new. When searching for a used car, look at all the trim levels; you might be surprised that you can afford a vehicle with more safety features than you hoped for, as well as more luxury than you planned on.

Most of today's brand new vehicles come equipped with the features that most people require. The majority of car stereos come with an auxiliary jack for an MP3 player or iPod. Heated seats are no longer available on just the most expensive vehicles, and adjustable seats, radio controls on the steering wheel, tilt and telescopic steering and many other features have been integrated into today's modern expensive and inexpensive cars. Knowing what features are available and on which cars can be confusing. Utilizing the car manufacturers' web sites is an easy way to shop and compare vehicles side by side, long before you ever head out for a test drive. Determining what features are included—and more importantly which are omitted—from certain models will help you to shorten your short list. Many auto makers' web sites also allow you to configure a vehicle to your specific requirements, giving you a good idea of all the options and final price. They can even calculate your monthly payments for traditional financing versus leasing. Remember, the interest rate to borrow the money, any extra insurance costs and other hidden fees need to be determined once you start visiting dealerships. (Think of the prices on the web sites as estimates.)

GROWING CONSUMER AWARENESS

Buyers also utilize the power of the Internet. Many shoppers do as much research as they can before ever setting foot in a showroom. Car sales people typically comment on the product awareness buyers now have before they head to the dealership. This is what sets apart good shoppers from average ones. The more informed you are, the better armed you will be to make a great decision. Besides the manufacturers' web sites, there are dozens of others you should visit to help prepare your short list. Everything from vehicle quality sites to crash-worthiness scores and independent reviews will help you narrow your selection.

Just as the public has preconceived ideas about products coming from certain countries, consumers also have biases about which manufacturers deliver quality product. But where do you find impartial information on this important measure? In my opinion, the most independent and consistent quality scores come from JD Power and Associates, and much of the information is available at www.jdpower.com. This company publishes two different studies every year. The first is called the initial quality study, which follows vehicles in their first 90 days of ownership. Vehicles and owners are chosen randomly from a wide variety of regions throughout the United States. The initial quality survey is very detailed and asks questions not only about vehicle repairs but the design, features and ease of use. If, for example, one model has a poor design on the interior, the electronics are hard to navigate and the owner had to take it back to the dealer for clarification, it will score lower in initial quality. Average scores are based on how many times a vehicle required dealership attention.

I know what you must be thinking: how can the quality of a vehicle be determined in just 90 days? In conducting this survey for many years and following up with three- and five-year dependability reports, JD Power and Associates has determined that the first 90 days of ownership is a good barometer of how well a vehicle will perform in the long term.

The company's web site also posts its dependability survey, which shows how a vehicle has fared over a three-year period. Unfortunately, JD Power has decided to no longer conduct a five-year dependability survey because too much of a vehicle's repair history is determined by how well it has been maintained, and not by its design problems. One thing to consider is that the three-year dependability survey is a snapshot of what was in the market three years earlier, and does not necessarily reflect the reliability you can count on in a brand new vehicle. New models can be introduced in that period that might be much better or worse than the previous version. This is why the initial quality survey is a gauge best used for brand new vehicles, and the three-year dependability reports for used products.

I am often asked about *Consumer Reports* and their vehicle quality scores. I tend to look at these as a secondary reference, and JD Power and Associates as my primary source. Unlike JD Power and Associates, *Consumer Reports* only surveys people who subscribe to its magazine or online service. The surveys are not random and they don't take into account people who aren't part of their subscription list. In my opinion, this approach skews the results. Imagine trying to conduct a political poll but only interviewing readers of a certain magazine? This would reflect the opinions only of those particular readers, not of the public's appetite for any politicians. The same is true for quality surveys. People of a certain type, often conservative, older men, subscribe to consumer magazines, and interviewing only these people for quality information often leads to very different scores. I still think it is worthwhile to have a look at the *Consumer Reports* scores, but when it comes to core quality, my first option is always JD Power and Associates.

For safety scores for new or used vehicles, there are two different web sites you must review before making a purchase: www.safecar. gov, the US government's safety crash-test site which I mentioned earlier, and the site of the Insurance Institute for Highway Safety (IIHS), www.iihs.org. This organization tests cars independently from the US government to gauge vehicle safety in relation to insurance claims. The IIHS uses slightly different tests. For instance, the IIHS performs a rear crash test to determine the safety of head restraints in rear collisions. It also conducts a frontal offset crash to replicate the types of crashes that often take place in real life and not just in the laboratory. I suggest you go to both sites and read how they conduct the tests. After looking up particular vehicles, you begin to get a very clear idea of how well they will do in collisions. Both are excellent resources and neither should be discounted.

Earlier in this chapter, I referred to the Automobile Journalists Association of Canada (AJAC) and its annual car of the year valuation. This group has been naming car of the year winners for the last several decades, and these can be viewed at www.ajac.ca. Keep in mind that the journalists don't evaluate quality or dependability; they only judge vehicles on design, ease of use, power, handling and overall appeal. The other thing to keep in mind is that AJAC members are experts in their field and throughout the year drive dozens of new cars. They have a good idea of what's available in the marketplace, what the trends are and which vehicles really are at the top of their class. When reviewing the AJAC winners, remember, the endorsement speaks to good design and leaders in a particular class; it is not a barometer of how vehicles perform years down the road. Auto reviewers are always driving brand new vehicles and these models don't have any historical information on dependability. Even though a model might have been around for several years, a new version might be significantly updated, so comparing it to the older version is not easy. Take my earlier example of some of the domestic manufacturers improving their products; if we always determined dependability and quality based on the old models, they would never improve. Auto makers improve their vehicles each time they release a new version, and in many instances the technology is often vastly different, so each new model has to be treated differently.

I always advise people to stay clear of brand new versions of a particular model for at least one full model year. After a new vehicle has been introduced to the market, there are often adjustments made in subsequent years based on consumer feedback. Remember the Hyundai van I referred to earlier? The issues we had with the first model were corrected in the second year. Such improvements made by manufacturers are ongoing.

You might have started with one short list, and after visiting the sites I have mentioned and auto review portals such as www.driving.ca, www.canadiandriver.com, www.edmunds.com, you'll get an idea of how vehicles stack up against others in that class. Taking the time to do some research, instead of just walking into a dealership and being enamoured with shiny paint and new car smells, will give you the satisfaction of knowing you have done the utmost in choosing your next car.

The web sites I've listed not only have information on new vehicles but also used ones, in some cases dating back over 10 years. Remember, though, that a review of a vehicle from 10 years ago is based on when the car was new, and not how it stacks up in the current crop of vehicles. Used car purchases are often dictated by supply in the marketplace, unlike the vast supply of new vehicles. Picking a used car often comes down to the best available version of that vehicle, at that particular time. But if you do research on a used vehicle well in advance of actually shopping, it will give you more time to wait for the one that best meets your needs.

I love nothing more than doing research on my next purchase. When I know I'm going to be in the market for a vehicle, whether new or used, I spend months poring over information. Only when I feel fully armed with enough knowledge to go shopping do I actually test drive vehicles. Car purchases are not made in a vacuum; I often consult other family members when it's time to go shopping. But if you follow the steps outlined in the previous and forthcoming chapters, and utilize the information you gain, I'm confident you will feel you've made the right decision.

Part**Four**
Shopping Around

9

How to get the most for your current vehicle

HOW MUCH IS MY CAR WORTH?

Chances are you own a vehicle. If you're considering buying a new or newer one, you're probably asking yourself what is the best strategy to get the most money for it. Should you sell it privately or trade it in? Both strategies have their advantages and weaknesses. There is no cut-and-dried formula to help you decide which is best, but there are some basic guidelines which will hopefully lead you to making the best decision for your circumstances.

TRADE OR SELL PRIVATELY?

If you're considering purchasing a vehicle at a dealership, here's how the trade-in scenario works. You will be offered the wholesale price for your car—not the price the dealer might sell it for off the lot. Dealerships are in business to make money and giving you top dollar for your trade leaves them little room for profit.

Unless your trade is less than three years old, the dealer is not likely to sell it. The car will be sold to a broker, who will re-sell it to used car dealers, or it will be auctioned to used car dealers. Your car is worth only as much as the used car dealers are willing to pay. I get e-mails every day from viewers across the country who have taken a vehicle into a dealer, been quoted a trade-in price and, much to their horror, they learn that their beloved vehicle is worth a whole lot less than they thought. There are outside influences that affect the car market, such as the price of gas, value of our dollar, depreciation, the availability of a particular model and the state of the economy.

For example, if a manufacturer had a special on a vehicle and sold thousands of them, the used market for that car can be saturated three or four years down the road. The established rules of supply and demand kick into place. If there is a surplus of inventory of used vehicles relative to buyers, prices will fall. The opposite is also true. If a certain popular model is in short supply, it will retain its value.

So, if a dealer is only offering the wholesale price for your trade-in, surely selling it privately instead is financially beneficial? This may sound like an obviously better strategy, but in reality it's not that simple.

A trade-in should not only be looked at as the amount you can get for your car but also *the ability to reduce the tax you pay on your new vehicle.* When you trade in a vehicle, the amount you get is put toward the purchase price of your new car and you pay tax only on the difference. If you're buying a new $25,000 car and your trade-in is $10,000, then you pay tax only on the outstanding $15,000. Let's take the province of Ontario for example. When you consider the 5% GST and the 8% provincial sales tax, you come up with a combined tax of 13%. When applied to this above example, the true value of the trade-in is not just $10,000, it's $11,300. Keep in mind that the more the used car is worth, the more tax you will save.

Now, let's estimate what your car is worth if sold privately. First, it will have to be prepared for sale. This might include having the car professionally polished and detailed, along with repairing any mechanical or cosmetic problems. Second, the vehicle will have to be advertised for sale. With web sites such as craigslist.org, the cost of advertising your used car could be very low or even free, but many times the best results still come from local newspapers, *The Auto Trader* and online used car portals such as driving.ca. The third factor is the hassle and time it takes to actually provide test drives, negotiate the sale and finalize the deal. For some, selling a used car is something they have done successfully in the past and feel comfortable with. But for others, having to take time out of their busy schedule, dealing with potential buyers, being stood up and deals falling through at the last minute, the ease of trading in seems much more appealing. In my experience, men seem much more comfortable with selling a car than many women. Not to say that women are incapable, it's just that many don't feel safe talking to strangers and escorting them on test drives.

Back to our example. The dealer has offered $10,000, and tax savings bring that up to $11,300. By using the standard rule of a 15% mark-up on the wholesale price, you would want to get $11,500 for your car if sold privately. Let's say the cost of detailing is $300; when you subtract $300, you have $11,200 or only $100 less than the amount you'd realize through the dealer. Keep in mind that you can often get more money for a car privately if the vehicle is very well maintained (and you can provide all service records—you should anyway) and represented, and the buyer meets you in person.

At the end of the day, it's a lot of work to sell a car. This is especially the case if the buyer wants to haggle over the price or insist that his uncertified cheque is good. And our example presumes your car will pass certification and that you don't need to make any expensive repairs that will eat into the amount of money you'll have left over.

All the vehicles that I have ever owned I sold privately, and I only had two instances that caused me frustration. I remember one situation where a fist fight almost broke out on my front lawn. The funny thing is, both these times involved selling my wife's car.

Back in 2001, we had the opportunity to buy a beautifully maintained vehicle from my uncle, so our three-year-old Honda Accord had to go. There were many people who came to take our impeccable Accord for a test drive, but there was one in particular who had total disregard for the fact they were driving someone else's property. After the test, this person backed our flawless Accord into the vehicle behind it, leaving two small holes in the bumper. (Because of that incident, I decided I would be the one parking the vehicle and only let potential buyers drive it once we were in a wide-open area.) When I pointed out that they had damaged the vehicle, they mumbled something about sorry and hightailed it out of there, never to be heard from again.

After a few days a very nice family arrived to have a look at the Honda, and once they realized I was the same person they watch on TV, they decided I had no right asking the price I was seeking. They said something along the lines of "You're rich, why don't you sell it to us for cheap?" Well, I've got news for you: I'm not rich and I had no intention of dropping my price!! The ironic thing is that this very same family ended up buying the Honda for the price I was asking. Other than the two holes in the bumper, that really was a nice ride.

Now for the near fist-fight story. For years, we had a little runaround car that my wife bought when she was just starting out after college. We liked it so much that we kept it, even after she got something better. It was a cute little Dodge Colt that I had taken over as my pickup and drop-off vehicle for getting the test cars for my reviews. I loved that little car. Sure it was dead slow, but it drove like new, was great on gas, easy to park and had a great stereo! But time moves on, and after we bought our first house we needed all the money we could get, and it was time for the trusty old Dodge Colt to go.

Little did I know what a goldmine we had on our hands. People were lined up at the door to take the car for a drive and put their money down. The playoffs came down to a mother who wanted to buy the Colt as a second car for her daughter, and a young woman starting out in her career. Both wanted the car badly, were willing to pay full price and made it very clear that they expected to end up with the keys. They even got into verbal sparring over who should drive the car home. The mother called first, and drove it first. The young woman arrived a little later, drove the car and really wanted it to the point that she became very pushy. I decided to use the old "first-come, first-served" approach and sell the Colt to the mother and daughter.

This didn't go down well with the young woman, who was incensed, and as time went on I could tell she was a spoiled brat who was used to getting her own way. She angrily stomped off, fuming about how I would dare sell it to someone else. I'm sure you have met this type of person, like a small child who always gets what they want. After my decision and after the car went home with its new buyer, I realized I had made the right decision in selling it to the much nicer family. In retrospect, I could have settled the situation a different way. Instead of "first come, first served" I should have sold it to the highest bidder. If the spoiled brat wanted it, she would have to pay for it. Oh well, live and learn.

I must have a sick and twisted sense of fun, because I quite enjoy buying and selling cars. I look at it as a kind of sport, but I know for many people there is nothing more agonizing than having to wheel and deal. If you don't have the stomach for what it takes to sell a used car, then maybe getting somebody else in your family to do it for you or trading in is the best idea.

FROM THE DEALER'S PERSPECTIVE

As I mentioned, you might want to prepare yourself for a shock if you find that the dealer's trade-in price for your beloved car is less than you expected. It's not just because the dealer wants to re-sell the car and make a profit, it's because often the dealer doesn't want to keep older cars or vehicles built by a different manufacturer since they can have a hard time getting rid of them. If, for example, you take your five-year-old Ford Taurus to the dealer and are offered only a few thousand dollars, it's easy to feel insulted. Sure, you maintained the vehicle properly, washed it regularly and treated it like a member of your family. But to a dealer, it's just another hunk of steel, plastic and glass—a hunk of steel, plastic and glass that they have to get rid of.

Only vehicles a few years "young" and in premium condition usually stay on the dealer's lot—the rest are either sold to brokers or sent to auction. Sometimes, when you are at a dealership scoping new cars, a sales person will call a broker to see what he can get for your car and have a price ready. If you're serious about buying a new car, the dealer knows the value of your trade and can provide you with a firm price. If they can't get a broker to purchase your car, it will be sent to auction. In that case, how does the dealer know what price he should offer to you for the Taurus? The dealer has at its disposal recent prices for all of the vehicles that have gone through auction. By looking up the recent values of a Ford Taurus, they can tell you roughly what the trade-in value is. You might have even heard people refer to the "Blue Book" price for a vehicle. The Kelly Blue Book is a service that publishes recent auction prices for vehicles in the United States. In Canada, we don't have the Blue Book, but we do have other services, such as the Black Book, Gold Book and a few others. Canadian Black Book is the largest in the country and publishes auction prices for dealers every two weeks. You may be asking yourself, "Do prices of vehicles really change so quickly that they need to publish the auction prices every two weeks?" The answer is yes. Depending on the number of cars available on the market at any given time and the number of potential buyers, this can have a dramatic impact on prices.

One of the most frustrating things to see is your used vehicle placed on the dealer's lot for thousands of dollars more than you received as a trade-in. It's like a slap in the face. Remember that the vehicle was traded at the wholesale price and the dealer is selling at the retail price. The dealer, unlike an individual seller, has many vehicles on the lot and also has the luxury of time to get that one buyer willing to pay top dollar. Dealers often place the used car on the high end of the retail price and then knock the price down as a prospective buyer negotiates. The dealer knows he probably won't get the full asking price, but if he gets close to it, he'll be happy. What you see advertised is rarely the final sale price.

Another reason a dealer marks up a vehicle from the whole-sale price is that the cars need to be refurbished. This may include mechanical repairs, new tires, touching up scratches, taking out dents and in some instances painting. The dealer also has overhead, sales commissions and interest to pay on the inventory sitting on their lot.

Car dealers love a good-quality used vehicle because there is a bigger profit margin; they can often mark it up and make more profit per unit than they can on a new car. Used cars are a constant source of revenue for dealerships, and that can work in your favour when negotiating. Since there's a bigger profit margin, there's also more room to negotiate. The difference between the Black Book price and the retail price is about 15%, so when you go shopping for a used car, know that there is probably about 15% mark-up and, in some cases, even more. Usually the used car department at the dealership is more used to wheeling and dealing on prices than staff selling new cars, so don't feel shy in offering less than the vehicle was advertised. You'll get a pretty good idea if the dealer is willing to deal by the response—be it a counter-offer or outright refusal—to your initial low offer.

There are times when a dealer pays too much for a trade-in, or the vehicle ends up sitting on the lot, so then they try to recoup the costs when re-selling it. In such instances, the dealer is often reluctant to discount the price at all, and you can even ask if they have "too much into" a vehicle for them to drop the price significantly. But remember, dealers get hungrier the longer a vehicle sits on their lot, so be sure to offer less than the advertised price and be prepared to negotiate. If the dealer doesn't accept your offer, leave your phone number and let them know that if they want to sell to give you a call. You'd be surprised how many times the phone will ring.

OTHER FACTORS THAT AFFECT PRICES OF USED VEHICLES

Have you ever been to the airport and rented a car? You've seen all of those shiny new vehicles parked waiting for drivers? All of those cars, once they have about 12,000 kilometres on the clock, are auctioned off. If you're trading in a vehicle just after a number of those rentals have gone through auction, it could affect the value of your vehicle. In the case of the Ford Taurus, there were literally thousands used by rental companies, and the effect their trade-in value had on the used car market was devastating. Because so many of these vehicles went through auction so often, it hammered the Taurus in the used market. This is just one example of what can happen at auction to affect the price of your used car. Auctions for car dealers are held across the country and in some cities as often as twice a week. Remember, people in the car business look at vehicles only as hunks of glass and steel to be bought and sold.

In chapter 7, I mentioned the SUV that we sent back after our lease was up. Well, another reason the market for that vehicle was so soft after three years is that so many people had the same plan as we did. The manufacturer had great lease rates, low payments and a good product, so many thousands of these SUVs were picked up on leases. Three years later, the market was flooded and prices dropped. Unfortunately, we don't live in a vacuum; other people and their decisions affect our property.

One of the other factors that can affect the price of vehicles going to auction is the cost of a litre of gas. When it was as high as $1.50, people were dumping full-size SUVs and pickup trucks as fast as they could. With so many going through the auction and so few people buying them, prices plummeted. In some cases, a dealer would take a full-size truck on trade and by the time it went to auction the value had decreased even further—that's how quickly the market was changing.

There is a way to find out before you go to the dealer roughly what your trade in is worth. The Canadian Black Book is not available to the public, but the companies that pay for that service make it available to you. For example, Toyota and General Motors subscribe to the Canadian Black Book and in turn allow the public to utilize their subscription to get an idea of trade-in values before heading to the dealer. If you did a search for the Canadian Black Book on your computer, you probably would come up empty-handed. But here's a little tip. Go to a web site such as Toyota.ca or GM.ca and look for a tab called "appraise my trade." This in turn gets you an internal link to the Canadian Black Book. Surprise, you can get an estimate of your vehicle's value! After entering information on your vehicle, the Canadian Black Book will give you a spread of possible prices. Prices at the low end are for vehicles that are in rough condition, and top dollar is obviously for those in very good condition. The Black Book price should be viewed only as an estimate of your vehicle's trade-in value, because there are fluctuations due to local market conditions. A convertible might be more desirable in

British Columbia, which typically has milder winters, and a pickup truck might be more desirable in Alberta, because of local demand.

So, what can you do to get the best possible trade-in price for your vehicle? One way is to take your car to several different dealers and get estimates of its value. This will give you a good idea of what somebody might pay. If one dealer is willing to pay more, take it as a sign the dealer wants your business. But be aware that some dealers will offer a higher trade-in value just to get your business and then not discount your new vehicle as much as another might. Getting you in the door and moving forward on a new car purchase is their goal, so be aware of a trade that seems too good to be true; you'll pay somewhere along the line! Dealers want to make money and will try to get it either from offering less for your trade and letting you think you're getting a great deal on the new car, or offering more for the trade and discounting the new vehicle very little.

OPPORTUNITY KNOCKS FOR OLDER CARS

If you're offered a low wholesale price, this tells you your car is going to auction. So you might want to take the time and effort to sell your vehicle privately. There can be a strong market for older used cars in good condition. After vehicles get to a certain age they have little attraction for used car lots, but that doesn't mean that they don't have a market. Lots of people want a solid, well-maintained vehicle and are willing to pay for one. In many instances, the prices for vehicles once they hit a certain age don't change that dramatically because the car has depreciated about as far as it can. I've bought vehicles that were seven years old, and after three years re-sold them for the same amount I paid for them, or slightly less. I've also sold older vehicles for more than I paid for them. It all depends on the market and what people are looking for. If your vehicle is an older model, advertising and selling it to a market that is more price-sensitive will often get you better results than trading in.

How do you come up with a price for an older vehicle? Looking through the newspaper, or searching similar vehicles online is a good way to get a barometer of what your vehicle is worth. Remember that the price posted in the newspaper and online is the asking price and not necessarily what the vehicle will eventually sell for; the Canadian Black Book can give you a good idea. By taking the wholesale Black

Book price and adding 15%, you should be able to estimate the retail market price. Once again, local conditions and market fluctuations will affect used vehicles that are being sold privately.

Just as the price of certain vehicles fell due to gas prices or other outside influences, you should be aware that you might have to adjust your price in order to sell. In my experience, it's a good idea to pick a price you feel comfortable with and stick with it for several weeks. If there's no action on the vehicle—the phone isn't ringing and nobody has come for a test drive—then you need to lower the price. I suggest you continue to monitor the prices others are charging for the same or similar vehicle and adjust accordingly. Lowering your price slowly over several weeks will usually result in a sale. On the other hand, I've had vehicles sit with no activity for several weeks, resisting marking the price down, and then suddenly the phone starts to ring. It could be a certain time of year when people are on vacation or just the way the moon and stars are aligned, but all it takes is for one person to be interested to make a sale. Sometimes, the waiting pays off.

I've had instances where I know the vehicle I own really isn't worth that much, but its usefulness is worth more than its cash value. In these cases, I've tended to keep the older car and continue to drive it instead of trying to sell it for very little. One of my vehicles is an old Volkswagen van that is worth maybe $3,000 in monetary terms, but much more in others. Sure, I certainly could use another $3,000, but I'd have a hard time trying to find such a vehicle that has been so reliable, functional and fun to own. The other great thing about keeping an old vehicle is it usually has hit the bottom of the depreciation curve; my old van has been worth the same amount for years!

The decision to trade in, sell privately or keep your old vehicle will often come down to the age of your used car. If it's relatively new, trading in will give you tax advantages on your new vehicle. An older vehicle will probably fetch the maximum when sold privately. And sometimes, just keeping an old car for sentimental reasons might also be an option. By doing a little online research for the value of your vehicle in the marketplace, you'll have a better idea of which direction to take. Regardless of how you dispose of your old car, one thing is always heart wrenching: the price you think your car is worth is usually far more than what somebody is going to pay for it. If you realize that going in, you probably will be more satisfied with the outcome. It's a tough reality, but that's the way it is.

The best way to recognize the value in your used car is to look at the new car market. The best selling cars in Canada are small compact or subcompact models, and these are also the vehicles that are the most coveted used. A used Honda Civic, Mazda3, Toyota Corolla, Toyota Yaris, Honda Fit, Hyundai Elantra and mid-size cars such as the Toyota Camry and Honda Accord will always fetch top dollar. In the SUV class, the Toyota RAV-4, Honda CRV, Ford Escape and Hyundai Santa Fe are all very popular new and used.

The fastest depreciating cars are the high-end luxury sedans such as the Mercedes S-Class or BMW 7 Series. Buyers of these models like new cars, and to sell the used product they have to drop the price to appeal to a different class of buyer.

Canadians love sensible, small reliable cars, and the used market can never get enough of them.

10 When is the best time to buy?

One of the most important factors in getting a good deal on a car is deciding when to purchase.

If there is a sleek new model that catches the public's interest, it will command a higher or a more consistent price than a vehicle that has been around for a long time. The same is true for other items we buy.

We've all been to a clothing store and seen the "sale" rack, typically filled with items from the end of season. For example, stores will want to get rid of heavy coats and sweaters at the beginning of spring. The opposite is also true: when you go into a store at the beginning of a season and find that one item you really want—it's rarely on sale. Our economy and what we pay for goods is based on supply and demand. Keep that "sale" rack in your mind when you think about vehicles.

There have been some extreme examples of vehicles being released into the market with such hype that they actually sell for more than the manufacturer's suggested retail price. Do you remember in the early 90s when the Mazda Miata was first introduced? That car single-handedly brought back the roadster to the marketplace, and the interest in it was so high that some dealers actually charged more than the vehicle was supposed to be sold for. After a while, as people became accustomed to seeing it on the road and the initial honeymoon passed, prices returned to normal levels.

Another example is the hot Nissan GT-R, released in 2008. The GT-R is a Japanese super car that was introduced in Canada in limited numbers. Those who wanted one had to pay more than the suggested selling price. I heard stories of dealerships asking $40,000 more than the sticker price and people actually forked over huge money to get one.

Buying a car in such an environment is never going to get you a good deal. But waiting for the vehicle to become more common will reduce the demand and price.

You have to ask yourself if owning the newest, latest and greatest model is what you need, or more a question of what you want. Most vehicle purchases are not just about your needs, they're also about fashion and the statement the vehicle makes about your personality. For some, driving in the latest car with all the leading-edge technology is what makes them who they are. For others, they're not bothered about being seen in a vehicle that is sexy or flashy; they might be more excited about getting a good deal. These buyers typically buy cars that are more sensible and cost less, and they tend to keep them longer. You have to decide what type of person you are and how much you're willing to pay to be in the latest and greatest vehicle.

You don't have to buy a boring, basic and out-of-date car to get a good deal. Sometimes, waiting for the right time to purchase can get you the vehicle that you aspire to own at a price that is easier to live with. It often comes down to timing.

Just as a clothing store wants to sell off their winter clothes before spring, car companies and dealerships want to sell an outgoing model before the new one arrives. When dealerships are motivated to move their product, they have to make it attractive to buyers. They can do this in a number of ways, such as reducing price, offering incentives or reducing the amount it costs you to borrow money. If you can get all three, that's like the Triple Crown in horse racing. Giddy up!

WHAT IT COSTS TO BORROW WHEN BUYING OR LEASING

Let's look at the cost of financing first, because most people don't realize that the most money you'll save when getting a new vehicle is on borrowing costs. Typically, people lease a vehicle over 48 months, and in the case of traditional financing, a loan can be as long as seven years. Paying interest on a vehicle, plus the taxes, over seven years can really add up. When comparison-shopping, you must calculate the costs associated with the loan and not just the initial purchase price.

Here is one of the first things you should look for when comparing vehicles on your short list. When manufacturers want to move product, they don't always drop the price, but make the cost to borrow attractive enough to interest buyers. Getting a vehicle when interest rates are being offered at 0% or 1.9% is a lot cheaper over a four- to seven-year period than 5% or 6%. Many buyers make the mistake of considering just the purchase price and not the total cost to carry the vehicle over the term of the loan.

One thing to watch for in advertising is the very tempting but often misleading monthly costs to get into a new vehicle. For example, a vehicle might be posted for $299 per month, which sounds great, but the loan might be at a high interest rate—and all they have done is make the term longer.

Low monthly lease payments are another way of making a vehicle attractive to buyers. Open the auto section in a local newspaper and you'll see monthly leases ranging from $199 to $499 per month for an average family vehicle. The car manufacturers and dealers know people have a limited amount of disposable income to put toward a car each month, and they tailor the lease payments to fit into an average household budget. What people often don't realize is the monthly lease payment can be quite misleading.

Many companies will have a low monthly lease payment, but they adjust the buyout at the end of the lease upwards. If you don't have any intention of buying the vehicle at the end of the lease, this works out well. But if you plan to keep the car, the lease-end balloon payment can be daunting. Another tactic is to offer a payment that is attractive, but including a hidden high interest rate. It's essential to look at not just the amount the vehicle costs per month, but also the interest rate, the buyout amount and the overall cost of ownership.

A member of my family was shopping for a new Honda Civic with the intent of doing what I just mentioned—lease for the first four years and buy it at the end of the term. When I asked if they had made a deal and taken the car home, I was shocked to find out that they hadn't done any of the things I just suggested. In fact, they actually thought that they had done a wonderful job of negotiating. You see, the only price they were interested in was the monthly lease payment, not the overall cost of ownership. When they went into the dealer to negotiate, they were told the cost of the car was $325 per month. Instead of asking how much the car cost and what the interest rate was and what the buyout amount would be, they focused only on the monthly payment. Here is the part that made them think they were actually being hard negotiators. My family member insisted that the $325 monthly price was too high and threatened to walk out of the dealership if they didn't drop the monthly price to a more palatable $275. As the story goes, the salesperson asked them not to leave and insisted he would plead his case with the sales manager. Sure enough, the salesperson came back and announced that they had negotiated a deal and $275 per month would be just fine. The buyers felt like masters of negotiation. Well, all the sales manager did was defer the cost of the vehicle from the monthly lease payment to the buyout. The buyers really hadn't done any negotiating; all they did was delay the financial pain. At the end of a four-year lease, when the buyout was to be paid, my family member decided to keep the car and make their lump sum payment. At the end of the day, the vehicle was no cheaper. In fact, they paid full retail.

If it had been me in the same situation, I would have negotiated the sale price and not just the monthly payment. Car dealers and manufacturers are great at adjusting payments to meet the average buyer's needs. They make it easy to meet the monthly payment, but in the end you don't save any money and often pay more for the same vehicle.

The Line-of-Credit Option

There is a way to make your own payment, if you have a personal line of credit. Buying a vehicle outright on your line of credit gives you the option each month to pay the minimum amount that is required by your bank, or more, depending on your borrowing agreement. Beware! This type of payment only works for people who are good with their money and are disciplined at paying off debt. Take my friend Ron: he decided to buy a vehicle this way and after about three years he hadn't paid off any principle, only the interest each month. What he ended up with was a vehicle that had depreciated but he still owed the full amount, including the taxes. What a mess. If he was good with his money, he would have applied a steady monthly payment to his line of credit and at least the amount the vehicle was worth, and the loan would have shrunk in lock step.

The main reason to buy a vehicle with a line of credit is to obtain the savings that many dealerships advertise on new vehicles. Companies will often have a cash purchase price, which is usually several thousands of dollars less than the amount you would pay if you financed the vehicle through the manufacturer. You need to figure out the cost to borrow the money on the higher amount, and see if the saving and interest costs from the line of credit will be better over a typical four- or five-year period. Basically, will the savings from the cash discount cover the interest?

I decided to buy our last vehicle on our line of credit because the cash deal we negotiated was very attractive, and the interest amount was lower than the manufacturer was willing to offer.

Speaking of interest rates, you should be aware that any line of credit has a floating interest rate. Over four or five years, the cost of borrowing will fluctuate. If you have room in your budget to absorb any changes in interest rates, then buying a car when there are attractive cash incentives might be worth a look. But do yourself a big favour: please pay more than the minimum amount each month. Don't be a Ron!

To reiterate, when you're shopping for a vehicle either online or at a dealership, it's essential to ask what the cost will be over the life of the loan or lease. Comparing these costs, along with any rebates or price reductions, will help you determine the best deal for you.

TIME TO SHOP AROUND

Let's get back to car prices and the rules of supply and demand. How do you know if one particular vehicle is more popular than another, and which ones have rebates and low interest rates? Hopefully, you're not in a rush to buy a car and you've taken several weeks (if not months) to do some research before buying. Reading this book suggests you are a sensible shopper and not an impulse buyer.

The best way to monitor prices and interest rates is in newspapers and online, which will give you an idea which vehicles are selling. Usually cars that aren't selling well are featured with more incentives and lower interest rates. Popular ones will be selling at or close to the manufacturer's suggested retail price, and their interest rates will be higher.

If you have established a short list, after doing all your research, you can now actively monitor vehicles' prices. Returning to the manufacturers' web sites and looking at their special offers, and actually building a car online, will give you key information on interest rates and rebates. Manufacturers often have regional incentives, and the best way to find these is to scan your local newspaper. Monitoring vehicle prices and rates over several months will give you a baseline of knowledge, so when you see a good deal you're actually able to recognize it.

This reminds me of when my wife and I were shopping for a house. Our real estate agent told us to monitor the market over several months on the MLS listings to get a feel for what the market was doing. Another great piece of advice he gave us was to look at homes that were more expensive than we could afford, and others that were less expensive. By knowing how the market was performing and seeing what was being offered we were able to appraise, on our own, what was good value. By utilizing the same principles when buying a car, you will be able to recognize a deal when you see one.

Okay, let's take this same approach and apply it to what motivates car companies and dealerships to sell at a discount. The best possible deal you will ever get on a car is typically when one model is being phased out and a brand new one is being introduced. But how are you to know when a car is about to be introduced? There's nothing more frustrating than buying a car in the summer only to find out three months later that a brand new model is ready to hit the market. When you're looking online at your short list of vehicles, search for the upcoming model year. For example, if you're considering a 2010 Ford Escape, you should also search the 2011 Ford Escape. You will find articles from auto enthusiast pages and industry web sites that describe the upcoming model. If there is an entirely new model about to debut, there will usually be quite a bit of information describing the changes, along with photos and statistics. If you notice that a brand new vehicle will soon be released, this indicates prices on the current model are about to be lowered or incentives and special financing could be introduced. If you're one of those people who like to have the latest and greatest, then this information might make you hold off until the new model arrives.

Remember, the Internet is your friend when it comes to shopping. Just as my wife and I looked at houses long before we purchased, we had knowledge when it was time to buy. By looking at current and upcoming vehicles, the information you glean will give you power when you need it.

A long-time friend of ours picked up a brand new Mazda3 two months before the 2010 model arrived. Unfortunately, I was unaware of her purchase until after the fact, and I can guarantee she didn't do any of the due diligence I have described. If she were aware that a brand new model was just about to arrive in dealerships, she would have had ammunition to purchase the vehicle at a discount or decide to wait until the new model came out so she could have the latest version. Even though she's thrilled with her car, knowing that she could have benefited from end-of-model discounts left her feeling that she overpaid.

The next best time to save money is during the end of year sell-off that happens when the upcoming models begin arriving on dealership lots. (You've heard the radio ads: "We have to make room, the 2010s are coming and the 09s have to go!") This is when manufacturers and dealerships are really motivated, and when they sweeten the pot. It is typically in the fall that the upcoming models begin to arrive, and as those new cars come in, the dealers want to move out the old ones. This is when you can save some money.

As the end-of-year sales events continue through the fall and into winter, the deals can improve but the selection of vehicles dwindles. If you have specific features and colours in mind, you should shop earlier rather than later. If you're not so selective, then delaying the shopping until late in the sales events might get you the best possible deal—but be aware that the vehicles left on the lot might be fully loaded, expensive versions.

One thing dealers never tell you is that they often get price reductions directly from the manufacturer to move out old stock. This means that the usually low margins they make on new vehicles can be greater on clearance models. Since factory rebates aren't always public knowledge, the dealer will try to get as close to the retail price as possible and keep the difference. Don't be afraid to ask for more of a discount on year-end models, because the dealers have more room to play with.

Other Money-Saving Strategies

There are other ways to save a few dollars on a new vehicle that many people don't consider. When a new car comes into a dealership and is used as a demonstrator, or demo model, the cost of freight and delivery is absorbed by the dealership. When the demo is resold, the new owner can save those costs, which can range anywhere from $1,000 to $2,500. Demo models also have to be reduced in price because they are no longer "new," but they usually have only a few thousand kilometres on them, which means they are almost new. The warranty coverage is not affected in any way, but the term will have begun when the vehicle first hit the road, not when you buy it. This can mean that the warranty will be a few months or weeks shorter than a brand new vehicle. Buying a demonstrator is also advantageous because you get to test drive the actual vehicle you might buy, not another on the lot.

Combining the savings of a reduced purchase price and not paying for freight and delivery is often an excellent way to get ahead financially. Many buyers often don't even think to ask if the vehicle they're test-driving can be purchased. Don't be afraid to ask for a list of demos that the dealership has on the road, and make an offer on one if it meets your needs.

Another great way to save some money is to buy a service loaner. These are the vehicles that dealerships lend to people when their own cars are in for servicing. Not all dealerships offer loaners, but those that do are a great source of less expensive, almost new vehicles for sale. Some dealerships sell these off at one time of the year, but others continually bring in vehicles and move out the ones that have been driven for a while. These vehicles tend to have more kilometres on them than demo models, but there are more savings to be had.

Most dealerships put basic, inexpensive models into their service loaner pool, but higher-end dealerships will put in several different types of vehicles so customers get a taste of what's available in the new car inventory. Imagine taking your compact car in to be serviced and as a loaner you get a bigger, more expensive vehicle. Not only do you get a service loaner but you're also on a test drive. Next time you are at a dealership, walk over to the service department and ask them what types of vehicles they have as service loaners. Once you know what's available, you can then ask the sales department if they will be selling any of these cars.

Buying a service vehicle is another great way to save money on a nearly new car with a remaining warranty. Loaners can be sold as a used car, so they might qualify to be certified, enabling you to get extended coverage.

The nice thing about buying a service loaner is *you* will be the only person who knows that other people drove it. It's not like there is a big red light on the roof that screams "Loaner." In fact, knowing that you got a great deal is a rewarding experience.

Another great time to buy a car is when the market is very slow. During the rapid economic downturn that began late in 2008 and into 2009, auto sales dropped like a rock and companies had to do something to keep some kind of traffic coming into dealerships.

They sweetened interest rates and kept them as low as 0%, or offered rebates, cash-only incentives, no payments for 90 days and many other enticements.

I can understand that in a recession many people don't want to buy a car; they're keeping their money tight to their chest in case something should happen to their job. For people who work in the public sector, with more secure jobs, this is actually the time they should consider buying a vehicle.

Have you ever heard of contrarians? These are people who do the opposite, or contrary, to the masses. When people are selling off a stock, they're buying, knowing it will eventually recover and make more money. For contrarians, the best time to buy something is when nobody else is. For nurses, doctors, teachers, firefighters, ambulance drivers, police officers and anyone working in a relatively recession-proof environment, a downturn is the perfect time to make the best deal. Again, those critical laws of supply and demand are always at play.

My best advice is that you should be making a short list and thinking about your next vehicle purchase well in advance of actually shopping. This gives you plenty of time to research current or upcoming models and monitor marketing trends such as incentives. If you watch the market over a longer period of time, the really good deals will become more obvious, and you'll know when you see a great deal. If you are a person who is not consumed by having the latest and greatest, you generally get a better deal than someone who has to have something before anyone else. For that privilege, you usually have to pay!

11 Making contact

Have you ever stood at the grocery checkout line and noticed a magazine, pack of gum, candy bar or horoscope book that you didn't plan to buy but purchased it anyway? These are called impulse buys. You had no intention of buying these items, but the fact they were placed in front of you somehow worked. You couldn't resist them because they were easy to purchase. Going shopping for a car is no different; sure, it's more expensive but there it is on its own little platform—the new flashy vehicle the dealer wants you to purchase—and will make it easy for you.

Car buyers do fall victim to the impulse purchase. Since you're reading this book, I gather you are a very sensible, practical shopper who would never fall prey to impulse buying. Right? I'm sure, just like me, you have friends who are not as prudent and have gone shopping for a vehicle and bought one on the spot. Maybe that intoxicating new-car smell overcomes their senses and they are bedazzled by the shiny paint, concert-class stereo system or persuasive (and pervasive) sales people helping them part with their money. Or all of the above.

Have you ever heard the term "buyer's remorse"? This occurs when the excitement of the moment overtakes common sense and a buyer makes a purchase, followed by the realization (usually two or three days later) that they made a rash decision and shouldn't have parted with their cash. Don't fall victim to buyer's remorse!

The most important thing on your side when you're shopping is time. Time to think, time to shop, time to negotiate, time to change your mind. If you're in a rush and haven't thought everything through, you might come away from a deal regretting it.

THE ANTIDOTE TO "DEALER-PHOBIA"

Walking into a car dealership, for many people, is akin to stepping on an airplane for those who are afraid to fly, or hanging over a railing on a tall building for people who are afraid of heights. Why don't we come up with a new name for this fear? Let's call it "dealer-phobia." The idea of being pressured by sales people or feeling confused by the vast array of options and not having a clear roadmap of how to buy a vehicle can be overwhelming. For people who are afraid of heights or flying, getting used to these situations ultimately relaxes and makes them more comfortable. To get over dealer-phobia, I suggest the same line of attack.

With this in mind, plus the fact we have already established a no-rush purchase timeline, heading out to visit dealerships with no intention to buy should be as easy as walking into any retailer, it's just that *this store* sells cars. Because you have time on your side and have no intention of purchasing, there is no pressure. Walk around, talk to people, get in and out of cars and make yourself at home. Getting familiar with the dealership's surroundings will help you get over dealer-phobia.

This is just like any other store. You are the customer and the sales people are there to serve you! Unfortunately, many people feel intimidated, like they shouldn't be there, they shouldn't touch the merchandise and they have to buy something. This isn't the case, and you shouldn't feel this way. Think about going into a clothing store to try on a sweater or a pair of jeans. Perhaps the fit isn't right, or maybe the colour, and you return the item to the rack. You have no obligation to buy and you move on to the next store. Car dealerships are no different. Try one on and if it doesn't fit, keep moving.

Another way to look at it is to remind yourself that buying a vehicle is about you and not the dealership. Keep this phrase in your mind like a mantra: "I am in charge! I am in charge! I am in charge!" You are in charge of when you visit the dealership, which vehicles you want to test drive, which one you ultimately purchase and how much you are willing to pay for it. What I'm really trying to do is empower you to believe that *you* drive the decision-making process. Unfortunately, many people forget *they are in charge.*

THE BUSINESS IS ABOUT CARS—AND PEOPLE

Since we have established that time is the most important thing on your side (okay, knowledge too), the best thing you can do is head out to dealerships long before you have any intention of purchasing a vehicle. This, along with your long-term monitoring of the market, will ultimately help you obtain the best possible price. The upside to walking around car dealerships and talking to people is you might actually meet some very nice people. You might make new friends and hopefully have long-term relationships with the people you buy from. Car dealers are in business to sell you not only one vehicle but many over your lifetime. If the dealership is reputable, the sales people knowledgeable and cheerful and service and maintenance are carried out to your satisfaction, the dealer knows you will spread the word to your friends and family. The dealership that meets your needs and makes you the most comfortable will probably continue to get your business. So make them work for it, and remember, "I am in charge!"

Once you've decided to visit some dealerships with no intention of buying, tell them that. Say something like, "I'm not going to buy a vehicle today, but I'm in the market and I want to see which dealership is the best fit for me." Trust me, a sales person worth his or her salt will do whatever it takes to convince you that their dealership is the one you should buy from exclusively. The staff should also try to sell himself or herself to you to build a rapport. If you get a lacklustre response, thank them for their time, tell them you'll consider them but you've got other dealers on your list. If that doesn't spur a snappy response, you know this particular dealership is not for you. You're not just shopping for a car, you're also looking for the support system that comes with your vehicle—from the sales people to the business manager and ultimately the service department. I'll cover these other people and their departments in a moment. Just like any other sector of commerce, car dealerships are in competition with one another, and you should use this to your advantage.

Not only should you visit dealerships of cars on your short list but also competing dealerships within those brands. For example, if you're considering a Ford Escape, make sure you visit several Ford dealers. Hopefully, your short list includes several different brands, and this will give you a good indication of which dealers really want your business.

If you haven't purchased a new vehicle in a long time, you might be surprised by just how sophisticated dealerships have become in relating to customers. Your memory of car sales people might be the stereotypical sleazy characters portrayed in movies. In reality, they are often re-trained in the latest techniques of customer service and are regularly updated on product knowledge. Dealerships that invest in their people and how they treat their customers typically have thriving businesses that benefit from excellent word of mouth.

Don't be afraid to talk to the sales people. Trust me, they won't bite. Sure they want to sell you a vehicle as quickly as they can, but the good ones will realize that patience could ultimately lead to a sale. If they're willing to take the time to talk to you and answer your questions without pressure, then they might just be worthy of your business. (Remember, "I am in charge!") If you don't click with a particular sales person, don't be rude, but move on to somebody else. A really good sales person will even take time after you've told them you are not in a rush to purchase. If they have been properly trained, they know that planting a seed can sometimes take months to grow. You might even want to say that you are interviewing different dealers and sales people to see who might be the right fit. What a crazy idea: the person buying a vehicle is actually in charge and the person selling the vehicle is there to serve you. Interview away!

If you make a habit of visiting dealerships when you have free time, maybe in the evening when they're a little quieter, you have a better chance of starting a relationship that can end up benefiting you. I have made acquaintances with many new and used car sales people, and in my travels I sometimes pop in just to say hello. You never know when you might bump into these people in the future. Just like in any other sales force, these people often change jobs and move locations, so the staff you meet at one dealership might ultimately sell you a vehicle at another. Having a friendly face to deal with makes the whole process a lot easier. I don't mean you should expect lifelong friendships or have them over for dinner; just get to know the players and feel comfortable with the process.

There are other reasons for making an ally inside a dealership: sometimes they let trade secrets out! The inside knowledge might be about a sales incentive that is about to end or another more attractive one about to begin. As an average consumer walking in off the street, you would have no access to this vital information. If, however, you become acquainted with several sales people at different dealerships you get a better lay of the land. I even like to joke with those I have connected with, saying, "You're going to give me an amazing deal on this car—right?" Or, "I'm not paying for any extra fees on this vehicle, right?" Often they will say something along the lines of "We'll look after you," or "You drive a hard bargain." It's the same in any business; if you know the people and have a relationship with them, you're more likely to be at the receiving end of any favours or special treatment.

One example might be getting a reduced cost on a set of winter tires and wheels for your new car. If you have a good relationship with the sales person you could ask them to include them for free or at least at the dealer's wholesale cost. Without that rapport, they are more than likely to sell you the tires at full retail. Which would you rather have?

I should also note that you need to keep a balance between staying in contact with the sales staff and pestering them. It's totally appropriate to ask questions, visit the dealership and even take a vehicle out for a test drive. But doing it to the point where you're intruding into their business might backfire. I have stopped in to say hello and make small talk for a few minutes, and then leave without interrupting the flow of the business. It's not always about doing the deal; it is mostly about building a relationship. Ask any person in sales and they'll tell you it's about relationships, so get out there and make contact, because it can work in your favour.

Another person that you should connect with inside a dealership is the business manager, since this is who you will ultimately encounter once you decide to buy a vehicle. This person puts together the financing and any other extended warranty or maintenance packages that you may require when you sign your deal.

As you're doing your due diligence and following the auto market online and in the newspaper, there may be incentives advertised that require some clarification. For example, a company might have a promotion such as "free gas for a year." The business manager might be able tell you whether you can transfer the value of that promotion into a discount. Or, you might require an explanation on how a particular lease works or if certain promotions or introductory finance rates can be combined. It's always good to get clarification on how you will finance your vehicle because, as I stated earlier, this is the area where you will save the most money. There is no better person in the dealership to talk to about these things than the business manager. So make a point of asking the sales person you have befriended to introduce you to the manager, and don't be afraid to ask questions.

There is one more very important thing you should ask the business manager long before you actually sit down to negotiate your deal: what fees does the dealership charge when you purchase a vehicle? What most people don't realize is that dealerships include hidden fees. Knowing what these are before the time of closing is good ammunition. You might even be so bold as to tell the business manager, "I'm interested in purchasing a vehicle from your dealership but I want to be assured that you're not going to be charging any hidden fees." If he or she realizes you have other dealerships on your short list, they may be motivated to waive fees they usually add to purchase agreements. Remember the mantra "I am in charge!" It's *your* money, it will be *your* vehicle and *you* will be the person who has to live with the final decision. Build the foundation to ensure you will get the best deal possible and are fully satisfied.

Another important area you should definitely visit inside a dealership is the service centre, also known as the "back end" of the business. After you purchase your car, this is the part of the dealership you will have the most contact with. Taking your vehicle in for regular maintenance or any required repairs can lead to frustration if the service personnel aren't courteous, make warranty repairs properly and deliver everything to you as promised. I suggest you introduce yourself to the service manager and ask about schedules, which days tend to be busier and if you can get a courtesy car. You want assurances that if you do have a problem with your vehicle, it's attended to in a timely fashion. I know of several high-volume dealerships that have waiting lists for service of more than two weeks. Having a courtesy car available is something you might not think about before you buy, but trust me, when your vehicle is in for service over an extended period of time, renting a second car can be expensive.

One thing to keep in mind, though, is that you don't have to go back to the dealership you bought your car from. In fact, you don't have to take your vehicle back to any dealership for regularly scheduled maintenance, as long as you maintain the vehicle to the schedule set out in your owner's manual. (If you don't follow the schedule, then your warranty can be voided.) If there is one particular dealership that you are keen on purchasing your vehicle from, it doesn't preclude you from going to another dealership for service. Keep in mind you typically get the best possible treatment if you return to the same dealership. It really is all about relationships, and having a relationship with the service department, just like your sales person, will go a long way to keeping you satisfied.

Remember, a car dealership is just like any other store. A vehicle purchase should be done on *your* terms and the only way you will develop the confidence to ensure that your terms are met is to take charge. All the people who work at the dealership are there to serve you. Don't feel pressured, don't feel you have to make any quick decisions and don't hesitate to walk out the door if you don't feel comfortable. If you do what I have suggested in this chapter, you will probably make contact with some very nice people—and they will want to help you and hopefully retain your business for years.

12 Why buy Canadian?

On September 21, 2007, the Canadian dollar hit parity with the US dollar, sending Canadians into fits over what we pay for everything, compared to Americans. There was no more obvious discrepancy in prices than vehicles. Canadians at that time were paying 10% to 30% more for the same vehicle in Canada than our neighbours to the south. The public outcry was so loud that many people took notice, from consumers who felt ripped off, to politicians covering their backsides, to car executives coming up with lame excuses and even to lawyers filing lawsuits, claiming market manipulation. People on all sides were scrambling to either take advantage of cheaper cars in the United States or trying to stop Canadians from doing so. Fortunately, the controversy led politicians to make many needed changes in the way Canadians shopped for cars in the US, but there are still several drawbacks to doing business south of the border.

BUYER BEWARE ALWAYS

Initially, there were several hurdles that Canadians had to clear to bring a car purchased in the United States across the border. These included getting paperwork from the manufacturer to get the vehicle through the Registrar of Imported Vehicles (RIV), the Canadian authority regulating vehicle importation. Many Canadians felt that by allowing auto makers to influence which vehicles would qualify for an importation left "the fox in charge of their henhouse." Manufacturers, on a whim, could state that a particular model was no longer admissible in Canada without having to really give any explanation. Some companies claimed that the bumpers fitted on US vehicles were different than on Canadian cars, and that significant modifications would have to be made. In speaking to several people directly involved with importing cars from the US, they told me that some manufacturers had different part numbers for

Canadian cars than American cars, but in essence they were exactly the same—the varying parts numbers were there only to make the vehicle unique and not fit for importation. It was all a pile of rubbish.

Another tactic to slow the flow of vehicles into Canada was so simple yet sneaky. Some manufacturers would drag their feet on providing necessary documentation for US cars, or they would charge exorbitant fees to complete the paperwork. I heard of one company charging $1,000 for a single document. Another stalling method involved the inspection of imported vehicles. Any car that comes into the country needs to be inspected, but the RIV would let the manufacturers dictate that only *they* could perform the inspection. Once again, the "fox" was in charge. In some instances, the fees the dealership would charge for the inspection were as high as several thousand dollars. Often the vehicle was simply put on a hoist and visually inspected. Several thousand dollars to just *look* at a car; no wonder the public was outraged!

Because of these shenanigans, several consumer advocacy groups emerged to lobby the Canadian government to change its archaic importation regulations. These groups campaigned to have vehicle standards harmonized between the United States and Canada. In fact, the Canadian government has since succumbed to public pressure and harmonized the bumper and immobilizer regulations between the two countries to enable to importation of all new American cars. Hurray!

Here is another example of how absurd the laws were. Some vehicles were not allowed into the country because they were deemed to be unsafe! For example, a $150,000 Mercedes-Benz that was perfectly safe in the United States was deemed unfit for Canadian roads. Are you telling me that a full-size, heavy and well-made German car should not be allowed into the country because it has slightly different bumpers? The whole situation was ridiculous, and because of the pressure mounted by these consumer advocacy groups and threats of legal action, the Canadian government changed the regulations. Not all of the roadblocks have been lifted, however. There are still forces behind the scenes slowing the movement of traffic across the border, and the auto makers reacted aggressively to keep buyers in Canada.

So, what did the car companies do to compete? At first they did nothing and suffered a decrease of 5% to 7% in their business in the four months from September to December 2007. In January 2008, many of the manufacturers came to market with massive incentives and low interest rates and a few of them even reduced their manufacturer's suggested retail price (MSRP). By reducing the MSRP, this signalled a level of defeat that their prices were too high and needed to be adjusted. From January 2008 through the summer of 2008, prices dropped an average of 8% across Canada, helping to stimulate car sales in the country. The move, in fact, inspired record sales, but it didn't slow the steady flow of US cars coming into Canada. With the strong Canadian dollar and the vast selection of vehicles across the border, many people took the time and energy to find a car in the US and import it into Canada. An entire industry emerged of small companies sourcing American vehicles and bringing them back to Canada to supply a vast array of dealerships. Some estimates, at the time, claimed that 20% of all the vehicles on used car lots were imported from the United States.

If Canadian sales were high then why, at the same time, were imports from the United States continuing to set record levels? The reason is that many of the cars we buy in Canada, with the newly adjusted MSRP, rebates and low financing, were now competitive. The vehicles we buy most of—compact cars and compact SUVs—now looked more attractive to buy in Canada, not the US. In contrast, the other end of the market that had the largest percentage discrepancy in sales between the two countries were the more expensive vehicles; they were *still* cheaper by up to 30% than their Canadian counterparts. It doesn't matter where our dollar is trading or what specific incentives are in place, there will always be examples of cheaper cars in the US. To be fair, there are times (when the loonie is low) when Canadian cars are cheaper. The auto market is always evolving, depending on conditions. And since Canadians benefit from buying cars at home when the dollar is low or buying in the US when the dollar is high, we get it both ways.

One of my family members purchased a vehicle from the US, and they claim they saved more than $10,000. A friend picked up a used, fully loaded all-wheel-drive Sienna minivan and saved $10,000 to $15,000. Another family member had a BMW X5 imported and saved at least $20,000. Remarkable savings!

Those were the glory days, and unfortunately for many the party ended too soon. As we all know, in the fall of 2008, the world financial markets came to their knees as we were hit by more and more bad news. The financial boom-times were behind us and the world economy came to a stop, halting the need for Canadian commodities, which in turn affected the strength of the dollar. Since the Canadian dollar was worth 20% less, the advantage of importing a vehicle from United States was greatly diminished and the flow of vehicles slowed to a trickle.

When the Canadian dollar strengthens again, and it will, should you be looking for a vehicle at your local dealership or surfing the Internet trying to find a deal south of the border? There are very good reasons to buy a vehicle in Canada, and in some instances very good reasons to shop in the US. It all comes down to your particular viewpoint and the kind of vehicle you purchase.

One thing many people don't realize when they shop in the US is the car might not be covered under warranty in Canada. Even if it does qualify for coverage in Canada, many dealerships are reluctant to put an out-of-country vehicle ahead of one they sold to a local customer. In the case of my friend with the fully loaded Toyota Sienna, he had a problem with the driver's door latch (common with that vehicle). Even though it was still under warranty, the Canadian dealership dragged its feet because they didn't know (or claimed not to know) how to process a warranty for a US vehicle. I have heard of other scenarios where dealers will repair an out-of-country vehicle, but they put you on the never-never plan. This basically gets your problem addressed when *they* have time, not on your schedule. I've heard of service dates being made three months down the road, not three days! Be aware that dealers want to look after their own customers first, and you can understand why they might feel a bit jilted that you didn't want to purchase one of their vehicles. If they can, they'll make it hard for you to get service, and that great deal you got south of the border might just turn into a big headache.

One of the biggest stumbling blocks when looking for a vehicle south of the border is that there is no option to finance the vehicle in Canada. As we know, most people purchase a vehicle over several years, utilizing low monthly payments. The only way to get the vehicle out of the United States is to pay for it in cash, but for many people that's just not possible. If you have a line of credit that you can use instead of relying on traditional vehicle financing, you might be okay. But for many people, paying for a car in cash is a deal-breaker. Some leasing companies will purchase the US vehicle on your behalf and then lease it back to you, but these types of deals are not widespread.

As stated earlier, the best way to get a deal is to minimize your cost of financing your purchase over a period of time. Unless you have a wonderful rate on your line of credit, some of the financial advantages of bringing a car in from the United States might be mitigated, compared to getting a wonderful interest rate from a manufacturer in Canada. Visiting your local dealership to purchase a vehicle, taking advantage of their low interest rates, a Canadian warranty and peace of mind and knowing you'll be treated fairly, is all much more tempting for some people than just saving a few bucks. On the other hand, saving tens of thousands of dollars is well worth the extra work and risk that comes with importing a vehicle from the US. It really comes down to your level of tolerance for inconveniences versus your desire to save money.

There is a mindset among many used car buyers that they want to buy a Canadian car over an American car. Not knowing the origins of a vehicle can sometimes lead to doubt about its past. For example, after hurricane Katrina, there were stories of unscrupulous vendors in the United States selling off vehicles that had been severely water damaged. Imagine seeing a great car online, buying and importing it to Canada only to find out that there are severe problems throughout. What recourse would you have in that situation? None. I know this sounds a bit dramatic (and it likely was more urban legend than anything), but it does illustrate the point that buying a vehicle from the US can be something of a mystery. Unless you're buying a fairly new vehicle from a reputable dealer and not off a faceless web page, you really have no way of knowing the history of the car. A service in the US called Carfax provides a vehicle history report, but if a car has not been through any one of the government reporting agencies, there is no way to determine its history.

Visiting the United States and buying a brand new car off the lot sounds much easier than it is in reality. I mentioned there are forces behind the scenes trying to stop you from buying a US car. Most car companies in the United States forbid sales to Canadians. This is totally in contradiction of the NAFTA agreement, which allows the free movement of goods across our border. However, the practice continues and as soon as most US dealerships find out you're a Canadian, they will quickly end the conversation by telling you that they'd love your business but are unable to sell you a new car. This blatant act of restricting commerce goes against the very principles of a free capitalist society, so much so that there have been several class-action lawsuits against some of the major auto makers claiming they are in collusion. The theory is that the Canadian arms of these multinational companies have asked the American divisions to impede the sale of US vehicles to Canadians to protect their home turf. None of this has been proven in court, and at this point is an allegation. However, something is going on and if it looks and smells like a rat, it probably is.

Whether you believe these companies have a right to restrict sales to Canadians, the reality is that you might have a hard time buying a brand new car from a US dealership. The best way to get a vehicle across the border and into Canada is to purchase a used car, circumventing the restrictions placed on dealerships. The irony is that these same dealers will sell you a used car but they can't sell you a new car! When people ask me about buying a new vehicle in the US, I tell them to not bother, but do a search online for vehicles that are a few months old. Since the American market is so massive, there are often cases of people buying a vehicle and trading it in again just a few months later. Maybe they couldn't afford the purchase after all, the vehicle was repossessed or they just had a change of heart. But the reality is there are some amazing, almost new, vehicles available in the United States at incredible savings. Because the Canadian market is only one-tenth the size of the US and we have much more conservative buying patterns, these kinds of deals are rarely, if ever available here.

One example I can give you is the BMW SUV I mentioned earlier in this chapter. Check out this deal. In June 2008 in Southern California, someone purchased a heavily optioned BMW X5 for roughly US$65,000. In August 2008, just two months later, the same person traded in that same vehicle at a Nissan dealership with only 4,000 miles on the odometer. Why anyone would buy a very expensive vehicle and trade it in only two months later is a mystery. But I can tell you that my Canadian family member scored an amazing deal on this vehicle. They purchased it from the Nissan dealer for just US$45,000, which worked out to C$47,000 with the exchange rate. There were transportation costs and importation fees but no duty since this particular BMW is made in an American plant. In total, the gently used SUV ended up costing slightly more than $50,000, compared to more than $70,000 for a brand new equivalent with equal options here in Canada. Keep in mind there are also huge tax savings; my family member saved about $2,500 by buying it at $50,000 instead of $70,000. Granted, the US vehicle was used, but even if you are conservative in your pricing estimations, the US vehicle is still $10,000 to $15,000 cheaper.

As I mentioned, there is a bit of a stigma against non-Canadian vehicles, and therefore some of the savings you gain from buying a vehicle in the US will need to be passed on when you go to sell your American vehicle. Any savvy shopper will not be willing to pay the Canadian retail price for your used vehicle when they know you didn't pay the Canadian retail price when you bought it. If you got a deal on the car, expect the next person in line to want a deal as well.

The only protection one might have against passing on savings to the next owner is if you've purchased the US car when the dollar was high and you sell it when the Canadian dollar is very low. For example, if you bought the vehicle when the Canadian dollar was at US$.98 and you sell it when the dollar is a US$.78, then that roughly 20% decrease in the value of our currency might offset the savings the prospective buyer might be looking for.

Also in relation to currency rates, when the Canadian dollar is low and the auto manufacturers have not been able to raise prices quickly enough, Canada has some of the cheapest cars in the world. When comparing prices of the best-selling car in Canada, the Honda Civic, with other parts of the world, we have cheap transportation. At the time of writing, a Civic in Canada starts at roughly $17,000; in Great Britain it's the equivalent of almost C$28,000 and in the US more than C$18,000.

I have several good friends who work in the used car market, and many of them tell me that it isn't worth shopping for a car in the US unless there's a minimum $5,000 savings over the same vehicle in Canada. Keep in mind this is the profit margin they want to make out of selling a used car and not what you might consider a cut-off amount. Once again, the most substantial savings come from financing, and any lack of warranty might quickly diminish any discount you might get from buying south of the border. A $5,000 savings might not be enough to justify importing a US car.

Deciding to look for a vehicle in Canada or the US is a personal decision based on many different factors, from warranty to financing, MSRP, ease of shopping close to home and supporting the Canadian economy. Think long and hard before you make such a decision.

As mentioned, the most savings come with the big-ticket luxury brands and in some cases the savings can be significant. One way to get around shopping for one of these products yourself is to engage a professional to do it for you. Make contact with reputable used car lots that deal mostly in top-notch products and ask them if they have any US cars for sale. Choose businesses that have been around for many years, if not decades. Friends or relatives might be able to recommend a specific dealership based on their own experiences. If not, use the Internet to find out as much as you can.

Many of the vehicles that you find on these higher-end used lots tend to come from the US, especially when the Canadian dollar is in our favour. As I mentioned in an earlier chapter, go into these businesses and get to know the key people, and after a while you will feel more comfortable with your choice of sales person. Most of these businesses will source a vehicle for you in the United States and do all the work buying, transporting, importing and prepping it for you. Get an agreement in writing, stating the fees they will charge you before the vehicle is imported.

The savings will likely not be as great if you use the services of an expert, but there is much less risk going this route. First, the network of contacts that an importing specialist has is vital in getting a car that is in good condition. They might charge you more for getting a US car, but they often obtain the vehicle at a wholesale price—not what you might pay if you tried it yourself. The cost to ship a car, along with many other services, is also cheaper for dealers than individuals. These people often have long-standing relationships with vendors in the US, and dealers have their own subculture and network that will be able to source cars that you might never know were available. They use wholesale lists and intranet sites, and they can often call in a favour to get the exact model you're looking for. I've had some friends pull cars up without any assistance, and others who have left all the work to an importer; getting someone else to handle all the work is often a lot less stressful.

This chapter is called "Why Buy Canadian?" and it can be looked at in two ways. Why buy a Canadian vehicle when there are cheaper American cars available? Or, why shouldn't you buy Canadian? I know that there are great deals to be had on either side of the border, and the amount of savings changes with the strength of our dollar. Conduct a lot of research before you decide to take the plunge on any vehicle purchase. Regardless of which side of the border you decide to shop, the same rule applies: buyer beware!

Part Five

Finishing Touches

13 Road tests

After interviewing prospective dealerships and sales people and having built a short list of potential vehicles, now the fun begins. Really, it should be fun. When you're out on a test drive, you're doing exactly the same thing I do as an automotive reviewer, but you are not doing it for publication, you're doing it for yourself. Trust me, test driving cars for a living is a lot of fun. So when you're putting a car through its paces, have some fun with it, but also have a critical eye.

Remember to include on your short list some vehicles you might not have considered, or maybe a brand you normally wouldn't have contemplated. Instead of a compact SUV, give some thought to a small station wagon, or a diesel instead of a traditional gasoline engine. By going outside of your comfort zone trying different vehicles, something might stand out that could change your mind about your purchase direction.

In the past, I've suggested certain types of vehicles to friends and family, and initially they turned up their noses at the idea of trying something they hadn't considered. What often happens is after trying something new they have a totally different opinion. When I write a review for *Driving Television*, I try to have an open mind about the attributes of each vehicle. If I had a closed mind and only focused on the cars that *I* drive personally, my reviews would be one-dimensional. Looking at a vehicle without prejudice will open your eyes to products that could ultimately lead to better long-term purchasing decisions.

INTERIOR "FIT" AND FINISH

What do I look for when I test drive a car? And what should you be looking for in your personal vehicle? The list is long, but let's start with the most basic of needs—do you fit? I've covered this in an earlier chapter but it's worth repeating. If you don't fit in a vehicle or you don't feel comfortable as a passenger, keep on looking.

The size and shape of the car will not change, and if you don't fit properly when it's brand new, that won't be any different over time. Make sure you can sit comfortably and reach all the essential features with ease. Don't go alone; take your family and take accessories such as baby seats, strollers, hockey bags and golf clubs—all the things you use on a regular basis, and see if those will fit too.

Something else you should consider when you're inside a prospective test car is the level of fit and finish compared to other vehicles you test. Many new buyers often overlook interior design and finish because they have no reference point to compare to. This is why taking time to shop is so important. Going to several different dealerships and driving several different vehicles on your short list will give you the kind of baseline knowledge you need to make an informed decision. For example, if I were trying to do a test drive of the Toyota Corolla without having driven its other main competitors, I wouldn't have anything to compare it to. The same is true when you're looking at a vehicle to buy. By going from one vehicle to the next you will get a sense of which ones have a better use of materials on the inside.

What's so important about the interior? The fit and finish is key because this is what you interact the most with on any vehicle. The feeling of the steering wheel in your hand, the functionality of the buttons and switches, the read-out of the gauges and information displays and how they all work is important and is what connects you to the car. One of the most important features on any new vehicle is the use of hard plastics. Manufacturers are trying to utilize softer materials on the dash, doors and any other surfaces that the interior occupants come in contact with. These materials give the impression of quality but more importantly they don't scratch easily compared to many of the hard plastics used by some auto makers. When I'm reviewing a vehicle, I tap on the surfaces of the interior to find out if they are soft-touch or hard plastic. Usually, less expensive vehicles are riddled with this less expensive hard plastic, but some manufacturers take more pride and effort with their interior finishes, and give the buyer a more upscale feel through the use of better materials. If the interior of the car literally feels cheap to the touch it gives the sense of a cheap product. Would you rather spend all of your time inside a car looking at something that is cheap or rich and luxurious? I can almost bet on the answer. We get so caught up on the exterior styling of a car, but in reality when you're driving, it's the interior that you look at, and it's just as important.

REALLY DRIVE THE CAR ON A TEST DRIVE

The term test drive is a little misleading because, for many people, it's a five-minute spin around a few blocks with a sales person in the passenger seat, and then back to the dealership. The kind of test drive I'm talking about is just that—testing your potential new car in the same conditions you will drive it. If you live in an urban setting and spend much of your time driving in stop-and-go traffic, then that's the kind of test drive you should emulate. On the other hand, if you're a person who lives in the suburbs or a rural area, you should take the car on the highway or a backcountry road and drive it in those conditions. In an earlier chapter, I mentioned that you should also review the dealership and the salespeople to see if they are a good fit for your needs. If you take the time to get to know potential sales people, they might let you take out a vehicle for a real test drive—and by "real" I mean a good, long test drive. When I test a vehicle for *Driving Television*, I keep it for a minimum of one week and in most cases two weeks. Don't expect any dealership to give you a vehicle for that long, but taking a car out for an hour is not out of the question. Some dealers insist their sales people accompany you, but it is so much more relaxed without an employee of the dealership riding along. In my opinion, this is a much better way to test drive a vehicle; it gives you a chance to really do the test without somebody talking in your ear or distracting you from what you want to achieve. Some higher-end dealerships that sell expensive luxury cars will often let you take a test car home overnight, allowing you a great chance to use the vehicle in your day-to-day life.

So what should you be looking for when you test a vehicle just like an auto reviewer? We've already touched on the interior, fit and finish, but now you should use the features that are in the car as you drive. You want to see if the interface between the car and the driver or any passengers is simple and easy. Many cars have a lot of electronic advancements but they are horrid to navigate, pun intended. Check to see if the navigation system is easy to program and operate. Can you easily manoeuvre through the radio and heat controls without too much difficulty? Granted, some of these features take some time to learn, but I have found that the most intuitive systems are best.

Another reason I want you to test a vehicle under normal day-to-day conditions is to get a feel for the power, brakes and steering. If you drive a lot on the highway, does the engine have enough power to pass when necessary? If you live in the city and manoeuvre in and out of traffic on a regular basis, is the steering too heavy or light? If you spend much of your time crawling along in bumper-to-bumper traffic, do the brakes grab and release smoothly? These types of attributes would be totally lost had you only taken one vehicle for a short five-minute drive around the dealership. By using the vehicle in the kind of conditions that you typically drive in, the good and bad points quickly surface.

If you spend a lot of time in rush-hour traffic, going to the dealership on a Sunday morning when there's nobody on the road is not a good test for your lifestyle. But taking that Sunday morning test drive along with another test drive in city traffic will give you a good reflection of the vehicle's abilities.

Testing the different vehicles on your short list several times—going from one vehicle to the next and back again—you will be able to build important baseline knowledge. How many vehicles do you get to drive in any given year? Two or three, maybe five or six? I can guarantee it certainly isn't in the dozens. Most people drive their personal vehicle and maybe their spouse's on a regular basis, but the only time you ever get to drive another car is when you rent one on vacation or on a business trip. Since you're so used to your own car, the idea of test driving several cars might be a little overwhelming at first. If I took you out of the car you've driven for 10 years and put you in a brand new 2010 model with all the latest electronic advancement, a more powerful engine and advanced safety electronics, you would be so thrilled with the experience that you might not want to consider anything else. But if I insisted that you get in and out of several different vehicles over several months to get accustomed to what's available in the marketplace, you would quickly learn what you like and don't like. I know many people who have gone to test a new vehicle, after driving their old car for a decade, and been so overwhelmed with the newness of the car that they purchased it without investigating any other options. Knowledge is power. The more knowledge you have about what's available—with several kilometres under your belt over a period of time—you too will be like a reviewer: able to give your opinion on what you like and don't like.

One objective for many potential buyers is trying an alternative to a regular gasoline car or truck. If you're in the market for a hybrid, diesel or a smaller turbo-charged engine, the first time you try these alternatives, the driving sensation might feel totally foreign. But after driving several, the uniqueness dissipates until the new power plant feels normal. Hybrids, in particular, have a unique feel that's hard to describe and at first can be off-putting. After a while, however, once you adapt, the sensation can be very rewarding. On the other hand, a hybrid might be so smooth and quiet that a performance-oriented driver will come to realize that it's not for them.

Many drivers are surprised when they try a vehicle equipped with a new clean-burning diesel engine, because it is so much more sophisticated than the diesels we drove decades ago. The power, lack of diesel smell and the smooth and quiet operation is often a pleasant surprise, and after a while many potential buyers realize diesel is a good option.

Whenever you're outside of your comfort zone, the tendency is to resist anything that's new—it's human nature. Adjusting to a new type of vehicle or engine will take time because drivers tend to like what they know. On the other hand, the newness might be so intoxicating they make a rash decision. So, take test drives and get used to the vehicles on your short list. The more time you spend behind the wheel, the shorter the list will become and hopefully you will whittle it down to one or two well-researched choices. If you've narrowed it down to a few different vehicles but you're still undecided, consider putting everything aside for a few weeks and then go back and test drive them again. You will have forgotten many aspects of each car, and the high and low points will jump out at you again.

Often, you are not just comparing vehicle attributes but also the price and financing in combination to determine the best vehicle choice. As I mentioned at the beginning of the book, every vehicle is a compromise, and the best designed and handling vehicle might be too expensive or use too much fuel, so in the end something has to go. Getting the right balance of design, price and appeal is difficult, but taking the time to think through the options will help you settle on the vehicle you really want to buy.

14 Doing the deal

Without question, this is the one part of buying a vehicle that almost every single person dreads. Some people, because of their occupation, negotiate on a regular basis, whether they're in sales or they work on contracts. Unfortunately, most of us don't have the skill set that enables us to get the best price possible. Being able to negotiate and come to a fair price is something that has to be learned, and hopefully by reading this chapter you will gain the confidence to go in and get a fair deal.

The reason I use the word "fair" is that dealers are in business to make money, not to give the vehicles away at cost. It might come as a surprise to many people, but new car dealers don't make a lot of money selling new cars. Canadians love small, inexpensive vehicles and those products have very small profit margins for the businesses selling them. Larger, more expensive luxury models tend to be more profitable but even these brands can have low profit margins. Dealerships make most of their money on servicing vehicles and selling used cars. As I pointed out earlier, the best deal you will get on any car is with manufacturer incentives and low financing costs. Negotiating the price of a vehicle is common, but the savings that can be gained are often quite low. Brands that are in high demand often don't discount much, if at all. Those that are struggling in sales will often be more open to negotiating a lower price. The Honda Civic is the best-selling car in Canada, and going into a Honda dealer and trying to negotiate thousands of dollars off the price will be almost futile. On the other hand, with so much bad news surrounding many of the domestic makers, there is a better chance of getting a discount on one of their products. I don't want to suggest that you shouldn't try to negotiate a discount, but you have to be realistic when there isn't a lot of money to be made by the dealership when you buy a car.

If you've already decided before you head into a dealership whether you're going to lease, finance or buy your vehicle outright, keep this information to yourself. Why? The simple answer is that you want to negotiate the price before you implement any terms on the agreement. Leasing a vehicle based only on the monthly payment and not on the original purchase price can often lead to spending more money in the long run. The more money you negotiate off the purchase price, the less your monthly payments will be. If you base your decision just on the monthly payments, not knowing the purchase price, you often will end up paying for a longer period of time or the full retail price.

NEGOTIATION STRATEGIES AND THE "$500 WALK"

So how do you negotiate a lower price on a car? One way is to shop a few different dealerships to get an idea of just how flexible they are. When you're actively searching for a car, you can play one off against the other and hopefully get the best deal possible. I'm a firm believer that you should "dance with the girl you brought," meaning if you have started a relationship with one dealer and a particular sales person, it isn't very fair to go down the street and buy from a dealer who hasn't worked to gain your business. On the other hand, you don't want to pay more than you have to, just so you can get the vehicle you want. If you have built a relationship, you should have confidence in what they tell you. If your sales person tells you there isn't much negotiating room for a particular car, then you know you can't get much off. But it shouldn't deter you from trying.

I'm sure you have seen the television shows about real estate where an "expert" helps people find and purchase a home. In these shows, the house of their dreams is often more expensive than they can afford. The tension mounts as the expert tries to buy their dream home at a price that is more manageable. The way they do this is to put in an offer below the asking price in hopes that the seller will take it. If not, the seller often puts in a counter-offer less than the asking price but above what the buyer originally offered. What usually happens is the buyer and seller go back and forth until they come to a price they agree on.

This back and forth negotiating is exactly how you should negotiate a new car purchase. There is nothing wrong with you putting in a low-ball offer to see if the seller is motivated. The worst thing that can happen is that the sales manager will say no! If that's the case, then you know you have to come back with a more realistic price. On the other hand, the sales manager might discount the car slightly to entice you to come up to his price. This is beginning to look like one of those real estate programs, don't you think?

Something else that happens in the real estate market that can be directly related to a car purchase is offering incentives for people to buy. This has been no more evident than in the current downturn in the housing market, with free upgrades such as granite counter-tops and stainless steel appliances to get people to buy a brand new home. There is nothing wrong with asking for upgrades on your new car. Maybe you want the dealership to throw in a full set of rubber floor mats for the winter, or a car alarm, maybe an upgraded stereo, back-up sensors and, my favourite, a set of spare wheels and winter tires. If they want your business, they will seriously con-sider your requests for additional equipment or services in lieu of a price reduction.

Getting a set of wheels and tires free might be unrealistic, but getting them at the dealership's costs is likely something they would consider. Installing a back-up camera or an upgraded ste-reo is something they do often, and to make a sale they will often include services as part of the deal. So just like a real estate agent, you should be able to negotiate either a lower price or additional equipment to close the deal.

Dealers will often give you a good price for your trade-in, but are reluctant to reduce the purchase price of a new vehicle at the same time. Dealers need to make money somewhere; remem-ber, they're a business, and they have to pay their employees and overhead. Getting a crackerjack trade-in price and a huge reduc-tion in the purchase price is not very likely. Dealerships want to make money on either your used car or the new car; they will be reluctant to give a reduction on both. This doesn't mean that it is inconceivable, it's just unlikely. Once again, this is why you need to negotiate the purchase price of the vehicle before you do anything else. Once you have reduced that to a satisfactory level, you should explain to the sales person that you want to trade in your existing vehicle. If they give you fair value for your trade and you have nego-tiated a reduction in purchase price, then you're as close to nirvana as you're ever going to get. If you do it the other way around, they might give you the same fair trade-in value but be reluctant to dis-count the new vehicle.

Another tactic many people use to get the best possible price is to negotiate with the sales person and then take some time to think about it. Dealerships don't like this tactic; this is the reason they want you to give them a deposit and negotiate the purchase all in one day. They don't want you to have second thoughts and they really want to stop you from shopping the street. If you get 8/10ths of the way through a transaction with one dealership and then walk out knowing what their best possible price is, only to walk down the street and try to get a better price from somebody else, that doesn't benefit the first dealer at all. They want you to stay with them and sign a deal all in one visit. There is nothing to stop you from shopping around, but the relationship with the dealership may be soured to the point that they don't want to deal with you anymore.

The more tactful way to use this negotiating tool is to get to a point in the transaction where you feel you're getting close on the price, and then take a break. There is absolutely nothing wrong with saying to your sales person that you want to go home and think about it for a while. Let them know you're very interested and you feel that you're close in price, but would like them to sharpen their pencil a bit more to close the deal. No dealership wants you to walk down the street and buy a car from somebody else. I almost guarantee that the sales person will call you within hours, not days, to get your business and often they will have made concessions.

My father used this technique many times, and he calls it the $500 walk. Just by mentioning you want to take a break and motion for the door, he feels he gets an instant price reduction of $500. This is the point in the transaction you will find out if there is much more room in your purchase price. If the dealership isn't going to move on the price, then you know you've reached the bottom. Taking a little time to think over your purchase, even if the dealership has shown their hand, isn't such a bad idea. It gives you a chance to really think over any purchase before you actually go through with it, and also gives the dealership time to come back with another offer.

One way the dealers try to keep you in the building and shopping with them is to ask for a deposit, and many times they will say it is non-refundable. Do not, under any circumstances, give a deposit to a dealership unless you have it in writing that it's fully refundable. There is absolutely no reason for a dealership to ask for a non-refundable deposit, and if they're not willing to put it in writing, then walk out the door and find another dealership! The only time that money is non-refundable is when you sign for the vehicle and drive off the lot. Up until then you should be able to change your mind and walk away without any financial ramifications.

REFUNDABLE DEPOSITS

Good dealerships do not pressure potential buyers into signing contracts and committing money before they are ready. You should be able to negotiate the price of the vehicle and work with the dealership on a deal without any deposit at all.

There are times, however, that you should consider giving a deposit, but it must be fully refundable. One example might be when there is low availability of a certain car and you want to ensure you don't lose out on the one vehicle you are interested in. I remember purchasing a vehicle for my wife, knowing exactly what we were looking for, going to our favourite dealership only to find out that there were only two vehicles left. What I did was place a $1,000 deposit on the car with my credit card. This was with the full understanding that if we didn't decide to go through with the purchase, I would get my money returned in full. Using a credit card is beneficial because if there is any problem with the dealership, and no transaction takes place, you can have the funds returned.

Placing a deposit on a vehicle prevents the dealership from selling it to someone else, usually for a limited time of three to five days. This gives you time to think about the purchase without fearing the car will be sold. If at the end of that period the transaction cannot be finalized, then the money is returned and the dealer sells the car to someone else. It really is like having your cake and eating it too; making a refundable deposit shows you are serious, without any risk to your bank balance.

Another way dealerships push potential buyers into making a decision is to state that there are only a few vehicles left. By placing a refundable deposit on a car, you remove the pressure to make a snap decision. Ask the dealership to show you their inventory data to confirm what they say is true. Once again, this comes back to the relationship. If you have taken the time to get to know your sales person and the dealership and believe they're being honest, then you will be more confident to make the right decisions based on fact, not on speculation.

Once you have come to terms on the price you're willing to pay for the car and the value of your trade-in, you can move forward with the final purchase. The sales manager will agree to the terms of the deal, and if you haven't yet put down a deposit, you will be required to at that time. Once again, make sure it is fully refundable.

The sales person then puts you in contact with the business manager, who helps to put the financing together through either the manufacturer's finance arm or the banks they work with. You should be aware that most dealerships try to include additional fees to your sales contract to help bolster their bottom line. Before you see the business manager, tell your sales person and sales manager that you will not be paying any extra fees. This should get a reaction! First, they will be a bit shocked that you would be so informed as to ask for no fees. Then they will say that you have to pay them, everyone does. At this point, state that paying fees is a deal-breaker, and you don't want to pay any more for the vehicle than the sales price, plus taxes. I guarantee that they will make a fuss but eventually they will take the fees out of the contract.

When you meet with the business manager, repeat that you're not willing to pay any extra fees. At this point, the business manager should agree but there might be certain fees that are out of their control. Sometimes the financing company implements charges in order to get the lease or loan processed and gain access to certain deals. There is nothing you, or the dealership, can do except pay. If there is a fee that is out of the dealership's control, ask to see it, don't just take their word for it.

The kinds of charges you shouldn't be paying for are documentation fees or processing fees that the dealerships include, making a few bucks on every transaction. If you state up front that you won't pay them, you will eventually get your way. I know this advice will be unpopular with dealerships, but I believe the dealers have to earn your business. If they do a good job on the sales end, they will make money on the subsequent servicing and future sales.

I'm not sure how these fees got started, but in my opinion they should be banned. (Can you imagine going to a grocery store only to find out that they have an additional fee to process your purchase!) This practice is also rampant in the airline business, where they advertise a fare excluding all the fees. By the time you pay for your airline tickets, the cost can sometimes double. The good news is that you have control over where you spend your money. When it comes time to get a vehicle, tell the dealership up front that you will not pay, so there is no surprise.

Back to the process of buying a car. The business manager should be looked at as an additional salesperson . . . you're not done yet with the push to spend more. You will be offered items such as undercoating, paint protection, extended warranties, service packages, fabric and leather protecting, window etching and many other up-sell features. Some of these products are worthwhile, but how do you know which ones you should choose? Let's have a look at some of the most popular items.

DEALERSHIP UPSELLS

Undercoating and rust protection: having your vehicle undercoated to prevent rust was a real concern decades ago when vehicle manufacturers didn't use rust-preventing techniques like galvanized steel and the extensive use of plastic. I remember my dad's Buick from the 1970s rusting after a few years, so back then it would have been a good idea to have a vehicle rust-protected. Today's cars are built to a totally different standard. Galvanized steel is used on the lower parts of the car where rust had been a problem in the past, especially on the lower sections of the doors, fenders and trunk lid. Also, plastic is now used extensively on the inside of the wheel wells and along the bottom of the vehicle, where the salty spray in the winter splashes up. Keeping salt and water away from steel greatly reduces the problem of premature rust perforation. Because of these advancements, the likelihood of a modern vehicle rusting out is much lower, to the point that I'm not a big advocate of buying rust protection from a dealership.

Many of the techniques dealerships use to prevent rust are very simple, if not primitive. They spray a thin layer of petroleum-based product on the underside of the car, which doesn't penetrate the nooks and crannies where salt water can penetrate. If you plan to keep your car for a long period of time, then getting rust protection might be a good idea. In my opinion, though, undercoating isn't the way to go. There are other forms of protection you can purchase after you get your new vehicle, even years later.

The person who runs my web site, www.motormouth.ca, went to buy a mid-size luxury SUV and called me from the dealership asking if he should purchase undercoating/rust proofing for his new vehicle. (His current vehicle was a 12-year-old Toyota minivan.) I asked him if his old vehicle had any rust on it. He said no. So he basically answered his own question. If his 12-year-old minivan had no rust, why would his brand new vehicle rust any quicker, especially with the latest manufacturing techniques? Just out of interest, I asked how much the dealership was going to charge for this rust protection. I almost fell out of my chair when he said $2,500! You have to be kidding me, I said. That's outrageous.

For people who live in parts of the country where the weather is harsh, getting rust protection might be a good idea if you plan to keep the vehicle for a long period of time. If you plan to only keep it for three to seven years, rust protection might not be worth the expense. That said, there are some excellent products you can have put on your car, and they don't have to be applied by the dealership at an exorbitant fee. Krown Rust Control and Rust Check are two very reputable companies that have been in business in Canada for many years and have proven to be very effective in combating rust. Unlike the one-time application dealerships subscribe to, these companies apply a thin liquid that creeps into every nook and cranny of a vehicle, pushing out the moisture that promotes rust. These systems are most effective when they are applied on an annual basis, but I have found in personal experience that after a few applications, this wonderful protection keeps your vehicle looking brand new. The good news is that this type of rust protection costs just $100 to $150 dollars a year, and will keep your vehicle fully protected. Even if you kept it for 10 years and had this rust protection applied every single year, you would still have spent only about $1,500.

This rust proofing/undercoating up-sell is a perfect example of the kind of products you can purchase yourself without having to involve the dealership. There might be some great rust-proofing techniques dealerships use that I'm not familiar with, but having driven in harsh, Canadian winters and using products such as Rust Check and Krown, I can wholeheartedly endorse them.

Another up-sell is paint protection for your shiny new vehicle. Protecting your paint is a great idea, but I have found that some of the products used to supposedly protect the paint, in the long run, look worse than had the paint been left alone. The only way you can really protect your paint, in the long run, is to take an interest in its condition—which means you have to wash your vehicle and apply a good cover of wax on a regular basis. I have my own vehicles professionally cleaned at least once a year, including a polish with a high-quality wax. Even when things like bird poop, tree sap, leaves, tar and road grime beat up the paint, the high-quality wax underneath provides the best layer of protection against these corrosive and harmful elements. If you notice any of these on your vehicle, it's wise to remove them as quickly as possible with a proper soap formulated for cars. Vehicles that look like they are brand new, even years after they've been on the road, are typically owned by people who take the time to clean and wax them on a regular basis. The paint protection dealerships sell, in my opinion, will not protect your paint if you don't make the effort to keep your vehicle clean. Good old soap and water is the best bet to keeping your car looking new.

If stone chips have beaten up your old vehicle, you might want to protect your new car with what is called a clear-bra. This is a thin, clear film that is applied to the front of a car to prevent stone chips and damage. Developed originally by 3M, this film is undetectable from a few feet away and might be a better investment than regular paint protection. Ask your dealership if they install this film or if they can arrange to have it done.

Seat protection, or what is commonly called Scotchgarding the interior, is another up-sell that doesn't have to be done at the dealership. It's a good idea to go to a reputable detailing shop and ask them how much they charge to have this protection applied. Many of the fabrics in today's new cars have coatings to help prevent stains from forming, so adding an extra layer of protection might be overkill. Once again, the best way to preserve your interior is to clean it on a regular basis with a mild soap and water or cleaners formulated for car interiors. If you see a spill, clean it up quickly to prevent a stain from setting in.

Leather seats have become popular for the easy wipe-down that can be done when a spill happens, but leather seats need annual care to maintain that supple look. I don't believe a one-time application at the dealership will protect leather seats for a long period of time; the only way to keep your leather looking new is to moisturize it regularly. Just like dry hands that can crack, leather needs to be moisturized. There are plenty of great leather care products on the market, just make sure they don't have any silicone—this can actually promote cracking. If you plan on getting your new vehicle detailed once a year, ask them to treat your leather seats at the same time.

Other items that the sales person might want to include are an extended warranty or service package. First the warranty. There are two basic extended warranties, the manufacturer's warranty and an after-market or third-party warranty. If you are absolutely certain you will keep your vehicle for a long time, outside of the standard warranty, you might want to spend the extra money to extend the coverage. If you're uncertain about how long you will keep the vehicle, then you might want to delay the purchase of an extended warranty.

Some manufacturers will sell you an extended warranty at a lower rate when the car is brand new, or give you the option to purchase it at a later date at higher cost. Buying an extended warranty from the manufacturer is your best bet, because when you bring your vehicle in for service, you don't have to deal with a third-party. Usually, the warranty work is done and the dealership takes care of the bill without you having to pay for the repair and wait to get reimbursed. There is also a greater chance the dealership will go to bat for any warranty work that needs to be done when they are dealing with their own company versus having to deal with third-party coverage. Some of the aftermarket warranty companies are very reputable, but others have questionable backgrounds—which means you have to do your due diligence to know which one is best to cover you in the long run.

Always ask if you have to buy the extended warranty at the outset of your new car purchase, or if you can bring the vehicle in, have it inspected and then have the extended warranty instated. If this is an option, you can drive your car for several years with the existing warranty and decide at a later date if you want to extend coverage on a pay-as-you-go system. The other option is to use the existing new car warranty, and when you reach the end of that period, decide whether you want to shop the market and get third-party coverage for your long-term needs. Some of these companies offer very competitive rates and will extend the warranty much farther than a factory plan. You need to ask lots of questions of the business manager, and if you're not satisfied with the answers, make sure *they* will do the homework to find out more before you sign off on your new car purchase.

Another package that might be presented to you when you close your deal is a maintenance package to cover repairs such as worn brakes. Once again, it comes down to how long you plan to keep your vehicle, how much you drive and what the cost of these regular service items are. It's very easy to walk down to the service department and ask how much brake service would typically cost for your vehicle and any other service items that are included in the maintenance package. With this information, you can easily compare how much the maintenance package will cost versus paying out of pocket. Several years ago when we were leasing a mid-size SUV, the business manager proposed a $750 maintenance package that included regular wear items such as brakes. A brake job on the vehicle we were just about to lease was well in excess of $750, and this package would have been money well spent if we were owners who typically drove plenty of mileage. In our case, we don't do a lot of mileage and due to the lease duration, we realized we probably wouldn't need any additional service before the vehicle had to be returned. If, on the other hand, we drove 25,000 to 30,000 kilometres a year, this package would have been a money saver. So, take the time to do the math, average your yearly driving and see if a maintenance package can save you money in the long run.

Other items include a credit protection package, which will ensure that if you are not able to pay for your vehicle or if you're laid off from work, the insurance will pay for your vehicle until you get back on the job. Some of these policies pay the difference between what your vehicle is worth and the amount you still owe. (For example, in the unfortunate event you become ill and the vehicle is worth $15,000 but you owe $20,000, then you and your family are still on the hook for the outstanding $5,000.) This type of credit protection bridges the gap between the value of the car and the amount outstanding. For the small cost of this credit protection, I believe it's money well spent. It will give you great peace of mind knowing that if anything should ever happen to your job or health, your car will not be an additional burden.

One of the companies that offer this protection is Walk Away Canada, and I have had the opportunity to interview the president and founder several times on my radio show. You might have seen TV commercials where car companies promote that if you lose your job within the first year of ownership you can return your vehicle. Hyundai was the first car company in the US to offer this product; in Canada, Toyota and Kia also have similar protection. Walk Away Canada is the company that put several of these packages together, and it has the same kind of protection available at dealerships that offer their services. The cost is only a few hundred dollars to protect you and your investment for several years, so ask your business manager when you're closing the deal if such a product is available.

There is a new up-sell that I'm hearing more about that seems to be a bit over the top. Some dealers are telling buyers that they have to have security numbers etched on the glass of their brand new vehicle. One gentleman contacted me to tell me his dealership insisted he absolutely had to have this security feature, and they were going to charge a fee of several hundred dollars. I don't know of any jurisdiction that mandates security codes etched into glass. This future owner got in touch with the regional sales manager and was told this practice was not something the manufacture mandated, and he should ask to be reimbursed for his money. Had this customer not been alert and asked pertinent questions, the dealership would have made a few hundred dollars at his expense.

The lesson here is that there really isn't anything you need to purchase on a brand new or even a used car other than the taxes due on completion. If the business manager says something is mandatory and you have to pay for it, this should raise a red flag. Ask plenty of questions and if you're not satisfied with the answers, take a break from the process and head off to another dealership to get verification one way or the other.

A perfect example of this was an e-mail I received from a frustrated new car owner who traded in a vehicle for an agreed price of $8,500. A few days later, as he was driving his brand new car, he heard an advertisement on the radio stating that any cash purchase on the model he just bought would get an additional $2,000 discount. When he got home, he pulled out his contract and sure enough, the dealership didn't give him $8,500 for the trade-in, they gave him $6,500 and applied the $2,000 cash discount to come up with the $8,500 figure. He was ticked, and rightfully so. I told him to go back and speak to the sales manager and general manager to get this resolved. In a subsequent e-mail, the owner told me the general manager couldn't reopen the contract but they were willing to give him $3,000 worth of services for the mix-up. He was not entirely satisfied, but the dealership did show goodwill to try to rectify the problem. The sales person might have given him the figure of $8,500 knowing full well that it was a combination of trade-in and rebate. He might have mentioned that to the owner, but in the rush of getting his new car, the customer might not have noticed. On the other hand, the sales person might have pulled a fast one, we'll never know. What *you* should know is that whenever you are signing a final sales document and driving off the lot, the deal is done and you have entered into a contract. Some provinces have a cooling-off period, which allows the owner to change their mind, but it's usually only a few days. You must read your sales contract very carefully and ask lots of questions. If you are not satisfied with the answers you're getting, stop. Buying a vehicle is a very expensive proposition and you don't want to be taken advantage of—and you certainly want to know exactly what your rights are. If there's something on your sales document that you don't understand, make sure you get it fully explained. If you see a fee or an amount on the sales form which looks out of line, don't proceed without speaking up. Once you have signed and taken the vehicle home, there is very little recourse.

Earlier in this book I mentioned the phrase "You are in charge." You should always keep this in mind throughout the full process of shopping and purchasing any new or used vehicle. Since you're the one who will be spending the money, you have the upper hand. Dealerships and the people who work inside them have to work for your business and you have to feel comfortable that they're putting your best interests first. It is also important that *you* take the responsibility to speak up and ask questions when something isn't quite right, because sometimes it can be just a matter of miscommunication and not the dealer trying to take advantage of you. For most people, the car business is foreign; they speak a different language and processes might not be familiar, so don't be afraid to ask and have dealers explain to you exactly what is taking place.

If you follow the steps in this book and have tried several different vehicles, narrowed your list and then finally decided on one vehicle, you will be so much farther ahead than people who have no direction at all. By doing research online and knowing what incentives there are and the prices asked, you will be able to spot good value when you see it. Taking the time to do your due diligence and test drive vehicles without being rushed will give you a clear head to think through your prospective purchase and come to a rational decision. When it's actually time to push the deal forward, don't be rushed—take charge and if you see something you don't like, speak up. You are in charge . . . remember that.

Buying a new or used vehicle is something almost all of us have to go through. Your attitude and the way you deal with everything along the way can make it a fun and exciting experience. Instead of looking at buying a car as a burden, hopefully, after reading *Motormouth*, you will see it as something that can be very rewarding. Good luck, and happy driving.

PartSix

Ratings

How to Read the Reviews

RATINGS

Ratings have been broken down into three main categories:

- "Worth consideration" means a vehicle might be worth looking at but it is not as strong a candidate as others.

- "Must try" means that the vehicle should be on your short list and is worth a test drive. For categories with many models rated as "Must try," the choices for the consumer are very competitive. Some buyers might find different aspects of certain models more suitable to their needs.

- "Top Pick" is the overall winner in a category.

PRICES

Prices have been rounded off to the nearest thousand. Prices can change at any time, so these are just a guide. The lower price is the starting price of the base model and the upper price is the starting price of the top model. Remember that these prices do not include optional equipment, so prices will vary depending on trim choices.

ENGINES

The engine choices and horsepower ratings listed are not always available on every trim level. For example, a 2.4L engine might be the base engine but on higher trim levels the same vehicle might also have a 3.5L V6 available, in addition to the 2.4L. It is a good idea to check the manufacturer's web site to get clarification on engine options at different trim levels. Horsepower ratings are supplied by the manufacturers and have not been independently verified.

WARRANTY

The warranty listed is the manufacturer's basic bumper–to–bumper warranty and does not include the extended powertrain warranty or any extra coverage for items like rust perforation or emissions.

Please check the manufacturer's web sites to get clarification on extra warranty coverage.

STANDARD SAFETY FEATURES

The safety features listed are the standard equipment on the base model. More expensive trim levels will often have more standard safety features. Check the manufacturer's web sites for clarification on individual models.

AVERAGE FUEL CONSUMPTION

This rating—the amount of fuel a model will consume during a year of use—is provided by Natural Resources Canada and is based on its testing performed on every vehicle sold in Canada. The manufacturers do not provide fuel ratings. The average fuel consumption per year is based on the posted city and highway fuel rating and then calculated at 55% city and 45% highway over 20,000 kilometres. This gives a good baseline comparison and is better than the posted fuel rating (supplied in the event average fuel consumption figures aren't available) because it allows potential buyers the ability to calculate fuel costs based on the current cost of gas. Keep in mind individual fuel consumption will change depending on the types of roads driven, weather, city or highway use and driving style.

INITIAL QUALITY SCORE

This is the published quality score from the JD Power and Associates' *Initial Quality Study* from 2009. Initial quality is based on vehicle problems within the first 90 days of ownership. JD Power and Associates has tracked vehicle ratings for decades and contends that the quality of a car in the first 90 days is a good barometer of quality over the life of the vehicle. For more information and to look up additional information, go to www.jdpower.com.

DEPENDABILITY SCORE

This is the published quality score from the JD Power and Associates' *Dependability Study* based on 2006 vehicles. This study tracks the dependability of vehicles after three years of ownership. Keep in mind that if a vehicle has been significantly updated in the last three years, the dependability score might not be applicable.

ACRONYMS

AWD: all-wheel drive
FWD: front-wheel drive
RWD: rear-wheel drive
ABS: anti-lock brakes
4X2: four-wheel drive with two-wheel drive availability
4X4: four-wheel drive
SUV: sport-utility vehicle
V6: six-cylinder engine, with two banks of three cylinders
V8: eight-cylinder engine with two banks of four cylinders

Subcompact Category

SUBCOMPACT CARS

Chevy Aveo

Rating	Basic car, basic price
Price	Sedan: $14,000 Hatchback: $14,000
Engine	1.6L 4-cylinder with 108hp
Standard safety features include	Front airbags. Optional: side airbags, anti-lock brakes (ABS).
Average fuel consumption	1382L/year
Warranty	3-year/60,000 km
Initial quality score	2/5
Dependability score	2/5

Pros: The Aveo is made in Korea by the General Motors subsidiary Daewoo. This four-door sedan or hatchback offers basic transportation for buyers who are bottom-line oriented. The ride is smooth and well dampened for such an inexpensive car.

Cons: The lack of standard safety features is a major drawback in the face of well-appointed cars like the Honda Fit and Nissan Versa. The interior is rather small, even for this class of car.

Honda Fit

Rating	TOP PICK
Price	$15,000-$20,000
Engine	1.5L 4-cylinder with 117hp
Standard safety features include	Front, side and curtain airbags, and ABS
Average fuel consumption	N/A
Warranty	5-year/100,000 km
Fuel rating	7.1L/100km (40mpg) city and 5.5L/100km (51mpg) hwy
Initial quality score	N/A
Dependability score	4.5/5

Pros: The Fit set the pace for standard safety equipment when it was first introduced, including front, side and curtain airbags along with ABS. Now more companies are including these features as standard equipment. The Fit is a study in how to use a small space very well. The rear seats flip and fold to provide many configurations for cargo and passengers and the whole passenger experience is like driving a larger car. The engine is spirited, even with the automatic transmission, and handling is above average, making the Fit a bunch of fun to drive. Buyers enjoy good value, great fuel consumption, reliability and a strong resale market. The Fit might be more expensive than others in this class but you get what you pay for. Excellent car!

Cons: For price-conscious buyers the Fit is more expensive than alternatives in this category, but it comes very well equipped. For these buyers the Fit might price itself out of their purchase decision.

Hyundai Accent

Rating	Must try
Price	Sedan: $14,000-$18,000 Hatchback: $13,000-$18,000
Engine	1.6L 4-cylinder with 110hp
Standard safety features include	Front airbags. Optional: ABS and side and curtain airbags.
Average fuel consumption	1354L/year
Warranty	5-year/100,000 km
Initial quality score	3.5/5
Dependability score	N/A

Pros: Hyundai has had a remarkable renaissance with a surge in sales, even in light of the recent economic downturn. Their cars offer amazing value and they continue to score very well in quality scores. The Accent is the cheapest car offered in Canada when Hyundai discounts the hatchback price to $9995! Even though the price is low, the Accent is nicely finished on the inside with simple trim and appointments, but remember this is basic transportation for cost-conscious buyers. Available in hatchback or sedan trim, the buyer can choose the level of interior trim depending on their budget. The Accent holds up very well in the used market so the value equation is even better.

Cons: The biggest knock on the Accent is the lack of standard safety features like side and curtain airbags, ABS and traction control. The top-of-the line sedan includes many of these features, but the price is close to $19,000, making other vehicles more attractive. The small 4-cylinder engine does sip fuel but, in some instances, the Accent can feel underpowered.

Kia Rio

Rating	Worth consideration
Price	Sedan: $13,000-$17,000 Hatchback: $14,000-$19,000
Engine	1.6L 4-cylinder with 110hp
Standard safety features include	Front airbags. Optional: ABS.
Average fuel consumption	1334L/year
Warranty	5-year/100,000 km
Initial quality score	2.5/5
Dependability score	2/5

Pros: Many buyers are not aware that Kia and Hyundai are the same company offering vehicles based on similar platforms. The Rio is based on the same platform as the Hyundai Accent, but differs in the configuration of doors and cargo. The Rio is offered as a five-door hatchback and sedan, where the Accent is only offered as a three-door hatchback and sedan. The Rio is a more sensible choice for buyers who need to carry people in the back seat, plus cargo. The Rio is a pleasant car to drive with a no-frills approach and thrifty fuel consumption.

Cons: Kia is improving in quality scores but doesn't meet the high level set by Hyundai. The lack of standard safety features is the main drawback, making other subcompacts like the Fit and Versa better choices.

Nissan Versa

Rating	Must try
Price	Sedan and Hatchback $13,000-$17,000
Engine	1.8L 4-cylinder with 122hp
Standard safety features include	Front, side and curtain airbags. Optional: ABS.
Average fuel consumption	1365L/year
Warranty	3-year/60,000 km
Initial quality score	2/5
Dependability score	N/A

Pros: The Versa is a subcompact car but it is larger than most in this class, and some might even consider it a compact. The interior is very well done for a vehicle of this price, the seats are comfortable, the back seat is roomy and the cargo area is bigger than many competitors. The engine is larger than others in this class, providing better performance but also able to achieve sensible fuel consumption. The Versa is a comfortable and practical design that will be perfect for buyers who want a slightly bigger car than a Toyota Yaris or Hyundai Accent.

Cons: The Versa is a very appealing car when ordered in a base trim, but the options can push the price up quickly. Just like the Nissan Cube, the lack of optional heated seats is an oversight.

Suzuki Swift

Rating	Cheap and cheerful
Price	$14,000-$17,000
Engine	1.6L 4-cylinder with 106hp
Standard safety features include	Front and side airbags
Average fuel consumption	1382L/year
Warranty	3-year/60,000 km
Initial quality score	N/A
Dependability score	N/A

Pros: The Swift is an interesting car because it is sold only in Canada and as a joint venture with General Motors. GM produces this car in Korea through its Daewoo subsidiary and packages it as a Suzuki Swift. It is also sold as a Chevy Aveo and, until recently, as the Pontiac G3. What this car offers is basic transportation to buyers who are bottom-line oriented. The Swift is a pleasant car to drive with good noise and vibration dampening with a simple and functional interior.

Cons: This subcompact car has limited cargo space behind the rear seats and the back seat is small. The lack of standard safety equipment is intended to keep the price down. There are several other cars in this class that include strong safety features and don't cost much more. Many buyers might think they are buying a Japanese Suzuki, when in fact they are buying a Korean-made Daewoo.

Toyota Yaris

Rating	Must try
Price	Hatchback: $13,000-$20,000 Coupe: $14,000-$20,000
Engine	1.5L 4-cylinder with 106hp
Standard safety features include	Front airbags. Additional airbags and ABS are optional.
Average fuel consumption	1254L/year
Warranty	3-year/60,000 km
Initial quality score	2.5/5
Dependability score	N/A

Pros: The Yaris is sold as a hatchback or sedan, making it accessible to a wide number of buyers. Though it may look small on the outside, the interior is actually quite roomy and the features on the inside are very functional. The small 1.5L 4-cylinder sips fuel yet is lively enough to please most drivers. The Yaris is a good alternative for buyers who might consider a hybrid vehicle because it is much cheaper to buy yet uses only slightly more fuel. These fun-to-drive cars have a very strong following in the used-car market, making them good value.

Cons: The interior features a speedometer and instrument cluster placed in the centre of the dashboard, which takes time to get used to. The base models lack side and curtain airbags, and ABS, so the starting price is misleading if you want to equip a Yaris to include these safety features. The Honda Fit, in comparison, has these features as standard equipment but the starting price is higher.

PREMIUM SUBCOMPACT CARS

BMW 1 Series

Rating	TOP PICK
Price	Coupe: $34,000-$42,000 Convertible: $40,000-$47,000
Engines	3.0L 6-cylinder with 230hp 3.0L turbo 6-cylinder with 300hp
Standard safety features include	Front, side and curtain airbags, ABS, traction and stability control
Average fuel consumption	3.0L engine, 1873L/year 3.0L turbo, 2011L/year
Warranty	4-year/80,000 km
Initial quality score	2.5/5
Dependability score	N/A

Pros: The BMW 1 series is a subcompact premium vehicle that competes mostly with the BMW-made Mini. Unlike the Mini, the 1 Series has large, powerful 3.0L 6-cylinder engines with head-snapping performance considering the size of the car. The remarkable thing about driving the 1 series is it doesn't feel small; in fact, it feels very much like the larger 3 Series. The interior is finished to a high level and the back seat is a usable size. Whether a coupe or convertible, the 1 Series is a blast to drive. The mini is like a go-cart and the 1 Series is like a small, precise performance car.

Cons: The base models are a good alternative to a Mini, but the higher-priced versions compete more with the larger 3 Series.

Mini Cooper

Rating	Must try
Price	Hatchback: $23,000-$38,000 Wagon: $26,000-$40,000 Convertible: $30,000-$44,000
Engines	1.6L 4-cylinder with 118hp 1.6L turbo 4-cylinder with 172hp 1.6L turbo 4-cylinder with 208hp
Standard safety features include	Front, side and head airbags, ABS, traction and stability control
Average fuel consumption	1.6L engine, 1260L/year 1.6L turbo, 1380L/year
Warranty	4-year/80,000 km
Initial quality score	2/5
Dependability score	3/5

Pros: The Mini is a premium subcompact car with amazing handling and surprising interior space, and it can be ordered with a host of features, trims levels and colour choices. The base model is one of the most fuel-efficient cars on the road, making it a rival to most hybrids. The funky interior is retro inspired and has a flair that few cars can rival. The Mini has one of the highest resale values of any car on the road, making the high sticker price easier to take.

Cons: The Mini is just that—mini. The small interior is perfect for a single person or couple, but this is no alternative for a family car. The interior may look funky, but it could be much more functional. The switch to a new engine supplier (Peugeot) in the latest model has resulted in a lower initial quality rating.

Volvo C30

Rating	This is no GTI
Price	$27,000-$32,000
Engines	2.4L 5-cylinder with 168hp 2.4L turbo 5-cylinder with 227hp
Standard safety features include	Front, side and head airbags, ABS, traction and stability control
Average fuel consumption	2.4L engine, 1800L/year 2.4L turbo 1800L/year
Warranty	4-year/80,000 km
Initial quality score	3/5
Dependability score	N/A

Pros: The C30 is a premium compact hatchback competing with well-established vehicles like the VW Golf GTI. Volvo is known for safety, and the C30 has the highest rating in this class of vehicle. The exterior design is similar to Volvos from the 1960s, but the interior is thoroughly modern. The seats are comfortable. Power is good but only on the turbo version.

Cons: The C30 has a small back seat and limited cargo area. The ride isn't as inspiring as the competition and the additional options can make a C30 expensive.

Compact Category

COMPACT CARS

Chevy Cobalt

Rating	Worth consideration
Price	$15,000-$25,000
Engines	2.2L 4-cylinder with 150hp 2.0L turbo 4-cylinder with 260hp
Standard safety features include	Front, side and curtain airbags. Optional: anti-lock brakes (ABS), stability and traction control.
Average fuel consumption	2.2L engine, 1446L/year 2.0L turbo, 1637L/year
Warranty	3-year/60,000 km
Initial quality score	3.5/5
Dependability score	3/5

Pro: The Cobalt has been one of the best-selling cars in Canada due to the attractive starting price and capable 4-cylinder engines. The Cobalt SS is one of the best values on the road for drivers who want a high-powered compact car. This is a good, basic car that has a strong following, especially when GM puts it on sale.

Cons: The biggest problem with the Cobalt is the weak resale value these cars command. The Japanese competition has a much stronger following in the resale market. The interior is functional, but not inspiring; there are better choices for fit and finish. The standard safety list could be stronger. The Cobalt is soon to be replaced by the Cruze, due out in 2010.

Ford Focus

Rating	Must try
Price	Sedan: $16,000-$19,000 Coupe: $17,000-$19,000
Engines	2.0L 4-cylinder with 140hp
Standard safety features include	Front, side and curtain airbags. Optional: ABS, stability and traction control.
Average fuel consumption	1448L/year
Warranty	3-year/60,000 km
Initial quality score	3.5/5
Dependability score	4/5

Pro: The Focus is often overlooked when buyers are shopping for a Toyota Corolla, Honda Civic or Mazda3, which is unfortunate because it is a solid competitor. Many car buffs complain that we don't get the sporty European Focus in North America, but this is still a good commuter car. (The Mazda3 is based on the European Focus platform, the top pick in this class.) The ride is smooth, the cabin is quiet and the handling is above average for this class. The optional Sync system delivers electronic goodies only available in cars costing much more. The solid quality scores prove that Ford can make a competitive product. The Focus is often on sale for much less than the posted sticker price, making it good value.

Cons: The lack of standard ABS puts the Focus behind the main rivals in this class. The perceived lack of quality hurts the Focus in the resale market. Ford used to make a hatchback and wagon in the Focus line, which is missed.

Honda Civic

Rating	Must try
Price	Sedan: $17,000-$27,000 Coupe: $17,000-$27,000
Engines	1.8L 4-cylinder with 140hp 2.0L 4-cylinder with 197hp
Standard safety features include	Front, side and curtain airbags, and ABS
Average fuel consumption	1.8L engine, 1300L/year 2.0L engine, 1734 L/year
Warranty	5-year/100,000 km
Initial quality score	4.5/5
Dependability score	3/5

Pro: The Civic has been the best-selling car in Canada for over 10 years because it has a unique blend of value, quality, gas economy and great resale value—and it is a fun car to drive. The interior offers a lot of space for back-seat passengers with a flat floor for easy entry, especially for children. The 4-cylinder engine is powerful enough for most drivers.

Cons: The latest Civic was introduced in 2006 and is due for a makeover, but not for the 2010 model year, so this could be the last year for the Civic in its current form. The dashboard features a digital readout that some drivers find distracting. The 2.0L Si version is powerful but not relaxing to drive; I call it "a cat on caffeine, ready to pounce." The standard-issue 1.8L engine is fine.

Hyundai Elantra

Rating	Worth consideration
Price	Sedan: $16,000-$24,000 Wagon: $15,000-$22,000
Engine	2.0L 4-cylinder with 138hp
Standard safety features include	Front airbags. Optional: ABS and side-curtain airbags.
Average fuel consumption	1442L/year
Warranty	5-year/100,000 km
Initial quality score	5/5
Dependability score	4/5

Pro: The Elantra is the highest-ranked compact car in initial quality according to JD Power and Associates for 2009. This is further proof that Hyundai is on a roll, winning car- of the year for the Genesis model and numerous quality awards. The Elantra is a competent sedan but a more appealing choice in the wagon version. Instead of a compact SUV, the wagon offers plenty of space, car-like handling and top quality. The 2.0L engine provides adequate power in sedan and wagon trim, plus good fuel mileage. Good basic interior layout with packages that will meet most pocketbooks.

Cons: The biggest knock on the Elantra is the lack of standard safety features like side and curtain airbags, ABS and traction control. The top of the line model includes many of these features, but the price jumps dramatically. If the Elantra were offered with these safety features as standard equipment, it would graduate to the "must try" rating.

Kia Forte

Rating	Worth consideration
Price	$16,000-$22,000
Engines	2.0L 4-cylinder with 156hp
	2.4L 4-cylinder with 173hp
Standard safety features include	Front, side and curtain airbags and ABS. Optional: traction and stability control.
Average fuel consumption	N/A
Fuel rating	2.0L engine, 8.3L/100km (34mpg) city
	5.8L/100km (49mpg) hwy
	2.4L engine, 9.2L/100km (31mpg) city
	6.2L/100km (46mpg) hwy
Warranty	5-year/100,000 km
Initial quality score	N/A
Dependability score	N/A

Pro: The Forte was introduced for the 2010 model year to replace the Spectra compact sedan. The Forte is sold as a sedan and coupe (the price of the coupe has not been released at the time of printing) and the Kia Soul has replaced the 5-door hatchback in this class of vehicle. The Forte brings a new level of interior features to the Kia compact range with better styling on the inside and outside, more dynamic drive and the optional 2.4L 4-cylinder engine. The addition of more standard safety features makes this car a much better value proposition.

Cons: Even though Kia has included more features into the mix, the starting price is no longer best in class when compared to the Corolla or domestic compact cars.

Mazda3

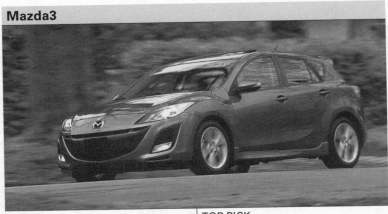

Rating	TOP PICK
Price	Sedan: $16,000-$23,000 Hatchback: (Sport): $17,000-$24,000
Engines	2.0L 4-cylinder with 148hp 2.5L 4-cylinder with 167hp
Standard safety features include	Front, side and curtain airbags, and ABS. Optional: traction and stability control.
Average fuel consumption	2.0L engine, 1473L/year 2.5L engine, N/A
Fuel rating	2.5L engine, 10.1 L/100km (28mpg) city 6.9L/100km (41mpg) hwy
Warranty	3-year/80,000 km
Initial quality score	N/A
Dependability score	2/5

Pro: Mazda follows up the original Mazda3 with an even better offering for 2010. This fun-to-drive compact gives drivers everything they could ever want in a small and cost-effective car. The interior materials and quality are second to none and the long list of standard and optional equipment is staggering. Sold as either a sedan or practical 4-door hatchback, the Mazda3 rivals the Civic for the best-selling car in Canada. The addition of an optional 2.5L engine provides power for those who want some fun in their daily commute. The Mazda3 gets Top Pick in the compact class due to the high level of interior finish, great handling and well-thought-out features.

Cons: Heated seats are only offered on the top trim level. The "smiley" front grille might not be for everyone, especially those who want an aggressive-looking car. The back seat can be rather cramped for tall passengers.

Mitsubishi Lancer

Rating	Worth consideration
Price	Sedan: $16,000-$40,000 Hatchback: $23,000-$35,000
Engines	2.0L 4-cylinder with 152hp 2.4L 4-cylinder with 168hp 2.0L 4-cylinder turbo with 237hp 2.0L 4-cylinder turbo with 291hp
Standard safety features include	Front, side, curtain and knee airbags, and ABS. Optional: traction and stability control.
Average fuel consumption	2.0L engine, 1637L/year 2.4L engine, 1755L/year 2.0L turbo, 2198L/year
Warranty	5-year/100,000 km
Initial quality score	2/5
Dependability score	3/5

Pro: Mitsubishi has been rewarded with stronger and stronger sales due in part to Lancer. It can be ordered with so many different configurations from basic sedan to sporty hatchback and flat-out turbo-charged rocket ships like the Lancer Evolution. The standard features are very attractive as is outside and inside design. The inclusion of knee airbags on a car of this price is worth noting. Every time I drive the Lancer I am pleasantly surprised by how fun it is to drive.

Cons: The interior design is worthy of the less expensive versions, but the high-powered Evolution doesn't have the interior finish of a car costing $40,000.

Nissan Sentra

Rating	Worth consideration
Price	$15,000-$23,000
Engines	2.0L 4-cylinder with 140hp 2.5L 4-cylinder with 177hp 2.5L 4-cylinder with 200hp
Standard safety features include	Front, side and curtain airbags, and ABS
Average fuel consumption	2.0L engine, 1411L/year 2.5L engine, 1542L/year 2.5L high-output engine, 1688L/year
Warranty	3-year/60,000 km
Initial quality score	3.5/5
Dependability score	3/5

Pro: The Sentra is offered with a solid 2.0L engine or potent 2.5L versions for buyers who are seeking performance in a small package. The Sentra, like the less expensive Versa, is very comfortable on the interior with soft seats, a long list of amenities and optional in-car entertainment features. It drives like a bigger, more expensive car and has good handling. This is a direct competitor to best sellers like the Civic and Corolla.

Cons: The Sentra suffers an identity crisis due to the popular Versa appealing to the same basic buyer. Which to choose? Both are excellent choices but the Sentra doesn't really offer anything more in the base trim except a larger engine. The 2.5L engine is overkill for most buyers.

Subaru Impreza

Rating	Must try
Price	Sedan: $21,000-$34,000
	Hatchback: $22,000-$46,000
Engines	2.5L 4-cylinder with 170hp
	2.5L turbo 4-cylinder with 224hp
	2.5L high-output turbo 4-cylinder with 265hp
	2.5L high-output turbo 4-cylinder with 305hp
Standard safety features include	Front, side and curtain airbags, ABS, traction and stability control
Average fuel consumption	2.5L engine, 1828L/year
	2.5L turbo, 1941L/year
	2.5 L high-output turbo, 2125L/year
Warranty	3-year/60,000 km
Initial quality score	2/5
Dependability score	4/5

Pro: Subaru includes all-wheel drive (AWD) on all of its vehicles, which makes this an attractive feature for Canadians who face harsh winter driving conditions. There are several variants to choose from, including base models all the way up to high-performance rally-inspired "pocket rockets." The basic cars offer good value due to a long list of standard safety features and AWD, making them the most sensible choice. Due to the design of the engine, Subaru was able to place it lower in the car offering above average handling, making the Impreza sensible and fun to drive. The interior is basic, yet functional and the seats are supportive. These vehicles have a very solid following and rarely last long in the used-car market, so they attract top dollar.

Cons: Subaru is not known for highly styled interiors and the Impreza does look a bit basic, even for the top model, plus the back seat is short on legroom. Beware—the turbo versions require expensive premium fuel to run at their best.

Suzuki SX4

Rating	Worth consideration
Price	Sedan: $17,000-$21,000 Hatchback: $17,000-$24,000
Engine	2.0L 4-cylinder with 143hp
Standard safety features include	Front, side and curtain airbags, and ABS. Optional: traction and stability control.
Average fuel consumption	1575L/year
Warranty	3-year/60,000 km
Initial quality score	3.5/5
Dependability score	N/A

Pro: The Suzuki SX4 has been flying under the radar for far too long; it unfortunately is not thought of when buyers are looking at vehicles like the Honda Civic, Toyota Corolla and Mazda3. What the SX4 brings to the table is a strong list of standard equipment, good road manners and the availability of AWD in the hatchback trim, making one of the least expensive AWD cars on the road. The interior is roomy, comfortable and the high roofline provides an open feeling. The 2.0L engine is powerful, making the SX4 a pleasure to drive.

Cons: The starting price might be a bit misleading, steering some buyers away when they should actually be looking closer at the true value of this well-equipped car. The AWD version is capable but competes with the more powerful Subaru models.

Toyota Corolla

Rating	Must try
Price	$15,000-$26,000
Engines	1.8L 4-cylinder with 132hp 2.4L 4-cylinder with 158hp
Standard safety features include	Front, side and curtain airbags and ABS
Warranty	3-year/60,000 km
Average fuel consumption	1.8L engine, 1318L/year 2.4L engine, 1619L/year
Initial quality score	N/A
Dependability score	4/5

Pros: The Toyota Corolla is a solid commuter car offering good value, solid resale and very good reliability, making it a favourite with Canadians. The latest version has a roomy interior, simple dashboard execution and many standard convenience features. The Corolla is very easy to drive, the ride is smooth and quiet, making it feel bigger and more expensive than it is. The top XRS version is sold with the larger 2.4L 4-cylinder for only those who need a bit more power; the standard 1.8L engine is more than adequate for everyday driving.

Cons: The electric power steering is rather vague feeling on the highway and the imprecise feel can make the Corolla wander. The larger 2.4L engine is overkill and the difference in additional power is not that noticeable, making the added expense not worth it.

VW City Golf /Jetta

Rating	Must try
Price	$15,000-$19,000
Engine	2.0L 4-cylinder with 115hp
Standard safety features include	ABS and front airbags. Optional: side and curtain airbags.
Average fuel consumption	1720L/year
Warranty	4-year/80,000 km
Initial quality score	N/A
Dependability score	N/A

Pro: The City Golf and Jetta are based on the previous model so the design dates back over 10 years. Even when compared to today's latest offering, these cars still hold up, offering above-average handling, good fuel consumption, a well-designed interior and good road feel. The low starting price puts these cars in the thick of the compact segment. Just because the origin of these cars dates back to the 1990s, they have been modified to suit today's drivers with a 6-speed gearbox and modern stereo interface.

Cons: The standard safety list could be better, but many of the features are available as options. The 115hp engine shouldn't deter any potential buys because the 6-speed transmission makes up for the lack of power.

VW Golf /Jetta

Rating	Must try
Price	Sedan: $22,000-$27,000
	Hatchback: $22,000-$29,000
	Wagon: $22,000-$29,000
Engines	2.0L turbo 4-cylinder with 200hp
	2.5L 5-cylinder with 140hp
	2.0L turbo 4-cylinder diesel with 140hp
Standard safety features include	Front and curtain airbags, ABS, and traction and stability control. Optional: side airbags.
Average fuel consumption	2.0L engine, 1700L/year
	2.5L engine, 1800L/year
	2.0L diesel engine, 1200L/year
Warranty	4-year/80,000 km
Initial quality score	3.5/5 (Jetta rating)
Dependability score	N/A

Pro: For buyers who want a taste of German engineering in a car that doesn't break the bank, the Jetta and Golf really are the only options. The Golf is the hatchback model and the Jetta is the sedan. Both come with a variety of engines, but the new clean diesel engine should be the model of choice because it offers a smooth and quiet ride and saves a bunch on fuel costs. These cars have a refined feel, with above-average handling and road manners, plus a solid list of standard safety features. The resale value of the diesel model is excellent, so buying one of these cars is a good choice for your pocketbook. The wagon is a great alternative to a compact SUV and the GTI/GLI versions are alternatives to buying a higher-priced Audi.

Cons: The Jetta and Golf command a premium over other cars in this class, and for buyers who couldn't care less about handling and performance, cheaper cars will better serve them. Buyers who would never have tried a diesel are missing out, this is a great alternative to a hybrid, plus it will outperform any comparably priced hybrid on the road.

PREMIUM COMPACT CARS

Acura CSX

Rating	A Honda Civic in Acura clothing
Price	$28,000-$35,000
Engines	2.0L 4-cylinder with 155hp
	2.0L 4-cylinder with 197hp
Standard safety features include	Front, side and curtain airbags, ABS, stability and traction control
Average fuel consumption	2.0L engine, 1533L/year
	2.0L high-output engine, 1734L/year
Warranty	5-year/100,000 km
Initial quality score	N/A
Dependability score	N/A

Pro: The CSX model is only sold in Canada and is based on the Honda Civic sedan. To make it an Acura, the CSX is fitted with a powerful 4-cylinder engine, premium interior and electronic and luxury features fitting of a luxury brand. It is a good-handling car with ample room in the back seat, just like the Civic.

Cons: Before the CSX there was the Acura EL, also based on the Civic, but the designers did a much better job of disguising that car. Not the case with the CSX. It looks exactly like the Civic from 10 feet away, and now that Honda has made the same powerful engine available in the Civic line, for less money, the CSX is losing relevance.

Audi A3

Rating	Worth consideration
Price	$32,000-$47,000
Engines	2.0L turbo 4-cylinder with 200hp 3.2L V6 with 250hp
Standard safety features include	Front, side and curtain airbags, ABS, traction and stability control
Average fuel consumption	2.0L engine, 1655L/year 3.2L V6, 1963L/year
Warranty	4-year/80,000 km
Initial quality score	2/5
Dependability score	2/5

Pro: Based on the same platform as the VW Rabbit/Golf, the A3 offers a more refined interior and the availability of AWD. The interior is very well finished with good materials. Handling is a nimble, as would be expected in a small compact German car. The turbo 4-cylinder is the engine of choice due to the power it provides and the good fuel ratings it achieves. The duel-clutch automatic is a marvel of engineering and it provides lightning-quick shifts up and down.

Cons: This is a not a big car, the back seat is cramped and the lower roofline compared to a 4-door VW Golf GTI makes the A3 a compromise. The price of the A3 makes the VW GTI a much better value, but you don't get the Audi badge!

Audi A4

Rating	Must try
Price	Sedan: $38,000-$51,000 Convertible: $53,000-$77,000 Wagon: $43,000-$47,000 **Note:** The S4 sedan information was not available at the time of printing.
Engines	2.0L turbo 4-cylinder with 211hp 3.2L V6 with 250hp 4.2L V8, with 420hp
Standard safety features include	Front, side and curtain airbags, ABS, traction and stability control
Average fuel consumption	2.0L engine, 1575L/year 3.2L V6, 2024L/year 4.2L V8, 2569L/year
Warranty	4-year/80,000 km
Initial quality score	3/5
Dependability score	4/5

Pro: The A4 is the most popular Audi model because it allows access to the luxury market at a price that many buyers can afford. The new A4 is much roomier than the last model, especially in the back seat. The interior is very well designed and finished with high-quality materials. The 2.0L 4-cylinder is the engine of choice because it provides almost the same performance as the V6 but it costs less and is cheaper to run. Handling is very sure-footed, thanks to the optional AWD. The S4 convertible is the last year for the V8; next year it will feature a supercharged V6.

Cons: The new A4 styling lacks much of the punch of earlier efforts; it is rather bland compared to the competition. The options on these cars can add up in a hurry so be prepared. The power steering is rather soft so the A4 can feel rather vague compared to the BMW 3 Series. There is no diesel offered in the A4 yet, so try the BMW 3 Series for a diesel option. The convertible features a soft top and not a retractable hardtop, which has become the norm in this class.

BMW 3 Series

Rating	TOP PICK
Price	Sedan: $35,000-$71,000 Coupe: $43,000- $70,000 Convertible: $56,000-$66,000 Wagon: $44,000
Engines	2.5L 6-cylinder with 200hp 3.0L 6-cylinder with 230hp 3.0L turbo 6-cylinder with 300hp 3.0L turbo diesel 6-cylinder with 265hp 4.0L V8 with 414hp
Standard safety features include	Front, side and curtain airbags, ABS, traction and stability control
Average fuel consumption	2.5L engine, 1842L/year 3.0L engine, 1873L/year 3.0L turbo, 1984L/year 3.0L diesel, 1475L/year 4.0L V8, 2556L/year

Warranty	4-year/80,000 km
Initial quality score	3.5/5
Dependability score	2.5/5

Pro: The BMW 3 Series is the Top Pick in the premium compact segment for several reasons. First, the basic 6-cylinder rear-wheel drive (RWD) design has been perfected for decades, getting better with every version. Second, the handling and driving dynamics are so good that every other maker in this category strives to mimic the 3 Series. Third, the 3 Series is sold in many configurations from basic sedan to coupe to convertible and useful wagon all the way to the high-performance M3. Fourth, the addition of a powerful clean diesel engine makes the 3 Series an alternative to buying a hybrid car. Fifth, many of the 3 Series models are available with AWD. Sixth, the resale value of these cars is very strong. BMW is not just a status symbol; it actually makes a superior product capable of igniting the passion for driving.

Cons: The back seat can be a bit cramped, especially for people with child car seats. All gas-models require expensive premium fuel to deliver the best performance.

Cadillac CTS

Rating	Must try
Price	Sedan: $40,000-$69,000 Wagon: N/A at time of printing
Engines	3.0L V6 with 270hp 3.6L V6 with 304hp 6.2L supercharger V8 with 556hp
Standard safety features include	Front, side and curtain airbags, ABS, stability and traction control
Average fuel consumption	3.6L V6, 1962L/year 3.6L AWD, 2064L/year 6.2L V8, 2602L/year
Warranty	4-year/80,000 km
Initial quality score	5/5
Dependability score	4/5

Pro: The Cadillac CTS is a great car. The quality scores are very high, the interior is as good as it gets in this class, and it has the power and handling to rival any German sedan. Available this year as a sport wagon, the CTS can provide superior handling plus extra cargo capacity. The available AWD is perfect for winter driving. The best choice is the direct-injection 3.6L V6 with just over 300hp, making the CTS a BMW rival. The Supercharged V8 is beyond belief, basically a 4-door Corvette. This car is proof that GM can make great cars!

Cons: Driving the CTS without AWD in the winter can be a handful. The sharp styling might distract potential buyers from how good this car is.

Infiniti G

Rating	Must try
Price	Sedan: $38,000-$47,000 Coupe: $45,000-$48,000 Convertible: $57,000-$61,000
Engines	3.7L V6 with 325hp 3.7L V6 with 328hp 3.7L V6 with 330hp
Standard safety features include	Front, side and curtain airbags, ABS, stability and traction control
Average fuel consumption	3.7L V6,1971L/year 3.7L V6 AWD, 2000L/year
Warranty	4-year/100,000 km
Initial quality score	5/5
Dependability score	4/5

Pro: The G sedan, coupe and convertible have taken the established pre-mium compact class by storm. The leader in this class is the BMW 3 Series, but the Infiniti products are almost as good for a lot less money. The powerful 3.7L engine is spectacular, the handling is sublime, especially in AWD trim and the interior is nicely finished. The computer interface is easy to use, plus the interior materials are all first rate. Infiniti cars have been scoring better and better quality scores so a G sedan is a good choice.

Cons: The only problem with the G is the lack of room for bigger people. Headroom is limited for drivers over 6 feet and the width of the driver cockpit is too narrow for large people. If the G were a tad bigger, it would easily win this class.

Lexus IS

Rating	Must try
Price	Sedan: $33,000-$66,000 Convertible: $52,000-$60,000
Engines	2.5L V6 with 205hp 2.5L V6 with 204hp 3.5L V6 with 306hp 5.0L V8 with 416hp
Standard safety features include	Front, side, knee and curtain airbags, ABS, stability and traction control
Average fuel consumption	2.5L V6, 1690L/year 2.5L AWD, 1839L/year 3.5L V6, 1901L/year 5.0L V8, 2195L/year
Warranty	4-year/80,000 km
Initial quality score	5/5
Dependability score	3/5

Pro: This entry-level luxury model is sold in several trim levels from basic sedan to high-powered sports sedan to classy convertible. Lexus has been on top of JD Power and Associates' quality study year after year, making any Lexus an attractive choice. The interior finish is second to none; the solid road handling and choice of powerful engines can make the IS an exhilarating experience. Competing with the BMW 3 Series and Mercedes C Class, the IS offers a distinctly "Lexus" approach to refinement. The availability of AWD on the base model makes for a good all-weather car. The convertible features a retractable hardtop design and unique exterior styling, the prettiest car in the lineup.

Cons: The IS is not a big car, so rear-seat passengers might be squished. The base IS250 is not that inspiring to drive; the IS350 is much more fun and the ISF is a rocket. The velvety approach to road feel can leave some drivers wanting more feedback, even on the ISF. Road feel is not as precise as the BMW 3 Series but on par with the Mercedes C Class.

Lincoln MKZ

Rating	Worth consideration
Price	$37,000-$40,000
Engine	3.5L V6 with 263hp
Standard safety features include	Front, side and curtain airbags, ABS, stability and traction control
Average fuel consumption	3.5L V6, 1935L/year 3.5L AWD, 2144L/year
Warranty	4-year/80,000 km
Initial quality score	2.5/5
Dependability score	5/5 (sold as Zephyr in 2006)

Pro: The MKZ is the Lincoln version of the popular Ford Fusion, bringing a higher level of interior finish and a more supple ride. The MKZ comes standard with a 3.5L V6 and can be ordered with AWD. If you are considering a fully loaded Fusion, the MKZ might be a better overall buy.

Cons: Lincoln has only had the MKZ in the market for a few years so it doesn't have the following of, say, the Cadillac CTS. The FWD design on the base model doesn't compete well with the RWD German cars or the CTS for handling and performance.

Mercedes B-Class

Rating	Unique car, unique transmission
Price	$30,000-$35,000
Engines	2.0L 4-cylinder with 134hp
	2.0L turbo 4-cylinder with 193hp
Standard safety features include	Front, side and curtain airbags, ABS, traction and stability control
Average fuel consumption	2.0L engine, 1620L/year
	2.0L turbo, 1760L/year
Warranty	4-year/80,000 km
Initial quality score	N/A
Dependability score	N/A

Pro: The B-Class is only sold in Canada and is not offered in the United States. This vehicle is typical of the fun-to-drive, thrifty and practical cars that rule the roads of Europe. Interior space is ample and the materials used are first rate. The turbo engine is the most effective, yet it still remains good on gas. The high seating position makes this compact crossover a real alternative to an SUV. In addition, the price tag makes this Mercedes attainable for many owners.

Cons: The continuously variable transmission gets the job done but it isn't the most fun to drive. The manual is better but many buyers will not consider a 5-speed manual.

Mercedes C-Class

Rating	Must try
Price	$36,000-$64,000
Engines	2.5L V6 with 201hp
	3.0L V6 with 228hp
	3.5L V6 with 268hp
	6.2L V8 with 451hp
Standard safety features include	Front, side and curtain airbags, ABS, traction and stability control
Average fuel consumption	2.5L engine, 1960L/year
	3.0L V6, 1980L/year
	3.5L V6, 2060L/year
	6.2L V8, 2820L/year
Warranty	4-year/80,000 km
Initial quality score	4/5
Dependability score	3/5

Pro: The latest C-Class has turned into a real contender for the BMW 3 Series. Until now, the C-Class was a soft, relaxed and rather boring car to drive, but the latest model changes all of that. The new platform and suspension changes make this Mercedes much more exciting to drive and the high-horsepower versions are a blast to drive. When compared to the BMW 3 Series the Mercedes are cheaper.

Cons: The back seat is rather cramped, making the Audi A4 a better choice for buyers who require more back seat room. The interior is rather basic looking and the materials used don't convey the same level of refinement that one might find in other premium compact cars like the Lexus IS or 3 series. Since the 3 Series offers a wagon and diesel option, it is a more rounded line than the C-Class.

Volvo S40/V50

Rating	Worth consideration
Price	S40 Sedan: $32,000-$40,000
	V50 Wagon: $33,000-$42,000
Engines	2.4L 5-cylinder with 168hp
	2.4L turbo 5-cylinder with 227hp
Standard safety features include	Front, side and head airbags, ABS, traction and stability control
Average fuel consumption	2.4L engine, 1800L/year
	2.4L turbo, 1800L/year
Warranty	4-year/80,000 km
Initial quality score	3/5
Dependability score	2/5

Pro: The S40 and V50 are based on the same platform as the award-winning European Ford Focus sedan. Handling is very good and the optional AWD system makes for a compelling package. The interior is very well designed with top-notch materials and the seats are very comfortable. The V50 wagon is a great alternative to buying a compact SUV. The turbo version is the engine of choice; the base motor lacks much punch.

Cons: The S40 and V50 are often overlooked in the premium compact class but they are very well designed. The Volvo image might be a drawback for buyers who want a more prestigious brand.

COMPACT CROSSOVER/TALL WAGONS

Chevy HHR

Rating	Worth consideration
Price	$20,000
Engines	2.0L 4-cylinder with 260hp
	2.2L 4-cylinder with 150hp
	2.4L turbo 4-cylinder with 172hp
Standard safety features include	Front and curtain airbags, ABS, traction and stability control
Warranty	3-year/60,000 km
Average fuel consumption	2.0L engine, 1690L/year
	2.2L engine, 1570L/year
	2.4L turbo, 1668L/year
Initial quality score	2.5/5
Dependability score	3/5

Pro: Obviously the world needs another vehicle that looks just like the PT Cruiser, so GM came up with the HHR. All kidding aside, these retro-styled compact crossovers offer a lot of interior space with three engine choices, including the high-output 2.0L turbo. New for 2010 is a panel-side version which is perfect for business use. Good, basic transportation for a family that wants space but not the cost of buying and running a compact SUV.

Cons: PT Cruiser owners will give you the evil eye!

Chrysler PT Cruiser

Rating	Worth consideration
Price	$19,000
Engine	2.4L 4-cylinder with 150hp
Standard safety features include	Front and side airbags, and ABS
Average fuel consumption	1753L/year
Warranty	3-year/60,000 km
Initial quality score	4/5
Dependability score	3/5

Pro: If you are in the market for a roomy compact crossover and don't want to spend a lot of money, then the PT Cruiser is worth a look. The unique interior can be configured in many different ways to accommodate several passengers or cargo. The engine does a good job and the PT Cruiser has proven to be very reliable. In fact, it tops recent quality scores.

Cons: The turning radius is horrible on this car, making quick turns tricky. The interior is funky looking but doesn't have the best layout. The exterior styling is overdue to be updated. Also look at the Kia Soul or Chevy HHR.

Dodge Caliber

Rating	Outside good, inside bad
Price	$13,000-$22,000
Engines	1.8L 4-cylinder with 148hp
	2.0L 4-cylinder with 158hp
Standard safety features include	Front and curtain airbags. Optional: ABS, stability and traction control.
Average fuel consumption	N/A
Warranty	3-year/60,000 km
Initial quality score	2.5/5
Dependability score	N/A

The Caliber is the Dodge version of the Jeep Compass and Patriot except it can be equipped with smaller engines, making it the least expensive of the bunch. See the comments for the Compass/Patriot.

Jeep Compass/Patriot

Rating	
Price	$15,000-$22,000
Engines	2.0L 4-cylinder with 158hp
	2.4L 4-cylinder with 172hp
Standard safety features include	Front and curtain airbags, ABS, stability and traction control
Average fuel consumption	2.0L engine, 1647L/year;
	2.4L AWD, 1787L/year
Warranty	3-year/60,000 km
Initial quality score	2.5/5
Dependability score	N/A

Pro: The Compass and Patriot are essentially the same vehicle but with different styling. Both offer an inexpensive option for buyers looking for AWD traction for winter at a low price. The cabin is roomy, as is the cargo area. There are some innovative features like an iPod or cell phone holder and chilled glove box. These vehicles are an option for buyers looking in the compact crossover segment.

Cons: The future of these vehicles is in jeopardy with the restructuring of Chrysler. The interior is riddled with hard plastic, making an inexpensive vehicle look cheap. The continuously variable automatic transmission takes time to get used to and doesn't provide much inspiration to drive. The engine can be noisy inside the cabin.

Kia Soul

Rating	TOP PICK
Price	$15,000-$22,000
Engines	1.6L 4-cylinder with 122hp 2.0L 4-cylinder with 142hp
Standard safety features include	Front, side and curtain airbags. Optional: ABS, traction and stability control.
Average fuel consumption	N/A
Fuel rating	1.6L engine, 7.7L/100km (37mpg) city 6.3L/100km (45mpg) hwy 2.0L engine, 8.6L/100km (33mpg) city 6.5L/100km (44mpg) hwy
Warranty	5-year/100,000 km
Initial quality score	N/A
Dependability score	N/A

Pro: The Soul is a unique compact crossover vehicle that blends the best features of a car with the utility of a compact SUV. The exterior styling is funky as is the interior. The volume seller will be the 2.0L versions, which come standard with traction and stability control. The interior is very roomy, especially the back seat and cargo area. The Soul has a solid list of standard features including heated seats on all models. This is a great little urban runabout, capable of filling many family needs at a price that is easy to handle.

Cons: The only complaint is the Soul can be a little noisy on the highway.

Kia Rondo

Rating	Must try
Price	$20,000-$27,000
Engines	2.4L 4-cylinder with 175hp 2.7L V6 with 192hp
Standard safety features include	Front, side and curtain airbags, ABS, traction and stability control
Average fuel consumption	N/A
Fuel rating	2.4L engine, 10.6L/100km (27mpg) city 7.5L/100km (38mpg) hwy 2.7L engine, 11.5L/100km (25mpg) city 7.7L/100km (37mpg) hwy
Warranty	5-year/100,000 km
Initial quality score	N/A
Dependability score	N/A

Pro: The Rondo is a tall-wagon crossover that competes nicely with a vehicle like the Mazda5. The interior is a wonderful example of what can be achieved in a small space. It can be ordered with an optional third row of seats making room for seven people. The third row of seats is perfect for small children or adults in a pinch. The Rondo is easy to drive and manoeuvre, making it a perfect city runabout for a family. The long list of standard safety features and creature comforts makes it a must try compact crossover.

Cons: Kia unfortunately has the reputation of making second-rate vehicle, when this is not true. The Rondo is proof of that. However, the misguided reputation might affect resale value.

Toyota Matrix

Rating	Must try
Price	$16,000-$28,000
Engines	1.8L 4-cylinder with 132hp 2.4L 4-cylinder with 158hp
Standard safety features include	Front, side and curtain air bags and ABS
Average fuel consumption	1.8L engine-1416L/yr 2.4L engine-1695L/yr
Warranty	3-year/60,000 km
Initial quality score	N/A
Dependability score	5/5

Pros: The Matrix is based on the Corolla platform, sharing many features with that car including engine and transmission. The Matrix offers buyers more flexibility due to the 4-door hatchback design and higher roofline; this results in a higher seating position and more cargo space. Toyota decided to bring back an AWD system after dropping it from the Matrix line-up for several years, making it an alternative to a compact SUV. The larger 2.4L engine is useful when matched to the AWD system, but for most drivers the base engine is adequate.

Cons: Just like the Corolla, the Matrix uses electric power steering, which tends to have a vague feel. The Matrix is a joint venture with GM, so buyers have the option to buy the Matrix or the Pontiac Vibe version (while Pontiac is still around). The Vibe has more standard features but has not proved to hold its resale value as well. Buyers who want to get a Matrix with similar safety features will have to spend more money.

COMPACT SUV/CROSSOVER

Chevy Equinox	
Rating	Must try
Price	$23,000-$35,000
Engines	2.4L 4-cylinder with 182hp
	3.0L 5-cylinder with 264hp
Standard safety features include	Front, side and curtain airbags, ABS, traction and stability control
Average fuel consumption	N/A
Fuel rating	9.2L/100km (31mpg) city
	6.1L/100km (46mpg) hwy
Warranty	3-year/60,000 km
Initial quality score	2/5
Dependability score	2/5

Pro: The Equinox is all-new for 2010 and a great deal of attention went into refining the interior, improving the ride, making the cabin as quiet as possible and making this crossover the most fuel efficient in its class. Often overlooked in this segment, this latest Equinox should be seriously considered as it offers much more interior space, especially in the back seat and cargo area, compared to the competition. If you want a compact crossover with healthy interior space and an eye to fuel consumption, then the 4-cylinder is your vehicle.

Cons: Unless you need this vehicle to tow a boat or trailer, opt for the 4-cylinder—it is that good. The only question about this new Equinox is the resale value, other than that GM did a nice job here.

Dodge Nitro

Rating	Worth consideration
Price	$21,000-$26,000
Engines	3.7L V6 210hp 4.0L V6 with 260hp 3-year/60,000 km warranty
Standard safety features include	Front and curtain airbags, ABS, stability and traction control
Average fuel consumption	3.7L engine, 2271L/year 3.7L engine 4X4, 2413L/year 4.0L engine 4X4, 2358L/year
Initial quality score	2.5/5
Dependability score	N/A

The starting price of the Nitro makes it an inexpensive option for buyers who want a compact SUV. The Nitro is the tougher-looking version of the Jeep Liberty, available in 4X2 and 4X4. Look for more comments under the Liberty.

Ford Escape

Rating	TOP PICK
Price	$24,000-$35,000
Engines	2.5L 4-cylinder with 170hp 3.0L V6 with 240hp
Standard safety features include	Front, side, and curtain airbags, ABS, traction and stability control
Average fuel consumption	2.5L engine, 1660L/year 2.5L engine AWD, 1910L/year 3.0L V6, 1958L/year 3.0L V6 AWD, 2078L/year

Warranty	3-year/60,000 km
Initial quality score	3.5/5
Dependability score	3/5

Pro: Some might be surprised that I have chosen the Ford Escape as the Top Pick in the compact SUV category, but there are some very good reasons for choosing this vehicle. First, it is the best-selling compact SUV in the country, so I'm not alone. Second, the starting price makes it much more accessible to more people than some of the higher-priced import units. Third, the base 4-cylinder engine gets very good gas mileage; in fact, every time I have tested this vehicle it gets very close to the posted ratings. Fourth, it can be ordered in many different configurations to suit every budget. Fifth, it is the only compact SUV to be offered as a hybrid. (See hybrid category.) The Escape is a simple but well-thought-out vehicle with a long list of standard features, making it an easy unit to buy and enjoy. Solid quality scores, too.

Cons: The Ford Escape sells very well, so there are a lot available in the resale market, which can affect the value. Plus, the stigma that domestic vehicles carry can affect the value compared to vehicles like the CR-V and RAV4.

GMC Terrain

Rating	Must try
Price	$23,000-$35,000
Engines	2.4L 4-cylinder with 182hp 3.0L 5-cylinder with 264hp
Standard safety features include	Front, side and curtain airbags, ABS, traction and stability control
Average fuel consumption	N/A
Fuel rating	9.2L/100km (31mpg) city 6.1L/100km (46mpg) hwy
Warranty	3-year/60,000 km
Initial quality score	2/5
Dependability score	2/5

The Terrain is the GMC version of the Chevy Equinox, so see comments on the Equinox.

Honda CR-V

Rating	Must try
Price	$28,000-$37,000
Engine	2.4L 4-cylinder with 166hp
Standard safety features include	Front, side, and curtain airbags, ABS, stability and traction control
Average fuel consumption	FWD, 1790L/year AWD, 1879L/year
Warranty	5-year/100,000 km
Initial quality score	4.5/5
Dependability score	5/5

Pros: The CR-V is based on the Civic platform and is powered by the same engine as the Accord, tried and true components that come together to make a good all-around compact SUV. Reliability is good and so is resale value. The CR-V is very smooth, refined and quiet, plus the seats are comfortable and outward visibility is good. The CR-V is a much more practical alternative to the Honda Element. The swing-up tailgate makes for easy access to the useful cargo area. The 4-cylinder engine delivers decent performance.

Cons: The CR-V is sold with front-wheel drive (FWD) as standard equipment and the cost of adding all-wheel drive (AWD) brings the price closer to $30,000. The 4-cylinder engine is good on fuel and has adequate power but under hard acceleration the engine can be loud and passing power could be better.

Honda Element

Rating	Not for families with small children
Price	$27,000-$32,000
Engine	2.4L 4-cylinder with 166hp
Standard safety features include	Front, side and curtain airbags, ABS, stability and traction control
Average fuel consumption	FWD, 1844L/year AWD, 1957L/year
Warranty	3-year/60,000 km
Initial quality score	3.5/5
Dependability score	5/5

Pros: The Honda Element was the first of the square compact utilities to come to North America from Japan, followed by the Nissan Cube and Scion. The boxy shape provides a cavernous interior with high roof and wide cargo area. The rear seats flip up to the side to allow for large cargo capacity and the side doors swing out (suicide doors) to offer a large entrance into the cabin. The interior is filled with plastic, even on the floor, for easy wipe down.

Cons: Single people or a couple who can utilize the versatile cargo area for outdoors activities and maybe pets is the best fit for the Element. The Element is not recommended for families, as the rear doors have to be opened by the front-seat occupants, so the driver might have to get out to open the passenger front door then the rear door to allow children to exit and enter. The boxy shape doesn't deliver the best handling and the 4-cylinder engine strains in headwinds and highway passing. The Honda CR-V is a much better option.

Hyundai Tucson

(Comments are based on 2009 model as the 2010 model had not been released at time of printing.)

Rating	Not tested
Price	$21,000-$31,000
Engines	2.0L 4-cylinder with 140hp 2.7L V6 with 173hp
Standard safety features include	Front airbags, ABS, traction and stability control. Optional: side and curtain airbags.
Average fuel consumption	2.0L engine, 1842L/year 2.7L V6, 1999L/year 2.7L V6 AWD, 2068L/year
Warranty	5-year/100,000 km
Initial quality score	2/5
Dependability score	4/5

Pro: The current initial quality score is surprising because Hyundai has won top honours in the past for quality for the Tucson. This compact SUV is offered in many different trim levels and has a price that will suit most buyers. For buyers who don't need a large vehicle, the Tucson has just enough room without being too cramped. The engines offer good power, especially the V6 option for those who do a lot of highway driving. A good, functional, compact SUV.

Cons: Unfortunately we do not have the information on the new 2010 model at the time of printing.

Hyundai Santa Fe

(Comments are based on 2009 model as the 2010 model had not been released at time of printing.)

Rating	Not tested
Price	$26,000-$37,000
Engines	2.7L V6 with 185hp 3.3L V6 with 242hp
Standard safety features include	Front airbags, ABS, traction and stability control. Optional: side and curtain airbags.
Average fuel consumption	2.7L V6, 2001L/year 3.3L V6, 2098L/year 3.3L V6 AWD, 2142L/year
Warranty	5-year/100,000 km
Initial quality score	4/5
Dependability score	3/5

Pro: The 2010 model will be updated with new front and rear styling and improved engine choices. The Santa Fe has proven to be a very reliable crossover, offering a high-quality interior and a smooth ride and handling. Plus, it is a value leader in its class. Any improvements for 2010 will make the already good Santa Fe even better. People who own these vehicles love them for their practical size and luxury-like ride and interior.

Cons: Unfortunately we do not have the information on the new 2010 model at the time of printing.

Jeep Liberty

Rating	Worth consideration
Price	$25,000-$28,000
Engine	3.7L V6 with 210hp
Standard safety features include	Front and curtain airbags, ABS, stability and traction control
Average fuel consumption	2413L/year
Warranty	3-year/60,000 km
Initial quality score	3/5
Dependability score	2/5

Pros: The second-generation Liberty is bigger than the first generation, making it a more useful size and helping to replace the market that the original Cherokee had years before. With a solid off-road performance and rugged design, this is a good choice for drivers who navigate country roads. The ride is surprisingly smooth and the V6 engine is a good match for this size Jeep.

Cons: As with all Jeep products the interior relies too heavily on hard, cheap-looking plastic. The 4X4 system is not meant for dry on-road driving, it is an on-demand type of system for true off-road or inclement weather situations. An AWD crossover is more suitable for most drivers.

Jeep Wrangler

Rating	Must try
Price	$20,000-$32,000
Engine	3.8L V6 with 202hp
Standard safety features include	Front and curtain airbags, stability and traction control
Average fuel consumption	2523L/year
Warranty	3-year/60,000 km
Initial quality score	2/5
Dependability score	3/5

Pros: The Wrangler and Wrangler Unlimited have no real competitors; there is no substitute for a Jeep! The go-anywhere attitude is what makes these vehicle appealing, especially for top-down cruising in the summer. The off-road capability is legendary and, now with a four-door version, this vehicle is available to a wider number of potential buyers. The interior is basic and functional; Jeep makes no excuses for what it is—simple.

Cons: The back seats of the four-door Unlimited version are not very comfortable. The roof is complex and hard to take down and put up. The removable hard panels on the roof can take time to re-install. The V6 lacks the low-end torque that the old 4.0L in-line 6-cylinder had.

Kia Sportage

(Comments are based on 2009 model as the 2010 model had not been released at time of printing.)

Rating	Not tested
Price	$21,000-$31,000
Engines	2.0L 4-cylinder with 140hp 2.7L V6 with 173hp
Standard safety features include	Front, side, and curtain airbags, ABS, traction and stability control
Average fuel consumption	2.0L engine, 1835L/year 2.7L V6, 2008L/year 2.0L engine AWD, 1935L/year 2.7L V6 AWD, 2079L/yr
Warranty	5-year/100,000 km
Initial quality score	3.5/5
Dependability score	3/5

Pros: The Kia Sportage is based on the same platform as the Hyundai Tucson compact crossover, and both are due to be updated for 2010. This vehicle has a strong track record for quality. The interior is basic, yet functional and the different configurations make it attractive to many families who need a basic SUV. Also look at the review for the Tucson.

Cons: Unfortunately we do not have the information on the new 2010 model at the time of printing.

Mazda CX-7

Rating	Worth consideration
Price	$30,000-$36,000
Engine	2.3L 4-cylinder turbo with 244hp
Standard safety features include	Front, side and curtain airbags, ABS, traction and stability control
Average fuel consumption	FWD, 2092L/year AWD, 2216L/year
Warranty	3-year/80,000 km
Initial quality score	3/5
Dependability score	N/A

Pros: The Mazda CX-7 is unique in two different ways. First, it is larger than most of the compact utilities offered around this price point. Second, it is equipped with a powerful 2.3L turbo 4-cylinder. For buyers looking to spend just a little bit more than they might for a CR-V or RAV4, the XC-7 offers a much more dynamic-looking vehicle with fine interior appointments. The turbo-charged engine is an alternative to spending top dollar on a V6-equipped compact utility. Handling is sure footed with the FWD version, but the AWD will be the choice for most Canadians looking for winter traction.

Cons: For buyers who are most concerned about price, the additional money for better performance and handling might not be worth it. Those buyers can easily be served by other compact utilities. Also, when fully equipped, the CX-7 starts to compete with some very worthy competitors. The turbo engine is designed to run on expensive premium fuel.

Mazda Tribute

Rating	Must try
Price	$23,000-$33,000
Engines	2.5L 4-cylinder with 171hp 3.0L V6 with 240hp
Standard safety features include	Front, side and curtain airbags, ABS, and traction, stability and rollover control
Average fuel consumption	2.5L engine FWD, 1660L/year 3.0L V6 FWD, 1958L/year 2.5L engine AWD, 1910L/year 3.0L V6 AWD, 2078L/year
Warranty	3-year/80,000 km
Initial quality score	2/5
Dependability score	3/5

Pros: The Tribute was co-developed with Ford, so also look at the comments for the Ford Escape. The Escape has become a top seller in the compact crossover market, providing no-nonsense, inexpensive transportation to millions of buyers, and the Tribute piggy backs on that popularity. The interior is basic yet very well thought out, the seating is comfortable for four adults, and the cargo area is useful. The 2.5L 4-cylinder is a worthy engine and for most buyers will fulfill their needs, plus it is very efficient. The Tribute/Escape is proof that domestic brands can make great products.

Cons: The Escape might be a better option because it is made in the same factory as the Tribute, has better styling, a lower starting price and an optional hybrid system.

Mitsubishi Outlander

Rating	Must try
Price	$25,000-$32,000
Engines	2.4L 4-cylinder with 168hp 3.0L V6 with 213hp 3.0L V6 with 220hp
Standard safety features include	Front, side and curtain airbags, ABS, traction and stability control
Average fuel consumption	2.4L engine, 1857L/year 3.0L V6, 2057L/year
Warranty	5-year/100,000 km
Initial quality score	3.5/5
Dependability score	5/5

Pros: This is a vehicle that continues to surprise not only auto journalists but also the buying public because of the well-thought-out interior and good driving dynamics. The Outlander when equipped with the V6 engine is so smooth and quiet and it can cruise on the highway with ease. The Outlander can come equipped with FWD or AWD and can even be ordered with three rows of seats. The high level of interior finish, long list of standard features and good road manners make it a must try.

Cons: Even though the Outlander can be ordered with three rows of seats, don't bother because there are so many other vehicles that offer more room for the same money; this is really a five-passenger SUV.

Nissan Rogue

Rating	Must try
Price	$24,000-$30,000
Engine	2.5L 4-cylinder with 170hp
Standard safety features include	Front, side and curtain airbags, ABS, traction and stability control
Average fuel consumption	FWD, 1649L/year AWD, 1727L/year
Warranty	3-year/60,000 km
Initial quality score	2.5/5
Dependability score	N/A

Pros: The Rogue was introduced to replace the X-Trail compact utility and it has been a hit with consumers looking for a versatile yet fuel-efficient vehicle. The Rogue features a continuously variable transmission, which helps make it a class leader in fuel efficiency. The sporty styling and well-executed interior gives buyers the sense that they are buying a more upscale vehicle. The Rogue is fun to drive and is available with FWD or AWD depending on buyer's requirements. With a starting price below most competitors there is no wonder it is a hit.

Cons: The now retired X-Trail was a very square crossover, providing lots of glass, excellent outward visibility and plenty of cargo space. The Rogue might have more panache than the outgoing model, but the rounded design limits the size of windows, reducing outward visibility, especially when changing lanes or parking. The sloped rear hatch also limits the cargo capacity. None of these design features should detract any buyers, but take note and make sure you have the room you require.

Subaru Forester

Rating	Must try
Price	$26,000-$37,000
Engines	2.5L 4-cylinder with 170hp
	2.5L turbo 4-cylinder with 224hp
Standard safety features include	Front, side and curtain airbags, ABS, traction and stability control
Average fuel consumption	2.5L engine, 1828L/year
	2.5L turbo, 1946L/year
Warranty	3-year/60,000 km
Initial quality score	2.5/5
Dependability score	4/5

Pros: Subaru did a total overhaul on the Forester in 2009, producing one of the best compact SUVs in the market. The starting price is very attractive because AWD comes standard, which is not the case for the competition. The "Boxer" design of the engine provides great power and torque, along with a low centre of gravity for above-average handling. The base engine is more than adequate for most drivers. Styling has been totally revamped to give the Subaru a more conventional utility look, making it more appealing. The interior is functional with adequate room for four people. The Forester has a very strong following and demands top dollar in the used-car market.

Cons: The interior is functional but a bit too bland, lacking any real finesse. Keep in mind that turbo versions need to use expensive premium fuel to run their best.

Suzuki Grand Vitara

Rating	Must try
Price	$26,000-$33,000
Engines	2.4L 4-cylinder with 166hp 3.2L V6 with 230hp
Standard safety features include	Front, side and curtain airbags, ABS, traction and stability control
Average fuel consumption	2.4L engine, 1961L/year 3.2L V6, 2149L/year
Warranty	3-year/60,000 km
Initial quality score	2/5
Dependability score	2/5

Pros: This compact SUV is very different from most vehicles sold in this class because it comes standard with AWD and a great list of standard safety features, but more important is its rugged truck-like chassis. The Grand Vitara is a combination of a crossover and truck-based SUV providing good on-road manners and capable of off-road duties and towing. This is a good choice for buyers who drive over rough country roads or need light off-road duty. There are several different trim levels to suit most pocketbooks, making the Grand Vitara a vehicle to try.

Cons: For buyers who only use their compact SUV to provide extra winter traction and commuting duties then the added ruggedness of the Grand Vitara is overkill.

Suzuki XL7

Rating	More bang for buck with other models
Price	$37,000
Engine	3.6L V6 with 252hp
Standard safety features include	Front, side and curtain airbags, ABS with traction and stability control
Average fuel consumption	2259L/year
Warranty	3-year/60,000 km
Initial quality score	N/A
Dependability score	N/A

Pros: The XL7 is another joint venture with General Motors. It is based on the Chevy Equinox platform but differs in two important ways. First, the XL7 is a three-row, seven-passenger vehicle, whereas the GM version is only offered with two rows of seats. The second is the standard exclusive 3.6L V6, which has impressive power and torque.

Cons: The XL7 was advertised as the cheapest SUV with three rows of seats until the base 4-cylinder Toyota Highlander was introduced. The interior is rather cheap looking and the third row of seats is cramped. The XL7 is losing relevance due to the introduction of vehicles like the Chevy Traverse and Ford Flex three-row crossovers. These products offer more room and are sold for a similar price.

Toyota RAV4

Rating	Worth consideration
Price	$24,000-$37,000
Engine	2.5L 4-cylinder with 179hp 3.5L V6 with 269hp
Standard safety features include	Front, side and curtain airbags, ABS, stability and traction control
Average fuel consumption	2.5L, 1655L/year 3.5L V6, 1843L/year
Warranty	3-year/60,000 km
Initial quality score	3.5/5
Dependability score	4/5

Pros: The RAV4 helped introduce the "cute ute" phenomenon to North Americans along with the Honda CR-V back in the late 1990s. Unlike the CR-V, the RAV4 has grown in size to accommodate up to three rows of seats on higher trim levels. The interior is nicely finished, the seats are comfortable and the engines are efficient. When equipped with AWD and the 3.5L V6, the RAV4 turns into a very sporty utility, capable of very quick acceleration and easy cruising speeds. The V6 might be overkill because the new 2.5L 4-cylinder is very versatile and less expensive.

Cons: The biggest problem with the RAV4 is that it is getting crowded by other Toyota products like the new Venza and larger Highlander. For buyers who only require a five-passenger vehicle, the Venza is a better choice. For buyers who need three rows of seats, the 4-cylinder Highlander might do the trick. The rear swing-out tailgate is annoying for buyers who regularly parallel park because the door opens, not to the curb but to the road and in tight spots cannot be fully extended. A swing-up tailgate is a much better design and all other manufacturers have adopted it.

VW Tiguan

Rating	Worth consideration
Price	$27,000-$38,000
Engine	2.0L turbo 4-cylinder with 200hp
Standard safety features include	Front, side and curtain airbags, ABS, traction and stability control
Average fuel consumption	1920L/year
Warranty	4-year/80,000 km
Initial quality score	3/5
Dependability score	N/A

Pros: The compact SUV market is very competitive and growing quickly. The Tiguan is one of the latest entries into this class and it offers a unique approach. Instead of offering a 4-cylinder and a V6 option, VW only offers a turbo 4-cylinder to help it appeal to a wide range of buyers. The powerful, yet efficient engine, matched with above-average handling, a simple interior and good looks, makes the Tiguan a compelling package. If you don't require a lot of space in the back seat or cargo area, then this sporty SUV should be considered.

Cons: If you require room, especially in the back seat, then the Tiguan is rather small. The handling and performance can't compensate for the lack of space. This is a great choice for empty nesters who need occasional cargo and passenger room. The turbo engine requires expensive premium fuel.

PREMIUM COMPACT SUV/CROSSOVER

Acura RDX

Rating	Must try
Price	$43,000-$46,000
Engine	2.3L turbo 4-cylinder with 240hp
Standard safety features include	Front, side and curtain airbags, ABS, stability and traction control
Average fuel consumption	2214L/year
Warranty	5-year/100,000 km
Initial quality score	3/5
Dependability score	N/A

Pro: The premium compact utility class is one of the fastest-growing segments and the Acura RDX was one of the very first in this class of vehicles. The fuel-efficient turbo 4-cylinder is powerful and versatile. The interior is classy and well equipped. Acura is known for a high level of electronic gadgets and the RDX does not disappoint. The RDX is tuned for a spirited ride and above-average handling, making it an alternative to the BMW X3.

Cons: Due to the nature of turbo-charged engines, the RDX can exhibit slight turbo lag when pulling away from a traffic light. The performance-oriented ride can be choppy over uneven pavement and isn't relaxing on long highway trips.

Audi Q5

Rating	Must try
Price	$43,000-$48,000
Engine	3.2L V6 with 270hp
Standard safety features include	Front, side and curtain airbags, ABS, traction and stability control
Average fuel consumption	2075L/year
Warranty	5-year/100,000 km
Initial quality score	N/A
Dependability score	N/A

Pros: The Q5 is one of the latest entries into the rapidly growing premium compact crossover segment, competing with the BMW X3, Mercedes GLK, Acura RDX, to name a few. The Q5 differs from those vehicles because it is slightly longer, providing a more spacious rear seat and cargo area. The interior is luxurious and very well thought out, which is the case with all Audi products. The V6 engine is powerful and the AWD system provides superior handling and all-weather traction. A good choice in this class.

Cons: Optional packages can add up in a hurry. There is no diesel engine offered yet.

BMW X3

Rating	Worth consideration
Price	$45,000
Engine	3.0L 6-cylinder with 230hp
Standard safety features include	Front, side and curtain airbags, ABS, traction and stability control
Average fuel consumption	2098L/year
Warranty	4-year/80,000 km
Initial quality score	4/5
Dependability score	3/5

Pros: The X3 was the very first entry into the premium compact crossover segment and it still has an advantage over many of the new models introduced to compete with it. The powerful 3.0L engine and superior handling make the X3 the vehicle of choice for performance-oriented drivers. The back seat is roomy, the interior is functional and the cargo space is easy to access.

Cons: Since the X3 was the first in this segment it is way overdue to be redone. The interior is functional but the new competitors have much nicer finish and materials. The X3 is a great handling vehicle, but the comfort level could be a lot higher.

Infiniti EX

Rating	Worth consideration
Price	$41,000
Engine	3.5L V6 with 297hp
Standard safety features include	Front, side and curtain airbags, ABS, stability and traction control
Average fuel consumption	2184L/year
Warranty	4-year/100,000 km
Initial quality score	5/5
Dependability score	N/A

Pros: The EX is based on the G sedan and Infiniti refers to the EX as a "personal luxury" vehicle—perfect for a couple or single person who requires the back seats and small cargo area for occasional use. The solid handling and powerful engine found in the G sedan makes its way into this premium compact. The interior is well thought out with a high level of finish.

Cons: The EX has limited appeal to buyers who might need the rear seats for kids or the cargo area for strollers etc. It can feel cramped on the inside. The Acura RDX or Mercedes GLK might be better choices for those who require slightly more room.

Land Rover LR2

Rating	Reliability?
Price	$45,000
Engine	3.2L 6-cylinder with 230hp
Standard safety features include	Front, side and head airbags, ABS, traction and stability control
Average fuel consumption	2360L/year
Warranty	4-year/80,000 km
Initial quality score	2/5
Dependability score	2/5

Pros: The LR2 is often overlooked in the premium compact SUV class in favour of the BMW X3, Mercedes GLK or Acura RDX to name a few. The LR2 has a unique approach because it has an in-line 6-cyinder instead of a V6, which provides good torque. This is especially helpful for off-road duties, which Land Rover is known for. The LR2 comes with a strong list of standard features, and buyers of these vehicles are very loyal to the Land Rover brand.

Cons: Land Rover has suffered with very disappointing quality scores for years; in fact most years they place dead last. The second and bigger problem with the LR2 is it looks almost identical to the much cheaper Ford Escape compact SUV. Nobody wants to spend $45,000 to look like a basic Ford!

Mercedes GLK-Class

Rating	TOP PICK
Price	$42,000
Engine	3.5L V6 with 268hp
Standard safety features include	Front, side and curtain airbags, ABS, traction and stability control
Average fuel consumption	2040L/year
Warranty	4-year/80,000 km
Initial quality score	N/A
Dependability score	N/A

Pros: Why is the GLK the Top Pick in the premium compact SUV category? Well, it comes with a high level of standard features and a nicely finished interior, standard V6 engine and AWD, and a ride that will appeal to a wide range of drivers. The main reason is the price. Who would have thought that Mercedes would be undercutting the market, but it has. The GLK can be fully equipped for roughly $50,000. The GLK is based on the C-Class sedan but is thousands of dollars cheaper when you compare a similarly equipped C-Class to a GLK. Yes, there are others in this class that have better handling or a higher level of finish, but the overall GLK package is compelling.

Cons: The back seat might be short on legroom for some passengers. There is no clean diesel offered at this time.

Volvo XC60

Rating	Worth consideration
Price	$45,000
Engine	3.0L turbo 6-cylinder with 281hp
Standard safety features include	Front, side and head airbags, ABS, traction and stability control
Average fuel consumption	2320L/year
Warranty	4-year/80,000 km
Initial quality score	N/A
Dependability score	N/A

Pros: The XC60 is yet another introduction to the premium compact SUV market. The XC60 shares the same platform as the capable Land Rover LR2. The luxury interior, powerful turbo engine and compact design will surely make the XC60 a sales winner for Volvo. The very latest safety features have been implemented into this new vehicle, including the ability to stop the XC60 automatically if no driver intervention takes place.

Cons: Not tested at the time of printing.

Mid-Size Category

MID-SIZE CARS

Buick Allure

Rating	Must try
Price	$33,000-$41,000
Engines	3.0L V6 with 255hp 3.6L V6 with 280hp
Standard safety features include	Front, side and curtain airbags, anti-lock brakes (ABS), stability and traction control
Average fuel consumption	N/A
Warranty	4-year/80,000 km
Initial quality score	3.5/5
Dependability score	5/5

Pros: The Allure is all-new for 2010, featuring bold new styling, impressive direct-injection engines and available all-wheel drive (AWD). The Allure is a striking car from all angles, and the interior rivals any car in this class for finish and materials. The latest direct-injection engine, mated to the 6-speed automatic transmission, makes for a powerful and fuel-efficient car. Buick has been at the top of vehicle dependability studies for years; in fact, Buick ranks number one in the latest JD Power and Associates study, and the Allure is the number one most dependable car sold in the U.S. GM has hopes that this new Allure will help to resurrect the Buick brand to a place of prominence. The design and quality of this latest Allure should help.

Cons: Will the stodgy image of Buick keep potential buyers away from dealerships, even if this is a great car? Time will tell. Resale value is always a concern.

Chevy Impala

Rating	Worth consideration
Price	$26,000-$36,000
Engines	3.5L V6 with 207hp 3.9L V6 with 230hp
Standard safety features include	Front, side and curtain airbags, ABS and traction control. Stability control is optional.
Average fuel consumption	3.5L V6, 1791L/year 3.9L V6, 1984L/year
Warranty	3-year/60,000 km
Initial quality score	4.5/5
Dependability score	3/5

Pros: These cars fly under the radar, but they seem to have a strong following because the Impala consistently shows up as one of Canada's top-selling cars. There is a lot to like about the Impala from the spacious interior and good handling to powerful engine options and a huge trunk. The interior is very well thought out and features are easy to use. The ride is smooth and very quiet, and the Impala is an easy car to drive for a long period of time. The quality scores are also reassuring.

Cons: The exterior styling is a little lacklustre, and maybe that is why it flies under the radar. Even though the front seats are spacious, the back seats could use a bit more legroom.

Chevy Malibu

Rating	Must try
Price	$24,000-$32,000
Engines	2.4L 4-cylinder with 169hp 3.6L V6 with 252hp
Standard safety features include	Front, side and curtain airbags, ABS, traction control and stability control
Average fuel consumption	2.4L engine, 1565L/year 3.6L V6, 2044L/year
Warranty	3-year/60,000 km
Initial quality score	4.5/5
Dependability score	3/5

Pros: When the latest Malibu was introduced it won North American Car of the Year, an award it deserved. Styling is strong on this large mid-size car, making it a sedan one would want to own. The interior is a good example of what GM can do right, featuring a nice contrast of materials and colours. The back seat is huge, almost limo-like. The 4-cylinder engine is surprisingly good, providing more than enough power. The remarkable thing about the Malibu is the ultra quiet interior and smooth, yet sure-footed handling. The safety features are excellent as is the quality score.

Cons: The hybrid version has been dropped due to lack of demand. The resale value of this current Malibu is still a question mark.

Chrysler Sebring

Rating	Hello rental car
Price	Sedan: $18,000-$25,000
	Convertible: $22,000-$31,000
Engines	2.4L 4-cylinder with 173hp
	2.7L V6 with 186hp
	3.5L V6 with 235hp
Standard safety features include	Front, side and curtain airbags and ABS. Optional: stability and traction control.
Average fuel consumption	2.4L engine, 1661L/year
	2.7L V6, 1836L/year
	3.5L V6, 2086L/year
Warranty	3-year/60,000 km
Initial quality score	4.5/5
Dependability score	3/5

Pros: A favourite with rental car companies, the Sebring has not been as popular as it once was, which is surprising given the very low starting price. With a range of engine choices and a reasonably track record, this mid-size sedan is roomy and comfortable. The convertible is very inexpensive and the optional retractable hardtop is worth a look.

Cons: The 2.4L engine is not the smoothest and most refined engine on the market, and the consequent interior noise is a major reason to avoid this engine. The V6 is a much better choice due to the lower noise and smoother power. The styling of this car is part of the reason that its popularity is waning.

Dodge Avenger

Rating	Hello rental car
Price	$17,000-$25,000
Engines	2.4L 4-cylinder with 173hp 2.7L V6 with 186hp 3.5L V6 with 235hp
Standard safety features include	Front and curtain airbags, ABS, stability and traction control
Average fuel consumption	2.4L engine, 1661L/year 2.7L engine, 1836L/year 3.5L V6, 2086L/year
Warranty	3-year/60,000 km
Initial quality score	3/5
Dependability score	N/A

The Avenger is the Dodge version of the Chrysler Sebring. Please refer to the comments for the Sebring.

Ford Fusion

Rating	Must try
Price	$21,000-$35,000
Engines	2.5L 4-cylinder 175hp 3.0L V6 with 240hp 3.5L V6 with 263hp
Standard safety features include	Front, side and curtain airbags, ABS, stability and traction control
Average fuel consumption	2.5L engine, 1732L/year 3.0L engine, 1980L/year 3.0L AWD, 2084L/year 3.5L V6, N/A
Warranty	3-year/60,000 km
Initial quality score	4.5/5
Dependability score	4/5

Pros: The Ford Fusion is turning a lot of heads; it is proof that an American car company can build a sedan that is as good as, if not better than, the Japanese in design and quality. The 2.5L 4-cylinder is a good powerplant for average drivers and the availability of AWD is something many competitors don't offer. The exterior styling is bold and the roomy interior is well thought out with a good use of materials. The quality scores for the Fusion rival those for the Toyota Camry and Honda Accord. The list of standard safety features is as good as the Honda Accord, the Top Pick in this class.

Cons: The poor image that North American cars have is a drawback to resale values. Maybe as people come to learn that the Fusion is a well-made car, the values will improve.

Honda Accord

Rating	TOP PICK
Prices	Sedan: $25,000-$37,000 Coupe: $28,000-$38,000
Engines	2.4L 4-cylinder with 177hp 2.4L 4-cylinder with 190hp 3.5L V6 with 271hp
Standard safety features include	Front, side and curtain airbags, ABS, traction and stability control
Average fuel consumption	4-cylinder, 1610L/year V6, 1813 L/year
Warranty	5-year/100,000 km
Initial quality score	3.5/5
Dependability score	5/5

Pros: The Accord has grown over the years and is now considered a full-size sedan in the United States. Styling is strong with upscale trim touches. The roomy interior is comfortable with more than enough room for four or five. Handling is above average with good feedback to the driver, the Accord is a "driver's" car, offering a wonderful combination of function and pleasure plus good fuel consumption, standard safety features and a strong track record for quality and resale.

Cons: Loaded versions can be expensive and might not be worth the extra money because the 4-cylinder motors offered are so good. The interface with the radio and navigation computer is overly complex and cluttered with buttons but the driver does adapt.

Hyundai Sonata

Rating	Must try
Price	$22,000-$33,000
Engines	2.4L 4-cylinder with 174hp 3.3L V6 with 249hp
Standard safety features include	Front, side and curtain airbags and ABS. Optional: traction and stability control.
Average fuel consumption	2.4L engine, 1625L/year 3.3L V6, 1809L/year
Warranty	5-year/100,000 km
Initial quality score	4/5
Dependability score	3/5

Pros: The Sonata is one of the least expensive mid-size sedans sold in Canada, yet it offers excellent quality and value for money. Recently updated to include better styling and interior finish, the Sonata is a pleasure to drive with the 4-cylinder or V6. The base models offer good value but the real value is the top models, constantly costing thousands less than comparably equipped cars. The Sonata constantly scores well in quality surveys, making it a good choice.

Cons: As with many other Hyundai products, the base model looks attractive but to get it similarly equipped to cars with a full host of safety features, the price ramps up.

Hyundai Azera

Rating	Must try
Price	$37,000
Engine	3.8L V6 with 263hp
Standard safety features include	Front, side and curtain airbags, ABS, traction and stability control
Average fuel consumption	2044L/year
Warranty	5-year/100,000 km
Initial quality score	3.5/5
Dependability score	3/5

Pros: The Azera is based on a larger Sonata platform providing a choice to buyers who want more refinement, options and power. The styling is conservative, yet classy; the interior has a strong list of safety and convenience features. The Azera is direct competition for cars like the Toyota Avalon and Lexus ES, at a much lower price. The Azera is sold with one well-equipped package that includes a powerful and spirited 3.8L V6.

Cons: There is nothing wrong with the Azera; in fact, it is a very nice car to look at and drive. The problem is it has become irrelevant now that the award-winning Hyundai Genesis sedan has been introduced. The Genesis has a more substantial luxury feel for a similar starting price as the Azera.

Kia Magentis

Rating	Must try
Price	$22,000-$28,000
Engines	2.4L 4-cylinder with 175hp 2.7L V6 with 194hp
Standard safety features include	Front, side and curtain airbags, ABS, traction and stability control
Average fuel consumption	2.4L engine, 1592L/year 2.7L engine, 1785L/year
Warranty	5-year/100,000 km
Initial quality score	N/A
Dependability score	N/A

Pros: The Magentis is based on the same platform as the Hyundai Sonata, offering similar engine choices, but what sets the Magentis apart is the inclusion of more standard safety features. This roomy and comfortable car has a nice level of interior finish, especially on the higher-end V6 models. When the current model was introduced in 2009, the size grew to more appealing dimensions, making it a good fit for many families.

Cons: Not a lot of thought went into making this Magentis any different from the Sonata. This proves that car companies cut and paste from one side of the business, just to fill a hole in another part of the business.

Mazda6

Rating	Must try
Price	$23,000-$34,000
Engines	2.5L 4-cylinder with 170hp 3.7L V6 with 272 hp
Standard safety features include	Front, side and curtain airbags, ABS and traction control. Optional: stability control.
Average fuel consumption	2.5L engine, 1670 L/year 3.7L V6, 2051 L/year
Warranty	3-year/80,000 km
Initial quality score	3/5
Dependability score	2/5

Pros: The Mazda6 was re-done for 2009 making it a larger, more powerful and more sophisticated sedan than the outgoing model. For drivers who want a good combination of practicality and passion in their daily driving, the Mazda6 delivers. The new 2.5L 4-cylinder and eye-popping 3.7L V6 have all the power one could want in an inexpensive sedan. The 4-cylinder is the vehicle of choice because the 3.7L is overkill. The updated styling inside, along with larger dimensions, helps provide a very pleasant experience.

Cons: Now that the Mazda6 has grown in size it might have lost its appeal to some buyers. The Mazda6 is not as revered as the Toyota Camry and Honda Accord so the market might not be as strong as those vehicles when it comes time to re-sell. With so much sharing of components from Ford, the Fusion might be a cheaper option.

Mitsubishi Galant

Rating	Not much to like here
Price	$24,000-$33,000
Engines	2.4L 4-cylinder with 160hp 3.8L V6 with 230hp 3.8L V6 with 258hp
Standard safety features include	Front, side and curtain airbags, ABS. Traction control is optional.
Average fuel consumption	2.4L engine, 1790L/year 3.8L engine, 2097L/year 3.8L high-output engine, 2148L/year
Warranty	5-year/100,000 km
Initial quality score	2.5/5
Dependability score	3/5

Pros: Sold with a 4-cylinder or V6, the Galant has something for most buyers, but it is the high-output 3.8L engine that is the star of the show. This engine has plenty of passing power, and the reworked suspension on this Ralliart model makes it an option for driving enthusiasts.

Cons: Other than the high-output Ralliart version, there isn't much to like about the Galant. The styling is dull and the interior is poorly designed and looks cheap. With so many great sedans in this mid-size class, the Galant doesn't stack up, making it a forgettable car.

Nissan Altima

Rating	Must try
Price	Sedan: $23,000-$30,000 Coupe: $27,000-$30,000
Engines	2.5L 4-cylinder with 175hp 3.5L V6 with 258hp
Standard safety features include	Front, side and curtain airbags, ABS. Optional: traction and stability control.
Average fuel consumption	2.5L engine, 1528L/year 3.5L engine, 1870L/year
Warranty	3-year/60,000 km
Initial quality score	5/5
Dependability score	3/5

Pros: The Altima is an excellent choice in the mid-size car class due to its long list of standard features, above-average handling and solid quality score. The interior is very well executed, offering high-quality materials and comfortable seats for all passengers. The 2.5L engine is worthy of the competition, and the optional 3.5L engine makes the Altima a rocket. The continuously variable transmission helps to provide class-leading fuel economy. The Altima received top marks in 2009 for initial quality from JD Power and Associates.

Cons: The lack of standard traction and stability control puts the Altima a half step behind the Top Pick Honda Accord. The coupe suffers from poor outward visibility, especially through the back window. Stick with the thrifty 4-cylinder; the V6 is overkill.

Toyota Camry

Rating	Must try
Price	$25,000-$38,000
Engines	2.5L 4-cylinder with 169hp
	3.5 V6 with 268 hp
Standard safety features include	Front, side, curtain and knee airbags, ABS, traction and stability control
Average fuel consumption	2.5L engine, 1603L/year
	3.5L engine, 1807L/year
Warranty	3-year/60,000 km
Initial quality score	5/5
Dependability score	5/5

Pros: The Camry is the best-selling mid-size car in Canada because of Toyota's reputation for quality, value and great resale value. The ride is relaxed and enjoyable due to the soft suspension and quiet interior, appealing to a wide range of buyers. The interior is simple and well executed, offering plenty of room for all passengers. With two versatile and efficient engines, the Camry does most things well, and the all-new 2.5L 4-cylinder provides more than enough power for the average driver. Not the most exciting car, but it delivers the goods, day after day.

Cons: Drivers looking for a bit of excitement might find the relaxed drive of the Camry a little too sedate, making the Honda Accord or Nissan Altima more appealing options. The dashboard and driver interface is basic to the point of being bland. The Camry is a good car but it suffers from being dull—more like an appliance.

VW Passat

Rating	Must try
Price	Sedan: $27,000-$35,000 Wagon: $29,000-$36,000 CC: $32,000-$45,000
Engines	2.0L turbo 4-cylinder with 200hp 3.6L V6 with 280hp
Standard safety features include	Front, side and curtain airbags, ABS, traction and stability control
Average fuel consumption	2.0L engine, 1700L/year 3.6L V6, 2060L/year
Warranty	4-year/80,000 km
Initial quality score	3.5/5
Dependability score	2/5

Pros: The Passat is a secret in the mid-size class of cars; it falls between two classes of vehicles. The Passat should be viewed as an almost entry-level luxury vehicle because it offers more standard power than most mid-size cars and a well-made interior. The lineup is attractive because it can be ordered as a useful and very large wagon, or drop-dead gorgeous CC "comfort coupe" (a sedan with the roofline of a coupe). The Passat is also a wise choice for any buyer who is looking at a more expensive Audi, due to similar engines and features, at a lower price. For example, the Passat CC is a nicer car than the smaller A4 and it costs less!

Cons: Optional features can push the price up in a hurry. The Passat is not offered with a diesel engine yet. Buyers who don't care about European handling and performance will be better served by a cheaper sedan.

PREMIUM MID-SIZE CARS

Acura TSX

Rating	Must try
Price	$35,000-$41,000 for the 4-cylinder. The price of the V6 TSX was not available at the time of printing.
Engines	2.4L 4-cylinder with 201hp 3.5L V6 with 280hp
Standard safety features include	Front, side and curtain airbags, ABS, stability and traction control
Average fuel consumption	2.4L engine, 1641L/year 3.5L V6, N/A
Warranty	5-year/100,000 km
Initial quality score	2.5/5
Dependability score	3/5

Pros: Many potential buyers are not aware that the TSX is based on the European Honda Accord, which is altogether different from the large Accord sold in North America. The big news for 2009 was the introduction of a brand-new model, and the even bigger news for 2010 is the introduction of a V6 engine. This was done to keep the interest of power-hungry buyers. The 4-cylinder version is so well balanced, the power is effortless and the car is a riot to drive, so the V6 will make it that much faster and more desirable. The TSX is a truly great car.

Cons: Some buyers have not warmed to the new exterior and interior styling; the older car had a simplicity that made it attractive. The computer interface can be overly complex and the dash materials look a bit stark. The 4-cylinder engine is one of the great motors available today, making it a perfect match for the TSX. The V6 is overkill, though I suspect it will sell well in the U.S.

Acura TL

Rating	Must try
Price	$42,000-$50,000
Engines	3.5L V6 with 280hp 3.7L V6 with 305hp
Standard safety features include	Front, side and curtain airbags, ABS, stability and traction control
Average fuel consumption	3.5L V6, 1951L/year 3.7L V6, 2082L/year
Warranty	5-year/100,000 km
Initial quality score	4.5/5
Dependability score	4/5

Pros: The Acura TSX is based on the European Honda Accord, and the TL is based on the larger North American Honda Accord. The latest model was introduced in 2009 with a host of improvements including extra power, interior features and, for the first time, all-wheel drive. The TL, when equipped with the larger 3.7L engine and AWD, is a wonderful luxury performance sedan capable of taking on the best from Germany. The TL has a strong following because it does most things very well and has a solid reputation for quality and resale value.

Cons: Unfortunately, the restyling that was done for the latest model has turned the TL into a car you will either love or hate. The polarizing design might keep some people away from enjoying how well this car performs. The base model without AWD can be a handful under hard acceleration due to the powerful 3.5L engine sending all the power to only the front wheels.

Audi A6

Rating	Must try
Price	Sedan: $63,000-$100,000 Wagon: $67,000
Engines	3.2L V6 with 255hp 3.0L turbo V6 with 300hp 4.2L V8 with 420hp 5.2L V10 with 435hp
Standard safety features include	Front, side and curtain airbags, ABS, traction and stability control
Average fuel consumption	3.2L V6, 1920L/year 3.0L turbo, 2040L/year 4.2L V8, 2240L/year 5.2L V10, 2600L/year
Warranty	4-year/80,000 km
Initial quality score	4/5
Dependability score	3/5

Pros: The A6 is often overlooked in the mid-size premium class in favour of the 5 Series from BMW and the Mercedes E Class, which is unfortunate. The exterior styling has recently been redone, making it a more cohesive design. The interior is one of the best in this class, featuring an easy-to-use and -understand computer interface. (BMW take note.) The back seat is very roomy and the wagon version has a cargo area that puts many SUVs to shame. The powerful engines and solid AWD system provide an unflappable ride and handling. The A6 is a beautiful car to look at and the luxury approach from Audi is one of the best in the world.

Cons: The S6 might look good on paper but in real life it doesn't provide the kind of invigorating drive that the price tag suggests. The 4.2L V8 is a much better choice for a fraction of the price.

BMW 5 Series

Rating	Must try
Price	Sedan: $56,000-$107,000 Wagon: $71,000
Engines	3.0L 6-cylinder with 230hp 3.0L turbo 6-cylinder with 300hp 4.8L V8 with 360hp 5.0L V10 with 500hp
Standard safety features include	Front, side and curtain airbags, ABS, traction and stability control
Average fuel consumption	3.0L engine, 1873L/year 3.0L turbo, 2037L/year 4.8L V8, 2250L/year 5.0L V10, 3003L/year
Warranty	4-year/80,000 km
Initial quality score	3.5/5
Dependability score	2/5

Pros: Drivers and other vehicle manufacturers place the BMW 5 Series, just like the smaller 3 Series, in high regard for its handling and driving dynamics. The feedback to the driver, along with the powerful engines, makes the 5 Series very hard to beat for buyers who want a performance-prestige sedan. The back seat is roomy, and even though this car is bigger in every dimension over the 3 Series, it is only slightly heavier, making the driving experience feel like you're in a smaller car.

Cons: The 5 Series could be a better car. The interior is very stark; some might even call it bland. The biggest concern is the iDrive computer interface system that takes a great deal of time to learn, plus other manufacturers in this class have much better and intuitive systems.

Cadillac STS

Rating	Worth consideration
Price	$61,000
Engines	3.6L V6 with 302hp 4.6L V8 with 320hp
Standard safety features include	Front, side and curtain airbags, ABS, stability and traction control
Average fuel consumption	3.6L V6, 2017L/year 3.6L AWD, 2050L/year 4.6L V8, 2280L/year 4.6L AWD, 2381L/year
Warranty	4-year/80,000 km
Initial quality score	2/5
Dependability score	3/5

Pros: The STS is a larger version of the excellent CTS. The larger interior, especially the back seat, is welcomed. Available in rear-wheel drive or all-wheel drive, the STS is a car that compares to many German performance sedans in terms of handling and power. The AWD system makes the STS a good all-weather performance sedan.

Cons: The STS isn't cheap, and the optional packages can add to the price very quickly, pricing this car out of the market it is aimed at.

Hyundai Genesis

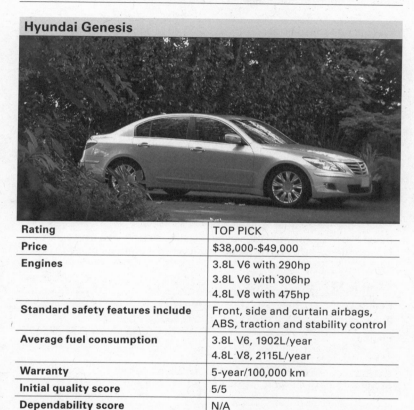

Rating	TOP PICK
Price	$38,000-$49,000
Engines	3.8L V6 with 290hp
	3.8L V6 with 306hp
	4.8L V8 with 475hp
Standard safety features include	Front, side and curtain airbags, ABS, traction and stability control
Average fuel consumption	3.8L V6, 1902L/year
	4.8L V8, 2115L/year
Warranty	5-year/100,000 km
Initial quality score	5/5
Dependability score	N/A

Pros: The Hyundai Genesis sedan took the auto industry by storm when it was introduced in 2009, winning several awards. This large rear-wheel-drive sedan has excellent driving dynamics for a luxury car with a spirited 3.8L engine and potent 4.8LV8. The price of the Genesis is what makes this vehicle a real winner, offering the same level of refinement that is typically found in cars costing twice as much. A beautiful car and at a price many people can handle. The coupe has the same name but is actually a very different car, putting emphasis on performance and not luxury. The Genesis scored top marks in the 2009 JD Power and Associates quality study in its very first year!

Cons: The only knock against the Genesis is that many people will not try it because it is a Hyundai, which is a shame because they are missing out on one of the true value luxury cars on the market.

Infiniti M

Rating	Must try
Price	$54,000-$69,000
Engines	3.5L V6 with 303hp 4.5L V8 with 325hp
Standard safety features include	Front, side and curtain airbags, ABS, stability and traction control
Average fuel consumption	3.5L V6, 2115L/year 3.5L AWD, 2282L/year 4.5L V8, 2331L/year 4.5L AWD, 2579L/year
Warranty	4-year/100,000 km
Initial quality score	5/5
Dependability score	4/5

Pros: The M sedan is based on a larger version of the amazing Infiniti G sedan. Both cars have excellent road-handling capability, especially in AWD trim. The V6 and V8 engines are powerful and refined. The interior is very well done, especially the computer interface system. The larger dimensions of the M sedan make it a much more comfortable car than the rather cramped G sedan. The M competes nicely with much more expensive German sedans.

Cons: The M sedan is overdue to be restyled, so look for a new one soon. The wonderful 3.7L engine found in the G is not offered in the M.

Jaguar XF

Rating	Must try
Price	$62,000-$78,000
Engines	4.2L V8 with 300hp 5.0L V8 with 385hp 5.0L supercharged V8 with 462hp
Standard safety features include	Front, side and head airbags, ABS, traction and stability control
Average fuel consumption	4.2L V8, 4180L/year 5.0L V8, N/A 5.0L supercharged V8, N/A
Warranty	4-year/80,000 km
Initial quality score	2/5
Dependability score	N/A

Pros: Jaguar was stuck in a rut, producing cars that looked exactly the same year after year. The XF was introduced to shake up the image of Jaguar—and it worked. The XF is a beautiful car and a real value in the category. The XF costs thousands less than many other cars in this class with V8 engines. The standard V8 is a willing partner and the supercharged versions are obscenely fast. The interior is stunning and very simple to use. Handling is very good and the XF is a pleasure to drive, a worthy competitor for anything that Japan or Germany can produce. It must be noted that Jaguar is No. 1 in vehicle dependability for all vehicles after three years, according to the JD Power and Associates dependability study.

Cons: The biggest problem Jaguar has is its image as a low-quality carmaker, when the exact opposite is true.

Lexus ES

Rating	Must try
Price	$41,000
Engine	3.5L V6 with 272hp
Standard safety features include	Front, side, knee and curtain airbags, ABS, stability and traction control
Average fuel consumption	1847L/year
Warranty	4-year/80,000 km
Initial quality score	5/5
Dependability score	5/5

Pros: Based on the same platform as the Toyota Avalon, the ES offers buyers a large comfortable interior and refinement that is found in cars costing much more. The ES is a beautiful car to cruise in, a perfect highway companion for any commute or road trip. The back seat is roomy and the trunk is also vast. I call the ES "The Japanese Buick" due to the laidback driving style and comfortable interior. The 3.5L V6 offers adequate power and is also efficient. The quality scores for this car are perfect, making it a solid choice for anyone who wants luxury and refinement in a large car for a reasonable price.

Cons: Not the most exciting car to drive and it is overdue for a refresh.

Lexus GS

Rating	Worth consideration
Price	$52,000-$64,000
Engines	3.5L V6 with 303hp 4.6L V8 with 342hp
Standard safety features include	Front, side, knee and curtain airbags, ABS, stability and traction control
Average fuel consumption	3.5L engine, 1847L/year 3.5L AWD, 1996L/year 4.6L engine, 2096L/year
Warranty	4-year/80,000 km
Initial quality score	5/5
Dependability score	3/5

Pros: A solid choice for any buyer who requires a large RWD or AWD sedan with good driving dynamics and a high level of interior finish. The GS competes with the well-established BMW 5 Series, but does it in a unique Lexus way that provides an insulated driving experience, coddling the occupants from any wind, road or engine noise. Two powerful engines are offered, although for most drivers the 3.5L V6 will be more than adequate.

Cons: Due to the sleek roof line, back-seat headroom can be limiting for tall people. Yes, the GS is a smooth operator but for drivers who require more road feel, the 5 Series is still the market leader.

Mercedes E-Class

Rating	Must try
Price	N/A at time of printing
Engines	3.5L V6 with 272hp
	5.5L V8 with 388hp
Standard safety features include	Front, side and curtain airbags, ABS, traction and stability control
Average fuel consumption	N/A at time of printing
Warranty	4-year/80,000 km
Initial quality score	4/5
Dependability score	2/5

Pros: The E-Class is all-new and now includes a coupe version to replace the CLK. This new model is a showcase for Mercedes-Benz technology and refinement along with unflappable driving dynamics. Look for a convertible version and diesel model to be included in this lineup.

Cons: Not available for testing at the time of printing.

MID-SIZE CROSSOVER/TALL WAGONS

Subaru Legacy/Outback

Rating	Worth consideration
Price	Sedan: $27,000-$42,000
	Wagon: $28,000-$31,000
	Outback $31,000-$44,000
Engines	2.5L 4-cylinder with 170hp
	2.5L turbo 4-cylinder with 243hp
	3.0L 6-cylinder with 245hp
Standard safety features include	Front, side and curtain airbags, ABS, traction and stability control
Average fuel consumption	2.5L engine, 1828L/year
	2.5L turbo, 2091L/year
	3.0L engine, 2125L/year
Warranty	3-year/60,000 km
Initial quality score	2.5/5
Dependability score	3/5

Pros: Subaru equips its vehicles with AWD, making them an attractive choice for Canadians who live in snowbelts. The Legacy is sold in different forms, including a sedan, a wagon and a crossover-wagon called the Outback. Due to the AWD system and low centre of gravity, the Legacy is a pleasure to drive, making it appeal to many drivers, including those who want a degree of performance. With three engines to choose from, there is something for most buyers. These vehicles tend to be a bit more expensive than others in this class, but the cars have great resale value and a strong following.

Cons: Subaru has done a good job of marketing the Outback models, appealing to buyers who want a more rugged-looking car. Keep in mind that most of the Outback's upgrades are cosmetic, with minor tweaks to the suspension and tires; in essence it is still a Legacy wagon. Savvy buyers should try the very capable Legacy wagon and save some money; plus, it is a better riding car. Subaru is not known for flashy interiors and the Legacy does suffer from being quite basic. Turbo versions need to be fed expensive premium gas to run at their best.

Toyota Venza

Rating	TOP PICK
Price	$29,000-$40,000
Engines	2.7L 4-cylinder with 182hp 3.5L V6 with 268hp
Standard safety features include	Front, side, knee and curtain airbags, ABS, stability and traction control
Average fuel consumption	2.7L engine, 1712L/year 3.5L V6, 1894L/year
Warranty	3-year/60,000 km
Initial quality score	N/A
Dependability score	N/A

Pros: The Venza is based on the Camry platform, which is also used for the Highlander SUV, so it falls somewhere in between these two vehicles, making it the Top Pick in the tall wagon/crossover segment. The Venza offers buyers plenty of options from basic 4-cylinder front-wheel-drive versions all the way up to V6 all-wheel-drive luxury models. The starting price is very attractive because the 4-cylinder engine is very capable for most needs, and FWD is perfect for city dwellers. The interior is roomy, well thought out, and offers better materials than found in the Camry. Cargo capacity is excellent and so is the legroom for rear-seat passengers. The Venza has a wide appeal from buyers of sedans to buyers of traditional SUVs.

Cons: Venza is a four-to-five-passenger vehicle, so it doesn't offer the room of a three-row SUV. The large 19- or 20-inch wheels look very stylish, but many Canadians will have to buy separate winter rims and tires. The large dimensions of the Venza might exclude buyers who want a tall wagon but don't want such a long wheelbase.

Volvo V70/XC70

Rating	Worth consideration
Price	$43,000-$52,000
Engines	3.2L 6-cylinder 235hp
	3.0L turbo 6-cylinder 281hp
Standard safety features include	Front, side and head airbags, ABS, traction and stability control
Average fuel consumption	3.2L engine, 2100L/year
	3.0L turbo, 2320L/year
Warranty	4-year/80,000 km
Initial quality score	2.5/5
Dependability score	3/5

Pros: The V70 and more rugged-looking XC70 are great alternatives to buying an SUV. The interior space makes them a wonderful place to spend time for all passengers. The unique built-in child booster seat is innovative. The cargo area puts many SUVs to shame. Handling is much better than an SUV, the drive smooth and the interior quiet.

Cons: The V70 is a sensible alternative to buying the more expensive XC70 because it is the same basic vehicle except for the more rugged look and modified suspension. Unfortunately, Volvo doesn't offer a turbo or AWD version of the V70, only the XC70.

MID-SIZE SUV/CROSSOVER

Dodge Journey

Rating	Worth consideration
Price	$18,000-$26,000
Engines	2.4L 4-cylinder with 173hp 3.5L V6 with 235hp
Standard safety features include	Front, side and curtain airbags, ABS, traction and stability control
Average fuel consumption	2.4L engine, 1921L/year 3.5L V6, 2259L/year 3.5L AWD, 2363L/year
Warranty	3-year/60,000 km
Initial quality score	2/5
Dependability score	N/A

Pros: Introduced in 2009, the Journey helped fill the hole created when Dodge stopped producing the base Caravan minivan. This inexpensive crossover has seating for up to seven people with three rows of seats. The interior is well thought out and can hold a surprising amount of cargo. This is an option for a family that doesn't want a van but still needs space. The option of AWD on the Journey makes up for the lack of AWD in the Grand Caravan lineup.

Cons: The interior is well thought out when it comes to seating and storage, but more effort should have been put into the dash materials and look. The pod that holds the instrument panel looks like it was an afterthought. This is too bad, because there is a lot to like about the Journey.

Ford Edge

Rating	Must try
Price	$30,000-$38,000
Engine	3.5L V6 with 265hp
Standard safety features include	Front, side and curtain airbags, ABS, traction and stability control
Average fuel consumption	3.5L V6, 2164L/year 3.5L AWD, 2315L/year
Warranty	3-year/60,000 km
Initial quality score	4.5/5
Dependability score	N/A

Pros: The Edge is based on the Volvo S80 platform that is also used for the Taurus and Flex. This provides a solid and sophisticated ride at a price that is easy to take. Offered with one engine choice and available with AWD, the Edge has been a hit with Canadians. The smooth, quiet ride and powerful engine make for a great commuter/family vehicle. With a long list of standard safety and convenience features, the Edge is good value. The interior is roomy, with space for five adults. If more space is needed, the Ford Flex is a longer version of the Edge in a funky, retro package.

Cons: In order to keep costs down, Ford scrimped a bit on the interior dash materials, giving them a cheap plastic look that lets the Edge down. The good news is that they have corrected this in the larger Flex.

Explorer

Rating	Stuck in the 1990s
Price	$35,000-$46,000
Engines	4.0L V6 with 210hp 4.6L V8 with 292hp
Standard safety features include	Front, side and curtain airbags, ABS, traction and stability control
Average fuel consumption	4.0L V6, 2772L/year 4.6L V8, 2641L/year
Warranty	3-year/60,000 km
Initial quality score	3.5/5
Dependability score	3/5

Pros: The Explorer is a truck-based SUV with standard 4X4 or AWD capability. It is offered with an available three rows of seats. With a long list of standard safety features and adjustments made to the track and suspension, the Explorer is very different from the problem-riddled versions sold in the 1990s. The Explorer is a throwback to when all SUVs were capable off-road and had a rugged persona.

Cons: The Explorer is losing relevance in today's competitive market as car-based crossovers are replacing truck-based SUVs. For buyers who want a mid-size, comfortable unit, the Ford Edge is a much better choice. If you don't require a vehicle for off-road or towing duty, you can do much more with your money.

Honda Pilot

Rating	Worth consideration
Price	$37,000-$50,000
Engine	3.5L V6 with 250hp
Standard safety features include	Front, side and curtain airbags, ABS, stability and traction control
Average fuel consumption	FWD, 2180L/year AWD, 2260L/year
Warranty	5-year/100,000 km
Initial quality score	N/A
Dependability score	3/5

Pros: The Pilot has recently been restyled and is now bigger and boxier than the older model. A boxy vehicle means a large, usable interior, and the Pilot doesn't disappoint. This vehicle is a solid alternative to a larger full-size truck-based SUV like a Chevy Tahoe because it is large enough on the inside for three rows of seats but uses a slightly more efficient V6 engine compared to V8s found in those larger vehicles. The 3.5L V6 is a very lively engine, making the Pilot quick and able to pass with ease.

Cons: While the Pilot is a useful vehicle it has some drawbacks. The vehicle feels big when you drive it, especially the width. Hard plastic is used liberally in the interior, which scratches easily, plus the interior is more a study of industrial design than a warm, inviting place to spend some time. The V6 engine at times drinks fuel like a V8. AWD pumps the price to almost $40,000.

Hyundai Veracruz

Rating	Great vehicle, but will people buy it?
Price	$37,000-$47,000
Engine	3.8L V6 with 260hp
Standard safety features include	Front, side and curtain airbags, ABS, traction and stability control
Average fuel consumption	2257L/year
Warranty	5-year/100,000 km
Initial quality score	2.5/5
Dependability score	N/A

Pros: The Veracruz was introduced to take on luxury crossovers like the Lexus RX350 and do it for a price that nobody could touch. Did they succeed? Yes. The Veracruz is a solid and luxurious vehicle with a powerful V6 engine, standard three rows of seats with room for 7 and available AWD. The packaging is compelling; plus the Veracruz is a handsome-looking vehicle. This crossover is proof that you don't need to spend huge dollars to get it all.

Cons: The only problem with this vehicle is image. The people who want a premium luxury crossover also like the badge that comes with them. A premium Hyundai? Maybe the Hyundai Genesis will help to change that.

Jeep Grand Cherokee

Rating	Long overdue to be redone
Price	N/A at time of printing
Engines	3.6L V6 with 280hp 5.7L V8 with 360hp
Standard safety features include	Front, side and curtain airbags, ABS, stability and traction control
Average fuel consumption	N/A
Warranty	3-year/60,000 km
Initial quality score	N/A
Dependability score	3/5

Pros: Coming in 2010 as a 2011 model, the Grand Cherokee will be all new. Based on a Mercedes ML platform, it will be equipped with a brand-new V6 or HemiV8. This new product is welcome due to the dated exterior and interior styling of the old model plus the lack of space that vehicle provided. This new product should have better on-road manners, but it will still be a capable off-road machine. It is a Jeep, after all.

Cons: Not tested at the time of printing. There is no word if there will be a new diesel engine for the 2011 Grand Cherokee.

Kia Sorento

Rating	Not tested
Price	N/A at time of printing
Engines	2.4L 4-cylinder 3.8L V6
Standard safety features	N/A
Average fuel consumption	N/A
Warranty	5-year/100,000 km
Initial quality score	N/A
Dependability score	2/5

Pros: The Sorento is all-new for 2010, boasting better on-road driving dynamics thanks to the shared platform with the Hyundai Santa Fe and Veracruz. Power will likely come from a 2.4L 4-cylinder and the wonderful 3.8L engine found in other Kia/Hyundai products. The previous Sorento was based on a truck chassis; this new model will have much better road manners.

Cons: Unfortunately, we do not have all the information on the new 2010 model at the time of printing.

Mazda CX-9

Rating	Must try
Price	Sedan: $38,000-$46,000
Engine	3.7 L V6L with 273hp
Standard safety features include	Front, side and curtain airbags, ABS, traction, stability and rollover control
Average fuel consumption	FWD, 2293 L/year AWD, 2404 L/year
Warranty	3-year/80,000 km
Initial quality score	2.5/5
Dependability score	N/A

Pros: The Mazda CX-9 is a secret gem in the mid-size crossover market. The 3.7 L V6 is powerful and smooth, the interior is very well finished, and ride and handling are well above average. Plus it is a great-looking vehicle. Mazda uses the slogan "zoom zoom" to advertise its products and that corporate philosophy is actually carried out in the vehicles it produces, even in a big crossover like this. For buyers who want three rows of seats and all the amenities of a big vehicle, but also enjoy the experience of driving, the CX-9 is a joy to drive.

Cons: Mazda has not been as sharp as other brands when it comes to pricing on the CX-9. In comparison, the Toyota Highlander is equipped with a FWD 4-cylinder version to get buyers into their product for less money ($33,000). The CX-9 is only offered with the very capable 3.7L V6, and in order to get AWD, the price jumps to almost $40,000.

Mitsubishi Endeavor

Rating	Long overdue to be redone
Price	$36,000-$43,000
Engine	3.8L V6 with 255hp
Standard safety features include	Front, side and curtain airbags, ABS, traction and stability control
Average fuel consumption	2344L/year
Warranty	5-year/100,000 km
Initial quality score	N/A
Dependability score	N/A

Pros: This mid-size SUV is based on the Galant platform, providing a smooth and capable on-road performance. The 3.8L engine is a willing companion for most light-duty work. The interior has plenty of room for five adults and a strong list of standard features.

Cons: The Endeavor is in tough with some serious competition that offers more features and does it for less money. With only a 4-speed automatic, no third-row seating option and awkward styling, the Endeavor is a crossover that is falling between the cracks.

Nissan Murano

Rating	TOP PICK
Price	$38,000-$48,000
Engine	3.5L V6 with 265hp
Standard safety features include	Front, side and curtain airbags, ABS, traction and stability control
Average fuel consumption	2081L/year
Warranty	3-year/60,000 km
Initial quality score	3/5
Dependability score	3/5

Pros: 2009 saw the introduction of the second-generation Nissan Murano, ushering in new styling, more features and more power. The Murano looks like no other mid-size SUV; the bold headlight design, futuristic shape and solid stance make it a standout in a very generic category. The interior is very well designed with easy-to-use computer interface and first-rate materials. The back seat is very roomy as is the cargo area. What sets the Murano apart from many mid-size SUVs is the sedan-like ride and handling. The powerful and quiet engine along with sophisticated ride and better-than-average handling appeal to a wide range of buyers. The engine is powerful, yet very efficient. The Murano is the Top Pick due to above-average handling, good fuel consumption, interior appointments and wonderful ride.

Cons: As bold as the styling is, some might not warm to the look. The starting price is slightly higher than others in this class, which might scare some buyers away from this very practical vehicle. I don't believe the price is too high; this really is like getting a premium SUV without the name and associated price tag.

Nissan XTERRA

Rating	Worth consideration
Price	$33,000-$37,000
Engine	4.0L V6 with 261hp
Standard safety features include	Front, side and curtain airbags, ABS, traction and stability control
Average fuel consumption	2403L/year
Warranty	3-year/60,000 km
Initial quality score	3.5/5
Dependability score	3/5

Pros: The XTERRA is based on a pickup truck platform, making it a favourite with buyers who require off-road capability and good on-road manners. 4X4 capability comes as standard equipment, along with a 2-speed transfer case for best off-road performance. The 4.0L V6 engine provides lots of torque for towing or crawling along back-country trails. The XTERRA has a strong following in the 4X4 community as a capable off-road unit without having to break the bank.

Cons: With all the rugged capability of the XTERRA, it has to compromise the on-road ride to some extent. If you don't require your mid-size SUV to do the hard work the XTERRA is capable of, then your money would be better spent on a smoother mid-size crossover.

Nissan Pathfinder

Rating	Worth consideration
Price	$37,000-$47,000
Engine	4.0L V6 with 266hp
Standard safety features include	Front, side and curtain airbags, ABS, traction and stability control
Average fuel consumption	2546L/year
Warranty	3-year/60,000 km
Initial quality score	2/5
Dependability score	3/5

Pros: The Pathfinder is based on a pickup truck platform so it is capable of more strenuous driving than a crossover might be capable of, like off-road duty or towing. The interior has three rows of seats for seating up to seven. The Pathfinder is a throwback to the original SUV, with a go-any-where attitude and standard 4X4 capability, including a 2-speed transfer case. The V6 engine is powerful, but due to lack of sales the V8 version has been dropped. This SUV is perfect for a family that needs to tow a trailer or requires a rugged truck.

Cons: Even though the Pathfinder looks big, it has limited legroom in the second and third rows, making a more practical crossover a better people mover. If you don't require the off-road ruggedness of a 4X4 truck-based SUV and the towing capacity it delivers, plus the fuel it burns, then keep on looking.

Subaru Tribeca

Rating	Expensive for what you get
Price	$40,000-$48,000
Engine	3.6L 6-cylinder with 256hp
Standard safety features include	Front, side and curtain airbags, ABS, traction and stability control
Average fuel consumption	3.6L engine, 2298L/year
Warranty	3-year/60,000 km
Initial quality score	3/5
Dependability score	N/A

Pros: The Tribeca entered the SUV market a few years ago with very polarizing front styling; either you loved it or hated it. More must have hated it because after just two years Subaru changed the styling to a more mass-appeal "traditional" SUV design. The good looks on the outside are followed up on the inside with a unique "wave" dash design that is easy to use and pleasant to look at. The Tribeca has optional third-row seating. Handling and performance are good and the standard AWD makes the Tribeca a good all-weather vehicle.

Cons: The Tribeca is more expensive than many vehicles in this class and the higher trim levels compete with premium brands. The seats are hard and can be uncomfortable, plus the third row of seats is rather small. The Tribeca has good handling and power, but the overall package could be better and for the price it should be better.

Toyota Highlander

Rating	Must try
Price	$33,000-$55,000
Engines	2.7L 4-cylinder with 187hp 3.5L V6 with 270hp
Standard safety features include	Front, side, knee and curtain airbags, ABS, stability and traction control
Average fuel consumption	4WD, 2145L/year
Warranty	3-year/60,000 km
Initial quality score	4/5
Dependability score	5/5

Pros: The Highlander was redone two years ago, making it a larger three-row SUV, capable of moving a family in comfort. The ride is smooth and quiet, the seats are comfortable, and the spacious cabin is very well designed. The second row of seats even has the ability to change from two separate seats into a bench—very clever. The third row is comfortable for children or adults on shorter trips. Toyota introduced a new 2.7L 4-cylinder FWD base model for 2010 to attract buyers who want a Highlander but can't stretch for the more expensive AWD V6 versions. This new more affordable option is terrific and I suggest you try the 4-cylinder first. Highlander is a relaxed driving vehicle with light steering, making it easy to manoeuvre.

Cons: The Highlander interior is pleasant to look at but many of the interior pieces utilize hard plastic, cheapening the overall effect. The ride is smooth and relaxing but the vagueness of the steering might leave some drivers wanting more responsiveness. For buyers who require a five-seat vehicle, the new Venza, which is based on the same platform as the Highlander, might be a better choice.

Toyota FL Cruiser

Rating	Worth consideration
Price	$31,000-$38,000
Engine	4.0L V6 with 239hp
Standard safety features include	Front, side and curtain airbags, ABS, and stability control
Average fuel consumption	2365L/year
Warranty	3-year/60,000 km
Initial quality score	3.5/5
Dependability score	N/A

Pros: The FJ Cruiser is a modern take on the iconic FJ40, which was introduced over 50 years ago. Styling is retro, yet thoroughly modern, featuring a white roof, flush windows and protruding bumpers. The FJ was purpose built to be a true off-road machine capable of taking on the toughest terrain and has proven to be very popular with buyers who tackle the outdoors. Even though it is at home off-road, its on-road manners are fantastic, offering a smooth and relatively quiet ride. The interior also has a funky, retro design that is easy to use. This is a perfect vehicle for anyone who wants to make a statement about what they drive.

Cons: Trying to make an old design into a modern vehicle has its drawbacks. Outward visibility is awful, especially with the rear window. Some off-road drivers have relayed horror stories of trying to back out of situations where they couldn't see! This poor visibility also makes it hard to park. The big 6-cylinder engine does a good job with power and especially low-end torque, but it has a large thirst for fuel. The buyer who will never utilize the true off-road prowess of the FJ will be spending a good chunk of money for the cool image it portrays.

Toyota 4Runner

Rating	Worth consideration
Price	$37,000-$49,000
Engine	4.0L V6 with 236hp
Standard safety features include	Front, side and curtain airbags, ABS, stability and traction control
Average fuel consumption	2365L/year
Warranty	3-year/60,000 km
Initial quality score	4/5
Dependability score	3.5/5

Pros: Can you remember back to the beginning of the SUV phenomenon? Trucks like the 4Runner, Nissan Pathfinder, Jeep Cherokee and Ford Explorer dominated the landscape. As time has passed the market has shifted away from these pickup-truck-based SUVs to more sophisticated crossover vehicles. Toyota has kept the 4Runner alive and plans to relaunch it with an all-new design soon. This is a truck for buyers who need a capable off-road SUV to move a family or tow a trailer.

Cons: The 4Runner is only worth consideration if you require a capable off-road, truck-based SUV. For the majority of buyers a more practical crossover like the Highlander will offer more interior room, good traction, better fuel consumption and a smoother ride. SUVs like the 4Runner are held over from the beginnings of the SUV craze, but are now a dying breed.

VW Touareg

Rating	Great diesel, pass on the gas
Price	$45,000-$54,000
Engines	3.6L V6 with 280hp 3.0L turbo diesel V6 with 225hp
Standard safety features include	Front, side and curtain airbags, ABS, traction and stability control
Average fuel consumption	3.6L V6, 2560L/year 3.0L diesel, 2040L/year
Warranty	4-year/80,000 km
Initial quality score	2/5
Dependability score	2/5

Pros: The Touareg shares the same platform as the more expensive Porsche Cayenne and the same 3.6L V6 engine as the base Cayenne. What makes the Touareg an interesting choice is the inclusion of a turbo clean-diesel engine that offers superior mileage and ample torque. The interior of the Touareg is stylish and provides plenty of room for five passengers. The Touareg is a very capable vehicle for off-road duties and towing, especially with the diesel.

Cons: The Touraeg suffers from below-average quality scores, and even though it shares many components with the Porsche Cayenne, the two vehicles are very different. Handling isn't the same and Porsche has a much stronger record with quality. Interior noise is a problem, especially at highway speeds.

PREMIUM MID-SIZE SUV/CROSSOVER

Acura MDX

Rating	TOP PICK
Price	$55,000-$64,000
Engine	3.7L V6 with 300hp
Standard safety features include	Front, side and curtain airbags, ABS, stability and traction control
Average fuel consumption	2418L/year
Warranty	5-year/100,000 km
Initial quality score	3/5
Dependability score	5/5

Pros: The MDX is the Top Pick in the luxury mid-size SUV class due to the value this vehicle offers. The wonderful and powerful engine, superior AWD system, three rows of seats, large interior and immaculate finish make it the best value in this class. The new exterior styling makes the MDX a more striking vehicle than the one it replaces. The high score for vehicle dependability also makes purchasing an MDX a good choice.

Cons: Even though the MDX offers three rows of seats as standard equipment, for those who don't require all the additional seating, this might be too much vehicle.

BMW X5

Rating	Must try
Price	$58,000-$71,000
Engines	3.0L 6-cylinder with 260hp 3.0L turbo diesel 6-cylinder with 265hp 4.8L V8 with 350hp
Standard safety features include	Front, side and curtain airbags, ABS, traction and stability control
Average fuel consumption	3.0L engine, 2333L/year 3.0L diesel, 1852L/year 4.8L engine, 2634L/year
Warranty	4-year/80,000 km
Initial quality score	3/5
Dependability score	3/5

Pros: The X5 was one of the very first vehicles in the premium mid-size SUV category and it is still a leader, offering buyers a sturdy, well-put-together vehicle with good handling. The AWD system is very capable for winter conditions and it also provides better driving dynamics. The interior is roomy and well finished, plus the seats are very supportive. The addition of the powerful and thrifty diesel engine now makes the X5 an alternative to buying a hybrid. The diesel is also faster than the regular 3.0L engine.

Cons: The optional third row of seats is one of the worst in the business, making the passengers feel like prisoners in the back. I would only consider the regular five-seat configuration. The interior is well finished but it lacks pizzazz. Base models are a bit misleading because a buyer will have to spend much more to get a well-equipped X5.

BMW X6

Rating	Must try
Price	$64,000-$78,000
Engine	3.0L turbo 6-cylinder with 300hp 3.0L turbo diesel 6-cylinder with 400hp 4.8L turbo V8 with 350hp
Standard safety features include	Front, side and curtain airbags, ABS, traction and stability control
Average fuel consumption	3.0L engine, 2484L/year 4.4L engine, 2871L/year
Warranty	4-year/80,000 km
Initial quality score	N/A
Dependability score	N/A

Pros: I consider the X6 a "sport" version of the BMW X5 due to the more aggressive styling, sloped roof and larger wheels. The X6 is a wonderful vehicle to drive due to sublime handling and wonderful turbo-charged engines. Even though this is a big vehicle, it drives like a much smaller crossover. Other manufacturers wish they could produce a vehicle that is as much fun to drive. The unique styling makes a statement, like few on the road can.

Cons: Due to the cropped roof and high hatchback design, the X6 has some drawbacks. The back seat only holds two passengers and the side windows are small. The cargo area is limited in height, plus the floor is high off the ground. The back window is small, making parking tricky; luckily back-up sensors are standard. The 3.0L engine turbo is so responsive and powerful, it makes the 4.4L V8 massive overkill in comparison.

Cadillac SRX

Rating	Must try
Price	N/A at time of printing
Engines	2.8L turbo V6 with 300hp 3.0L V6 with 265hp
Standard safety features include	Front, side and curtain airbags, ABS, stability and traction control
Average fuel consumption	2919L/year
Warranty	4-year/80,000 km
Initial quality score	4/5
Dependability score	4/5

(Not tested at the time of printing.) The SRX is all-new for 2010, featuring a bold new design running on a brand-new platform. With a new turbo-charged engine and standard 3.0L V6, the SRX should be quite spirited to drive. Aimed at other premium mid-size SUVs like the Lexus RX350, this new Cadillac looks like nothing we have seen from GM before.

Infiniti FX

Rating	Must try
Price	$52,000-$60,000
Engines	3.5L V6 with 303hp 5.0L V8 with 390hp
Standard safety features include	Front, side and curtain airbags, ABS, stability and traction control
Average fuel consumption	3.5L engine, 2184L/year 5.0L engine, 2515L/year
Warranty	4-year/100,000 km
Initial quality score	3.5/5
Dependability score	N/A

Pros: If you are in the market for a mid-size luxury SUV but still crave the handling of a sports sedan, then the Infiniti FX is a wonderful choice. There is the heart of a sports car inside this stylish SUV ready to pounce at any moment. The above-average handling, powerful engines and AWD system make the FX a treat to drive. The interior is finished with the highest level of materials and can be equipped with an astounding level of electronic gadgets. The large wheels and pronounced front styling make a bold statement. A great choice if you can't stomach the price of a German premium SUV.

Cons: The drawback to the FX is the lack of cargo carrying capacity inside the stylish rear hatch. The rear seats also have a slightly claustrophobic feel due to the sloping roofline.

Land Rover LR3

Rating	Reliability?
Price	$54,000
Engines	4.0L V6 with 216hp
	4.4L V8 with 300hp
Standard safety features include	Front, side and head airbags, ABS, traction and stability control
Average fuel consumption	4.0L V6, 2920L/year
	4.4L V8, 2960L/year
Warranty	4-year/80,000 km
Initial quality score	N/A
Dependability score	2/5

Pros: The LR3 is a large truck-based SUV capable of serious off-road duties, but is used mostly by families that want a premium vehicle. The three rows of seats offer a lot of space for all passengers. The interior is functional and easy to clean down. Buyers of Land Rover products are some of the most vocal champions of the brand; they have a very strong following.

Cons: Land Rover has suffered with very disappointing quality scores for years; in fact, in most years their products place dead last. The interior may be functional but it could also be seen to be rather plastic and basic.

Range Rover/Range Rover Sport

Rating	Reliability?
Price	Range Rover: $93,000-$110,000 Range Rover Sport: 71,000-$85,000
Engines	4.4L V8 with 300hp 4.2L supercharged V8 with 390hp 4.4L V8 with 305hp 4.2L supercharged V8 with 400hp
Standard safety features include	Front, side and head airbags, ABS, traction and stability control
Average fuel consumption	4.4L V8, 2900L/year 4.2L supercharged, 2960L/year
Warranty	4-year/80,000 km
Initial quality score	3/5
Dependability score	N/A

Pros: The Range Rover and Sport models have beautifully finished interiors, making them a favourite with well-heeled buyers. Their rugged, go-anywhere design has made them champions off-road, but they still provide a smooth and refined on-road feel. The buyers who own these vehicles absolutely love them for their ultra-luxury interiors and solid and safe-feeling driving dynamics.

Cons: As noted above, Land Rover has suffered with very disappointing quality scores for years. The image of a gas-guzzling luxury SUV is turning some buyers away from this status symbol.

Lexus GX

Rating	Poor handling, outdated design
Price	$61,000
Engine	4.7L V8 with 263hp
Standard safety features include	Front, side, knee and curtain airbags, ABS, stability and traction control
Average fuel consumption	2709L/year
Warranty	4-year/80,000 km
Initial quality score	5/5
Dependability score	5/5

Pros: The GX is a true truck-based SUV capable of off-road duty or for towing requirements. It is tuned to provide the Lexus experience that buyers expect, with seating for up to six passengers.

Cons: The market is moving away from truck-based SUVs to crossover vehicles that provide a smooth ride and plenty of room. The truck platform for the GX doesn't make it a very good-handling vehicle; in fact, the body roll when cornering can be unnerving. The third row of seats folds up to the side of the windows and doesn't fold into the floor, reducing cargo space. The back gate swings out and not up, making the vehicle hard to load when parallel parked. The GX is long overdue for an overhaul.

Lexus LX

Rating	Better choice for the money
Price	$83,000
Engine,	5.7L V8 with 383hp
Standard safety features include	Front, side, knee and curtain airbags, ABS, stability and traction control
Average fuel consumption	2907L/year
Warranty	4-year/80,000 km
Initial quality score	5/5
Dependability score	N/A

Pros: The LX is the Lexus version of the Toyota Land Cruiser that is sold in many other parts of the world. A host of luxury refinements, like air suspension, and a powerful engine make for a solid performer on- and off-road. This is a premium vehicle and people who buy an LX know that they are part of a small, privileged group. The LX is a good alternative to a Range Rover.

Cons: The LX is designed for a world market, so some features that would make it appealing to a Canadian market like xenon headlights and a power rear tailgate are omitted. The headroom in the back seat is limited as is the legroom in the third row of seats. The Toyota Sequoia is a better all-around package because it offers more room, a 6-speed automatic instead of a 5-speed, and is a lot cheaper.

Lincoln MKX

Rating	Ford Edge in Lincoln clothing
Price	$41,000
Engine	3.5L V6 with 265hp
Standard safety features include	Front and side-curtain airbags, ABS, stability and traction control
Average fuel consumption	2315L/year
Warranty	4-year/80,000 km
Initial quality score	3.5/5
Dependability score	N/A

Pros: Built on the same platform as the Ford Edge, the MKX offers more standard features and standard AWD. The interior is open and spacious for up to five passengers. The smooth ride and capable V6 engine makes the MKX a more luxurious option to the Edge.

Cons: Yes, the MKX has a few more features over the Edge, but not much work went into differentiating the two vehicles. They look similar except for the chrome grille and the interior is only slight better than the dowdy Edge. The drive train is exactly the same, so why bother to spend the extra money? Consider a fully loaded Edge as a better buy.

Mercedes M-Class

Rating	Must try
Price	$59,000-$97,000
Engines	3.0L turbo diesel V6 with 210hp
	3.5L V6 with 268hp
	5.5L V8 with 382hp
	6.2L V8 with 503hp
Standard safety features include	Front and side-curtain airbags, ABS, traction and stability control
Average fuel consumption	3.0L diesel, 2040L/year
	3.5L V6, 2520L/year
	5.5L V8, 760L/year
	6.2L V8, 3500L/year
Warranty	4-year/80,000 km
Initial quality score	3/5
Dependability score	2/5

Pros: The M-Class was one of the very first premium mid-size SUVs, and over the years Mercedes has made some superb improvements. The ride is very smooth and quiet and the 7-speed automatic makes it feel like the vehicle is floating down the road. Interior space is good for all passengers and the rear cargo area is well designed. The M-Class isn't trying to be something it isn't—a three-row SUV. The addition of the clean diesel engine makes the M-Class a serious alternative to a hybrid SUV, plus it has a load of torque. Diesel engines provide great power, great fuel consumption and they are very durable.

Cons: The only knock on the M-Class is it might be too refined and smooth for drivers who want a little more road feel.

Porsche Cayenne

Rating	Must try
Price	$55,000-$150,000
Engines	3.6L 6-cylinder with 290hp
	4.8L V8 with 385hp
	4.8L V8 with 405hp
	4.8L turbo V8 with 500hp
	4.8L turbo V8 with 550hp
Standard safety features include	Front and side-curtain airbags, ABS, traction and stability control
Average fuel consumption	3.6L engine, 2580L/year
	4.8L V8, 3180L/year
	4.8L turbo, 2940L/year
Warranty	4-year/80,000 km
Initial quality score	3.5/5
Dependability score	N/A

Pros: The Cayenne turned the Porsche world on its head when it was introduced, because many Porsche enthusiasts thought Porsche had no business building an SUV. Now that it has been out for several years, it makes up the bulk of Porsche sales. It is the SUV of choice for buyers who desire handling and power. (The BMW X6 is a close second.) The Cayenne is surprising because it is capable of doing things that most sedans cannot, including being able to go to the racetrack. No kidding! The interior is finished with high-quality materials and offers plenty of room for five people. The Cayenne is powerful, smooth, refined and has superb handling.

Cons: Everything on a Porsche is extra so the base price is misleading; you need to pay a lot more to get a well-equipped vehicle. Earlier versions had troublesome quality issues but the latest models are very reliable.

Volvo XC90

Rating	Must try
Price	$48,000-$71,000
Engines	3.2L 6-cylinder 235hp
	4.4L V8 with 311hp
Standard safety features include	Front, side and head airbags, ABS, traction and stability control
Average fuel consumption	3.2L engine, 2500L/year
	4.4L V8, 2740L/year
Warranty	4-year/80,000 km
Initial quality score	3.5/5
Dependability score	2/5

Pros: In the premium mid-size SUV class, the XC90 stands alone with a long list of features and innovative options. The interior is very comfortable; in fact, the front seats are almost like recliners. The optional third row of seats actually offers usable space for kids; the seats fold flat into the floor with ease. The second row of seats has a unique integrated child safety seat. Driving dynamics are average, but the optional V8 makes the XC90 a bit livelier.

Cons: The XC90 is overdue to be redone. The resale value of the XC90 isn't as strong as some other vehicles in this class.

Full-Size Category

FULL-SIZE CARS

Buick Lucerne

Rating	Worth consideration
Price	$43,000-$50,000
Engines	3.9L V6 with 227hp 4.6L V8 with 292hp
Standard safety features include	Front, side and curtain airbags, ABS and traction control. Stability control is optional.
Average fuel consumption	3.6L V6, 1986L/year 4.6L V8, 2301L/year
Warranty	4-year/80,000 km
Initial quality score	4/5
Dependability score	5/5

Pros: The Lucerne is a full-size front-wheel-drive sedan with seating for five or six. It comes with a large V6 or optional V8 engine. Buick models are known for their comfortable, smooth and quiet ride, and the Lucerne does not disappoint. This is an alternative to buying a Cadillac or Lincoln MKS. The interior is very relaxing and inviting, a car you could drive for hours. The dependability score is perfect, giving buyers peace of mind.

Cons: The Lucerne is due for some revisions and the addition of a 6-speed automatic will help with fuel economy and drivability.

Chrysler 300

Rating	Worth consideration
Price	$23,000-$42,000
Engines	3.5L V6 250hp
	5.7L V8 with 340hp
	6.1L V8 with 425hp
Standard safety features include	Front airbags, ABS, stability and traction control. Optional: side and curtain airbags.
Average fuel consumption	3.5L V6, 2071L/year
	3.5L AWD, 2160L/year
	5.7L V8, 2205L/year
	5.7L AWD, 2257L/year
	6.1L V8, 2714L/year
Warranty	3-year/60,000 km
Initial quality score	3.5/5
Dependability score	4/5

Pros: The Chrysler 300 is a unique car because it is built on a Mercedes-Benz platform and has Mercedes technology integrated throughout the car. It is a very nice car to drive. Powered by a very capable V6 or optional high-horsepower V8 engine, there is a 300 for all pocketbooks. Styling was revolutionary when the car was introduced and continues to turn heads. Due to the rear-wheel-drive or all-wheel-drive configuration, the 300 has good balance, making it a wonderful highway car that can handle corners well.

Cons: Chrysler has not updated the 300 and it is getting long in the tooth. The interior is filled with hard plastic and the design is basic. Look for a new 300 to be introduced soon.

Dodge Charger

Rating	Worth consideration
Price	$22,000-$35,000
Engines	2.7L V6 190hp
	3.5L V6 210hp
	5.7L V8 with 368hp
	6.1L V8 with 425hp
Standard safety features include	Front and curtain airbags, available ABS, stability and traction control
Average fuel consumption	2.7L V6, 1936L/year
	3.5L V6, 2071L/year
	5.7L V8, 2205L/year
	6.1L V8, 2714L/year
Warranty	3-year/60,000 km
Initial quality score	2.5/5
Dependability score	N/A

Pros: The Dodge Charger is based on the same platform as the Chrysler 300 sedan. The Dodge is slightly less expensive and can be ordered with different engine sizes and outputs. Read the Chrysler 300 comments.

Cons: The Charger is due to be replaced soon with a new 2010 or 2011 model.

Ford Taurus

Rating	Worth consideration
Price	$25,000-$37,000
Engines	3.5L V6 with 263hp
	3.5L turbo V6 with 365hp
Standard safety features include	Front, side and curtain airbags, ABS, stability and traction control
Average fuel consumption	N/A
Warranty	3-year/60,000 km
Initial quality score	3.5/5
Dependability score	4/5

Pros: Ford has made a major push with the introduction of the all-new 2010 Taurus. Formerly called the Ford Five Hundred, this new Taurus looks much more attractive with bold exterior styling and a totally new interior that competes with cars costing much more. Powered by a 3.5L V6 or turbo-charged version, the Taurus has more than enough power. The Taurus is based on the same platform as the Volvo S80, Ford Edge and Flex, providing a very capable and sophisticated ride.

Cons: Let's hope that Ford can stick with one name for this new and stylish car instead of changing it every few years. Unfortunately, the Taurus name carries a lot of bad baggage, which will probably affect resale values.

Nissan Maxima

Rating	Worth consideration
Price	$38,000
Engine	3.5L V6 with 290hp
Standard safety features include	Front, side and curtain airbags, ABS, traction and stability control
Average fuel consumption	1881L/year
Warranty	3-year/60,000 km
Initial quality score	4/5
Dependability score	2/5

Pros: The Maxima was totally redone for 2009 with advancements to exterior and interior styling and an increase in power. The previous model resembled the less expensive Altima sedan, cheapening the top-of-the line Maxima. The new distinctive styling is strong, the interior is very well thought out, and the potent V6 offers more power than most drivers will require. The Maxima uses a continuously variable transmission, so the Maxima has impressive fuel ratings for a full-size car.

Cons: With a starting price of almost $40,000, the Maxima is competing with premium brands, yet it doesn't have the same badge appeal of a premium car. The unique transmission helps provide great fuel consumption, but at low RPMs it can "bog down" the powerful V6 engine, causing vibration. The 290hp engine delivers power to the front wheels, so when pushed hard the Maxima tends to grab ruts in the road, causing what is called torque steer. The Maxima is a great cruising car and a joy to drive, but it falls into a bit of a no-man's-land of large non-premium sedans.

Toyota Avalon

Rating	TOP PICK
Price	$29,000-$46,000
Engine	3.5L V6 with 268hp
Standard safety features include	Front, side, knee and curtain airbags, ABS, stability and traction control
Average fuel consumption	1807L/year
Initial quality score	3.5/5
Dependability score	4/5

Pros: The Avalon is built on an elongated Toyota Camry platform, making it a more upscale version of that car. For buyers who are considering the Lexus ES, the Avalon has similar features at a more affordable price. The ride is smooth, the engine is powerful and handling—surprisingly—is sure-footed. The Avalon is a real "sleeper" in the Toyota lineup.

Cons: The reason the Avalon is a real sleeper is due mainly to the stodgy styling and lack of panache on the interior. Sure it drives well and has a powerful engine, but it looks dull. The interior has a wide and spacious dashboard, but it looks futuristic and not in keeping with the conservative image of the rest of the car. Warmer accents with wood might help.

PREMIUM FULL-SIZE CARS

Acura RL

Rating	The cheaper TL is a better car
Price	$66,000-$71,000
Engine	3.7L V6 with 300hp
Standard safety features include	Front, side and curtain airbags, ABS, stability and traction control
Average fuel consumption	2251L/year
Warranty	5-year/100,000 km
Initial quality score	5/5
Dependability score	5/5

Pros: The RL is based on an elongated TL platform, which is based on the Honda Accord. The interior is beautifully finished with a high level of refinement and materials. The standard AWD system provides great traction but also helps make the RL a responsive-handling car. The amazing quality score for initial quality and dependability speaks to how well this car is made. The RL isn't popular, but it is a fabulous used-car bargain.

Cons: The Acura RL is expensive for what is essentially a larger Acura TL. It has the same engine, AWD system and is built on the same platform, but it isn't as much fun to drive as the TL. The lack of a larger V8 engine makes it an also-ran in the premium sedan class.

Audi A8

Rating	Must try
Price	$95,000-$166,000
Engines	4.2L V8 with 350hp 5.2L V10 with 450hp 6.0L W12 with 450hp
Standard safety features include	Front, side, knee and curtain airbags, ABS, traction and stability control
Average fuel consumption	4.2L V8, 2240L/year 5.2L V10, 2800L/year 6.0L W12, 2740L/year
Warranty	4-year/80,000 km
Initial quality score	N/A
Dependability score	N/A

Pros: The A8 is often overlooked in this class of car and I believe it is one of the best due to the smooth ride, powerful engines and luxurious, yet easy-to-use interiors. The classy styling will ensure that the A8 will look current for years to come. The long wheelbase version provides limousine-like comfort.

Cons: At this price, the decision often comes down to style, so even if this is a good car a buyer might only want a Mercedes for the "badge appeal." The W12 and V10 engines are overkill; the V8 is more than enough power for most buyers

BMW 7 Series

Rating	Must try
Price	$105,000-$113,000
Engine	4.4L turbo V8 with 400hp
Standard safety features include	Front, side, knee and curtain airbags, ABS, traction and stability control
Average fuel consumption	2403L/year
Warranty	4-year/80,000 km
Initial quality score	3/5
Dependability score	3/5

Pros: BMW introduced an all-new 7 Series in 2009 to much warmer welcome than the car received in 2002 when the last model was unveiled. The previous overly styled exterior has returned to a much more traditional, conservative design that is appealing to 7 Series buyers. The introduction of a turbo V8 produces lightning-quick acceleration for such a big car. Sold as a standard sedan or long-wheelbase version, the interior is a joy to ride in for all passengers.

Cons: EXPENSIVE!! The iDrive computer interface system has been improved but it isn't as intuitive as other cars in this class. The Lexus LS460 might not have the dynamic performance of the 7 Series, but it is much cheaper.

Cadillac DTS

Rating	Worth consideration
Price	$55,000-$68,000
Engines	4.6L V8 with 275hp
	4.6L V8 with 292hp
Standard safety features include	Front, side and curtain airbags, ABS and traction control. Stability control is optional.
Average fuel consumption	2301L/year
Warranty	4-year/80,000 km
Initial quality score	3/5
Dependability score	3/5

Pros: The DTS is a full-size five- or six-passenger sedan that appeals to the traditional Cadillac buyer who might not like the edgy styling of their other cars. If you are interested in an ultra-smooth and soft ride with massive plush seats, then this is your car. The "living room" on wheels analogy is perfect here. The DTS is a joy to drive on a long trip, putting the miles behind you with ease.

Cons: The DTS is due for a makeover, not just in terms of styling but mechanically. Stability control is not offered on lower-trim models and the lack of a 6-speed automatic (a 4-speed is standard) puts the Lucerne out of step with others at this price.

Lexus LS

Rating	TOP PICK
Price	$77,000-94,000
Engine	4.6L V8 with 357hp
Standard safety features include	Front, side, knee and curtain airbags, ABS, stability and traction control
Average fuel consumption	4.6L V8, 2157L/year 4.6L AWD, 2268L/year
Warranty	4-year/80,000 km
Initial quality score	5/5
Dependability score	5/5

Pros: The LS is the Top Pick in the full-size luxury sedan category for several reasons. First, it is a joy to drive, with a smooth and sophisticated ride that provides a good balance of performance and luxury. Second, the price tag is thousands less than a comparable German luxury sedan. Third, the quality scores for the LS have been at the top of the pack for years, and those who have owned a premium sedan know the technology incorporated into these vehicles can be very expensive to fix. Fourth, there are several different configurations of LS to choose from, including the ultra-luxurious LS hybrid.

Cons: Buyers who want a performance luxury sedan will be better served with a BMW 7 Series.

Lincoln MKS

Rating	Worth consideration
Price	$44,000-$46,000
Engines	3.7L V6 with 273hp
	3.5L turbo V6 355hp
Standard safety features include	Front, side and curtain airbags, ABS, stability and traction control
Average fuel consumption	3.7L V6, 2131L/year
	3.7L AWD, 2211L/year
Warranty	4-year/80,000 km
Initial quality score	N/A
Dependability score	N/A

Pros: The Lincoln MKS was introduced to replace the Lincoln Continental sedan and to also help resurrect the brand to its former glory. Based on the Ford Taurus platform, the MKS is offered with front-wheel drive or all-wheel drive and has a solid 3.7L engine. New for 2010 is the EcoBoost turbo V6, with substantial power. Lincoln as a brand continues to have very strong quality scores, consistently near the top of all cars. The MKS is a pleasant car to drive with lots of room for all passengers and a ride that eats up bumps roads with ease.

Cons: The MKS is a nice car but it isn't going to win over buyers from other established luxury brands. The interior is rather plain and the buttons small on the centre console. The smooth ride won't win over any German car fans but will appeal to the older tradition luxury buyer. Existing Lincoln owners, or those who own a Buick or a Lexus, might consider this car.

Mercedes S-Class

Rating	Must try
Price	$108,000-$234,000
Engines	4.6L V8 with 335hp
	5.5L V8 with 382hp
	5.5L V12 with 510hp
	6.2L V8 with 518hp
	6.0L turbo V12 with 603hp
Standard safety features include	Front, side and curtain airbags, ABS, traction and stability control
Average fuel consumption	4.6L V8, 2380L/year
	5.5L V8, 2480L/year
	5.5L V12, 3120L/year
	6.2L V8, 3080L/year
	6.0L turbo, 3220L/year
Warranty	4-year/80,000 km
Initial quality score	5/5
Dependability score	2/5

Pros: Other than the Mercedes-built Maybach, the S-Class could well be the most prestigious luxury sedan on the road. With luxury amenities that coddle the passengers and provide comfort for the driver, the S-Class is a joy to drive or be driven in. The top models are frighteningly quick but are very expensive.

Cons: The more modest base models are very nice, but a vehicle like the Lexus LS has similar refinement for a lot less money. High-end sedans like the S-Class are wonderful when new and under warranty, but can become technical headaches as they age and become very expensive to repair.

Porsche Panamera

Rating	Must try
Price	$115,000-$155,000
Engines	4.8L V8 with 400hp
	4.8L turbo V8 with 500hp
Standard safety features include	Front, side and curtain airbags, ABS, traction and stability control
Average fuel consumption	N/A
Warranty	4-year/80,000 km
Initial quality score	N/A
Dependability score	N/A

Pros: The Panamera is being greeted with the same disdain that the Cayenne SUV did when it was introduced, but the Cayenne went on to be the most successful of Porsche products. The Panamera is built in the same factory as the Cayenne and shares many components with that vehicle. It has not been tested yet, but I can't wait.

Cons: Unfortunately the Panamera has not been tested, but you don't need to drive it to know that it is ugly. The forced Porsche styling makes it look like a frog from the back. It might grow on me, but I'm not sure.

Volvo S80

Rating	Worth consideration
Price	$50,000-$65,000
Engines	3.2L 6-cylinder 235hp
	3.0L turbo 6-cylinder 281hp
	4.4L V8 with 311hp
Standard safety features include	Front, side and head airbags, ABS, traction and stability control
Average fuel consumption	3.2L engine, 2100L/year
	3.0L turbo, 2280L/year
	4.4L V8, 2340L/year
Warranty	4-year/80,000 km
Initial quality score	3.5/5
Dependability score	4/5

Pros: What many people don't realize is that the S80 platform is used by Ford for the Edge, Flex, Taurus and Lincoln MKX and MKT. Land Rover also uses it for the LR2. This is a very solid platform capable of providing a smooth and sophisticated ride along with solid safety scores. The interior of the S80 rivals any vehicle in this class; in fact Volvo seats might just be the most comfortable on the market. The V8 makes the S80 a quick car.

Cons: The S80 has been flying under the radar, which could be attributed to the stodgy Volvo image. The suspension has been tuned for optimal comfort but in some instances makes the car a bit sloppy in the corners.

FULL-SIZE SUV/CROSSOVER

Chevy Suburban

Rating	Worth consideration
Price	$50,000-$70,000
Engines	5.3L V8 with 315hp
	6.0L V8 with 352hp
Standard safety features include	Front and curtain airbags, ABS, traction and stability control
Average fuel consumption	5.3L V8, 2532L/year
	6.0L V8, 2625L/year
Warranty	3-year/60,000 km
Initial quality score	3/5
Dependability score	3/5

Pros: This full-size SUV is based on the Silverado pickup truck chassis, so it offers a rugged option for large families that need to tow a trailer. The powerful engines and 6-speed automatic gives the best balance of power and efficiency. A well-equipped Suburban is an alternative to paying for an expansive Cadillac Escalade. The ride is surprisingly good for a truck and the quiet interior makes driving very relaxing.

Cons: The full-size SUV is going out of favour with many buyers due to high gas prices and environmental concerns. The third row of seats is surprisingly small for such a huge truck. For buyers who require plenty of room but don't need to tow, then a full-size crossover is a better option. Check out the Chevy Traverse as an alternative.

Chevy Tahoe

Rating	Worth consideration
Price	$47,000-$70,000
Engine	5.3L V8 with 320hp
Standard safety features include	Front and curtain airbags, ABS, traction and stability control
Average fuel consumption	5.3L V8, 2532L/year 5.3L 4X4, 2562L/year
Warranty	3-year/60,000 km
Initial quality score	4/5
Dependability score	3/5

Pros: The Chevy Tahoe is a slightly shorter version of the Chevy Suburban full-size SUV. Offered with one engine instead of two, the Tahoe is a very comfortable, smooth and quiet truck.

Cons: See Suburban comments.

Chevy Traverse

Rating	Must try
Price	$35,000-$50,000
Engine	3.6L V6 with 281hp
Standard safety features include	Front, side and curtain airbags, ABS, traction and stability control
Average fuel consumption	3.6L engine, 2153L/year 3.6L AWD, 2233L/year
Warranty	3-year/60,000 km
Initial quality score	N/A
Dependability score	N/A

Pros: With drivers looking for an alternative to a minivan or full-size truck-based SUV, then a full-size crossover like the Traverse is a wonderful option. The interior is roomy and comfortable for all three rows of seats. The Traverse is remarkably easy to drive and to manoeuvre for such a big vehicle. The cost to buy a crossover is less than a big truck but more expensive than a minivan, but you have to pay to look good! Also look at the comments for the GMC Acadia and Buick Enclave.

Cons: The interior is a bit basic compared to the Ford Flex, and since this vehicle is also sold as a GMC Acadia and Buick Enclave, it has less individual identity.

Ford Flex

Rating	TOP PICK
Price	$34,000-$41,000
Engine	3.5L V6 with 265hp
Standard safety features include	Front, side and curtain airbags, ABS, traction and stability control
Average fuel consumption	3.5L engine, 2164L/year 3.5L AWD, 2313L/year
Warranty	3-year/60,000 km
Initial quality score	2/5
Dependability score	N/A

Pros: The Flex is based on the Volvo S80 platform that is also used for the Taurus and Edge. Even though the Flex looks nothing like the Ford Edge, it is essentially a longer version of that vehicle, capable of seating six or seven passengers with three rows of seats. This is the Top Pick in the full-size crossover segment due to the interior space for all passengers, high level of finish, and the smooth and sophisticated ride. The Flex offers an option to buyers who might be considering a minivan or full-size truck-based SUV. This large crossover can haul around a family in style and do it more efficiently than a truck.

Cons: The only problem with the Flex is the polarizing styling that leaves some potential buyers cold. I love the looks, very different.

Ford Expedition

Rating	Must try
Price	$38,000-$54,000
Engine	5.4L V8 with 300hp
Standard safety features include	Front, side and curtain airbags, ABS, traction and stability control
Average fuel consumption	N/A
Warranty	3-year/60,000 km
Initial quality score	2.5/5
Dependability score	3/5

Pros: Based on the solid F-150 pickup truck chassis, the Expedition is an excellent choice for a large family who might need the ruggedness of this big vehicle for towing. The interior is comfortable and luxurious on higher trim models. What is surprising is just how smooth and relaxed the ride is considering the truck platform. The 6-speed automatic gets the most out of the big and powerful V8. Styling has been tweaked to make the Expedition look smaller than it is.

Cons: The Expedition is about as good as it gets in the full-size SUV class and would have been Top Pick, except General Motors now offers hybrid versions of their big trucks.

GMC Acadia

Rating	Must try
Price	$37,000-$48,000
Engine	3.6L V6 with 288hp
Standard safety features include	Front, side and curtain airbags, ABS, traction and stability control
Average fuel consumption	3.6L engine, 2153L/year 3.6L AWD, 2233L/year
Warranty	3-year/60,000 km
Initial quality score	N/A
Dependability score	N/A

Pros: With drivers looking for an alternative to a minivan or full-size truck-based SUV, then a full-size crossover like the Acadia is a wonderful option. Also see comments for Chevy Traverse and Buick Enclave.

Cons: Check comments for Chevy Traverse and Buick Enclave.

GMC Yukon

Rating	Worth consideration
Price	$50,000-$70,000
Engines	5.3L V8 with 320hp
	6.0L V8 with 352hp
	6.2L V8 with 403hp
Standard safety features include	Front and curtain airbags, ABS, traction and stability control
Average fuel consumption	6.0L V8, 2625L/year
	6.0L 4X4, 2037L/year
Warranty	3-year/60,000 km
Initial quality score	3/5
Dependability score	3/5

The Yukon is the GMC version of the Suburban and Chevy Tahoe. Please check the comments for both of those vehicles.

Kia Borrago

Rating	Nice first effort
Price	$37,000-$44,000
Engines	3.8L V6 with 276hp
	4.6L V8 with 337hp
Standard safety features include	Front, side and curtain airbags and ABS. Optional: traction and stability control, knee airbag.
Average fuel consumption	3.8L V6, 2276L/year
	4.6L V8, 2457L/year
Warranty	5-year/100,000 km
Initial quality score	3/5
Dependability score	N/A

Pros: The Borrego made its entrance into the mid-to-full-size SUV market last year, just as gas prices spiked. With fewer people opting for a truck-based SUV, the Borrego has to cut through the pack. This is an alternative to buying a Nissan Pathfinder or similar vehicle. The V6 and potent V8 offer brisk acceleration and ample towing capacity. The interior is simple and well thought out and includes a strong list of standard features. This is a very good first attempt by Kia into this market and the V8 engine is superb.

Cons: Yes, there is a still a place for powerful, truck-based SUV. People with large families who need to tow a trailer are a perfect example. If you don't require a vehicle with these capabilities, then a full-size crossover will provide more room and use less fuel.

Nissan Armada

Rating	Worth consideration
Price	$55,000
Engine	5.6L V8 with 317hp
Standard safety features include	Front, side and curtain airbags, ABS, traction and stability control
Average fuel consumption	2929L/year
Warranty	3-year/60,000 km
Initial quality score	2.5/5
Dependability score	2/5

Pros: The Armada is a full-size SUV based on the Titan pickup truck platform. This vehicle competes with luxury SUVs—the Cadillac Escalade and Lincoln Navigator to name two. As a luxury SUV goes, it is very well equipped, sold with only one option package, so it more than competes with the established trucks in this class. Even though the basis is a truck, it has a refined ride and is a pleasure to drive. The V8 engine and slick transmission do a great job making this big vehicle feel nimble. Good value in the full-size luxury market.

Cons: The appetite for big truck-based SUVs is waning in the face of environmental concerns and the high cost of fuel. There will always be a place for a capable truck for those who have large families and require a truck for towing, but if you just need a people-mover, then a full-size crossover will do the trick.

Toyota Sequoia

Rating	Must try
Price	$48,000-$65,000
Engines	4.6L V8 with 310hp 5.7L V8 with 381hp
Standard safety features include	Front, side, knee and curtain airbags, ABS, stability and traction control
Average fuel consumption	2887L/year
Warranty	3-year/60,000 km
Initial quality score	N/A
Dependability score	5/5

Pros: The Sequoia is a full-size SUV built on the same pickup truck chassis as the Tundra, offering buyers an alternative to buying a domestic product. The large interior is capable of carrying eight, making it popular with buyers who need a vehicle of this size for towing or going off-road. The introduction of a new, more efficient 4.6L V8 in addition to the larger 5.7L motor gives buyers options depending on their needs. The 6-speed automatic and 4X4 capability makes the Sequoia a worthy competitor.

Cons: The Sequoia isn't cheap and the higher trim levels quickly add up. The power of the 5.7L V8 is intoxicating, making this big truck feel like a sports car, but all that power comes at a cost, not only to buy, but in fuel. If you don't require a full-size truck for towing, then a cheaper and more efficient crossover will do the trick.

PREMIUM FULL-SIZE SUV/CROSSOVER

Audi Q7

Rating	Worth consideration
Price	$54,000-$74,000
Engines	3.6L V6 with 280hp
	4.2L V8 with 350hp
	3.0L turbo diesel V6 with 225hp
Standard safety features include	Front, side and curtain airbags, ABS, traction and stability control
Average fuel consumption	3.6L V6, 2555L/year
	4.2L V8, 2779L/year
	3.0L diesel, 2199L/year
Warranty	4-year/80,000 km
Initial quality score	2.5/5
Dependability score	N/A

Pros: If you are in the market for a full size, three-row SUV with a high level of luxury features, then the Q7 will not disappoint. The addition of a powerful diesel engine provides economy but does not sacrifice torque. The interior is second to none; Audi does some of the most luxurious and well-thought-out interiors in the business. The ride is smooth and refined, making it a great companion for long trips. Styling is aggressive and refined at the same time; it looks like no other vehicle in this class.

Cons: The Q7 is a big vehicle, which makes it hard to manoeuvre for some drivers. The options can add up in a hurry, so be prepared for sticker shock. The same diesel engine is available in the small VW Touareg, so buyers who want a diesel might be able to save money by choosing the VW.

Buick Enclave

Rating	Must try
Price	$43,000-$50,000
Engine	3.6L V6 with 288hp
Standard safety features include	Front, side and curtain airbags, ABS, stability and traction control
Average fuel consumption	3.6L engine, 2153L/year 3.6L AWD, 2284L/year
Warranty	4-year/80,000 km
Initial quality score	2.5/5
Dependability score	N/A

Pros: If you require a vehicle that can carry seven or eight people comfortably, but don't like the look of a minivan and don't require a rugged full-size SUV, then the Enclave is a perfect alternative. With sophisticated looks and luxury amenities, the Enclave has a car-like ride, it very easy to drive and manoeuvre, and in general a joy to drive. Crossover vehicles are the direction the auto market is moving and the Enclave is on the leading edge.

Cons: The Enclave shares the same platform with the GMC Acadia, Chevy Traverse and, until recently, the Saturn Outlook. All four are very similar to drive with only slight modifications for styling and interior appointments. The problem is some of the cheap-feeling plastic pieces on the doors are the same across the entire line.

Cadillac Escalade

Rating	Worth consideration
Price	$83,000-$94,000
Engine	6.2L V8 with 403hp
Standard safety features include	Front, side and curtain airbags, ABS, stability and traction control
Average fuel consumption	2919L/year
Warranty	4-year/80,000 km
Initial quality score	4.5/5
Dependability score	3/5

Pros: The Escalade is the pinnacle of full-size decadence. Built on the same full-size pickup truck chassis as the Chevy Suburban, Chevy Tahoe and GMC Yukon, this is the "top dog" in terms of trim and options. The large V8 engine provides plenty of towing capacity for a large family on the move.

Cons: As fuel prices rise and environmental concerns mount, more practical crossovers or hybrid versions are replacing these big trucks. Look up the comments on the full-size hybrid models from General Motors in the hybrid category.

Infiniti QX

Rating	TOP PICK
Price	$72,000
Engine	5.6L V8 with 320hp
Standard safety features include	Front, side and curtain airbags, ABS, stability and traction control
Average fuel consumption	2965L/year
Warranty	4-year/100,000 km
Initial quality score	3.5/5
Dependability score	N/A

Pros: The QX56 is based on the Nissan Titan pickup truck chassis and is the slightly more luxurious version of the Nissan Armada. This is a true full-size unit with seating for seven or eight passengers; the QX is an alternative to buying a domestic full-size luxury truck like a Cadillac Escalade or Lincoln Navigator. The QX is perfect for a large family that has the need to tow a trailer, but it is less expensive than many of the domestics and comes fully loaded.

Cons: The Nissan Armada is almost as luxurious for less money. If you do not require the truck-based ruggedness and towing capacity this big truck delivers, then a full-size crossover will carry as many people and use a lot less fuel.

Lincoln MKT

Rating	Must try
Price	N/A at time of printing
Engines	3.7L V6 with 268hp
	3.5L turbo V6 with 355hp
Standard safety features include	Front, side and curtain airbags, ABS, stability and traction control
Average fuel consumption	N/A
U.S. fuel rating	13.8L/100km (20mpg) city
	10.2L/100km (27mpg) hwy
Warranty	4-year/80,000 km
Initial quality score	N/A
Dependability score	N/A

Pros: The MKT is a full-size luxury crossover built on the same platform as the Ford Flex. Lincoln takes an already wonderful product (Top Pick in the full-size crossover category) and infuses more luxury and refinement. At the time of printing the vehicle was not available for testing, but I did see the MKT at the Detroit Auto Show and it looks spectacular and the interior is sumptuous. With more available power than the Flex, the MKT should be a more dynamic vehicle to drive.

Cons: Not available to test at the time of printing.

Lincoln Navigator

Rating	Ford Expedition in Lincoln clothing
Price	$62,000-$65,000
Engine	5.4L V8 with 310hp
Standard safety features include	Front, side and curtain airbags, ABS, stability and traction control
Average fuel consumption	2315L/year
Warranty	4-year/80,000 km
Initial quality score	3.5/5
Dependability score	N/A

Pros: The navigator is the Lincoln version of the Ford Expedition full-size truck-based SUV. With more luxury touches, standard 4X4 and good towing capacity, this is a solid family vehicle for those who need to tow a trailer.

Cons: The Expedition and the Navigator are based on the capable F-150 truck chassis, so all you really get with the Navigator is more bling. To be honest, the Expedition does everything as well as this truck, it can be fitted with similar luxury features and it costs less. The new MKT is a better choice for large families who need lots of room but don't tow and want a luxury brand.

Mercedes R-Class

Rating	Must try
Price	$55,000-$56,000
Engines	3.0L turbo diesel V6 with 215hp 3.5L V6 with 268hp
Standard safety features include	Front, side and curtain airbags, ABS, traction and stability control
Average fuel consumption	3.0L diesel, 2020L/year 3.5L engine, 2520L/year
Warranty	4-year/80,000 km
Initial quality score	3.5/5
Dependability score	2/5

Pros: Mercedes was well ahead of the pack when it designed and produced this full-size crossover vehicle; now there are several new products to compete with this trendsetter. The large interior offers plenty of room for all passengers over three rows and the R-class is finished to the same high standards as any product in the Mercedes lineup. The diesel engine is the preferred choice for better fuel consumption, lower emissions and the torque needed to move this large vehicle.

Cons: Styling is awkward; the R-Class looks too much like a minivan or even a hearse to appeal to a wide range of buyers. The good news is there will be an updated model due out sometime in 2010. The rear doors are massive, making it hard for small children to open them without banging against something.

Mercedes GL-Class

Rating	Must try
Price	$69,000-$89,000
Engines	3.0L turbo diesel V6 with 210hp
	4.7L V8 with 335hp
	5.5L V8 with 382hp
Standard safety features include	Front, side and curtain airbags, ABS, traction and stability control
Average fuel consumption	3.0L diesel, 2160L/year
	4.7L V8, 2839L/year
	5.5L V8, 2880L/year
Warranty	4-year/80,000 km
Initial quality score	3.5/5
Dependability score	N/A

Pros: If an M-Class is too small and the R-Class looks too much like a mini-van, then the GL-Class is here to provide seating over three rows of seats and a rugged exterior design. The GL-Class is an extended version of the M-Class, complete with the same-looking dash and many of the same features. The diesel engine is a wonderful choice for buyers who want to reduce the amount of fuel they use. This engine is more than capable of moving this large vehicle around. The smooth ride and refined interior make the GL a roomy alternative to the other Mercedes products.

Cons: The GL-Class is larger than the M-Class but not as big as other full-size SUVs, so if interior space is important, then many of the domestic brands offer more room.

Convertibles and Coupes Category

CONVERTIBLES UNDER $35,000

Chrysler Sebring	
Rating	Inexpensive convertible
Price	Sedan: $18,000-$25,000
	Convertible: $22,000-$31,000
Engines	2.4L 4-cylinder with 173hp
	2.7L V6 with 186hp
	3.5L V6 with 235hp
Standard safety features include	Front, side and curtain airbags, ABS. Optional: stability and traction control.
Average fuel consumption	2.4L engine, 1661L/year
	2.7L V6, 1836L/year
	3.5L V6, 2086L/year
Warranty	3-year/60,000 km
Initial quality score	4.5/5
Dependability score	3/5

Pros: A favourite with rental-car companies, the Sebring has not been as popular as it once was, which is surprising given the very low starting price. With a range of engine choices and a reasonable track record, this mid-size sedan is roomy and comfortable. The convertible is very inexpensive and the optional retractable hardtop is worth a look.

Cons: The 2.4L engine is not the smoothest and most refined engine on the market, and the interior noise with this engine is irritating. The V6 is a much better engine choice due to the lower noise and smoother power. The styling of this car is part of the reason that its popularity is waning.

Ford Mustang

Rating	Must try
Price	Coupe: $24,000-$49,000
	Convertible: $30,000-$52,000
Engines	4.0L V6 with 210hp
	4.6L V8 with 315hp
	5.4L supercharged V8 with 500hp
Standard safety features include	Front and side airbags, ABS, stability and traction control
Average fuel consumption	4.0L V6, 2077L/year
	4.6L V8, 2301L/year
	5.4L V8, 2614L/year
Warranty	3-year/60,000 km
Initial quality score	4/5
Dependability score	2/5

Pros: With the new Chevy Camaro and Dodge Challenger re-entering the market, Ford has updated the Mustang for 2010 with some nice improvements to packaging. The retro styling has been improved with a bulging hood, aggressive front end and sequenced rear turning signals. The interior has a level of quality never seen before in a Mustang. All engines are smooth and, in the case of the V8s, very powerful. The GT is one of the best value sports coupes on the road. A great car and it is obvious that Ford has been making improvements to this car year after year for over 40 years.

Cons: The back seat is small, but who cares? This car is all about style.

Mazda MX-5 (Miata)

Rating	TOP PICK
Price	Sedan: $29,000-$40,000
Engine	2.0L 4-cylinder with 167hp
Standard safety features include	Front and side airbags, ABS. Optional: traction and stability control.
Average fuel consumption	N/A
Fuel rating	9.2L/100km (31 mpg) city 7.1L/100km (40 mpg) hwy
Warranty	3-year/80,000 km
Initial quality score	3/5
Dependability score	5/5

Pros: The Mazda MX-5 is one of the best cars on the road, and dollar for dollar might just be the most fun car on the road. Each version is improved, making an already great car even better. New for 2010 is an all-new front design incorporating Mazda's "smiley" grille. Handling is perfectly balanced, the 2.0L engine is always up for some fun, plus the available retractable hardtop makes this car usable in most weather conditions. The MX-5 has proven to be very reliable, and due to its strong following, the car demands a strong resale price—if you can find one for sale.

Cons: It is too bad that the MX-5 (Miata) has been given the name "chick car," because this is preventing many male buyers from ever trying this wonderful machine.

Mini Cooper

Rating	TOP PICK
Price	Hatchback: $23,000-$38,000 Wagon: $26,000-$40,000 Convertible: $30,000-$44,000
Engines	1.6L 4-cylinder with 118hp 1.6L turbo 4-cylinder with 172hp 1.6L turbo 4-cylinder with 208hp
Standard safety features include	Front, side and head airbags, ABS, traction and stability control
Average fuel consumption	1.6L engine, 1260L/year 1.6L turbo, 1380L/year
Warranty	4-year/80,000 km
Initial quality score	2/5
Dependability score	3/5

Pros: The Mini is a premium subcompact car with amazing handling and surprising interior space—and it can be ordered with a host of features, trims levels and colour choices. The base model is one of the most fuel-efficient cars on the road, making it a rival to most hybrids. The funky interior is retro inspired and has a flair that few cars can rival. The Mini has one of the highest resale values of any car on the road, making the high sticker price easier to take.

Cons: The Mini is just that—mini. The small interior is perfect for a single person or couple but this is no alternative for a family car. The interior may look funky, but it could be much more functional. The switch to a new engine supplier in the latest model has produced a lower-quality score.

Mitsubishi Eclipse

Rating	Worth consideration
Price	Coupe: $26,000-$35,000 Convertible: $32,000-$38,000
Engines	2.4L 4-cylinder with 162hp 3.8L V6 with 265hp
Standard safety features include	Front, side and curtain airbags, and ABS. Optional: traction and stability control.
Average fuel consumption	2.4L engine, 1812L/year 3.8L V6, 1777L/year
Warranty	5-year/100,000 km
Initial quality score	2/5
Dependability score	2/5

Pros: This stylish car is available as a coupe or convertible with two engine choices. With so few convertibles available under $35,000, the Eclipse provides an option, plus it has a 2+2 configuration for carrying extra cargo or passengers in a pinch. The interior is sporty looking with a high centre console making the interior feel like a true cockpit. The 3.8L engine is powerful, but the 4-cylinder is no slouch either.

Cons: Some buyers might be attracted to the sweeping lines and flowing interior, but others might perceive the design to be too busy. The interior is cramped, especially the back seat. The Eclipse doesn't feel like a sports car, rather a touring car, especially in the convertible version.

VW Beetle

Rating	Fun car, limited market
Price	Coupe: $22,000-$25,000 Convertible: $27,000-$32,000
Engine	2.5L 5-cylinder with 150hp
Standard safety features include	Front and side airbags, ABS, traction and stability control
Average fuel consumption	1780L/year
Warranty	4-year/80,000 km
Initial quality score	3.5/5
Dependability score	2/5

Pros: For buyers who want to make a statement with a fun, roomy and funky car, the Beetle is worth a look. This is also an alternative to a Mini for attitude and quirkiness. The Beetle may look dainty but in truth is a capable handling car. The 2.5L engine is up to the job.

Cons: The glory days of the Beetle are behind it, and with the introduction of the retractable hardtop Eos, the Beetle convertible has become almost irrelevant. This is only a car that a potential buyer "has" to have; you either want one or you don't.

CONVERTIBLES $35,000-$55,000

Audi TT

Rating	Must try
Price	Coupe: $47,000-$57,000 Convertible: $50,000-$61,000
Engine	2.0L turbo 4-cylinder with 200hp 2.0L turbo 4-cylinder with 265hp 3.2L V6 with 250hp
Standard safety features include	Front, side and knee airbags, ABS, traction and stability control
Average fuel consumption	2.0L engine, 1606L/year 3.2L V6, 2034L/year
Warranty	4-year/80,000 km
Initial quality score	3/5
Dependability score	N/A

Pros: The original Audi TT was one of the most influential cars ever produced because it changed the way car interiors have been designed ever since. Not only is the interior stylish, the latest version has an equally handsome exterior. The TT is an easy-to-drive coupe or roadster, and now with the introduction of the TTS, the performance is invigorating. The latest car might not be as revolutionary as the original, but remember a car like the TT only comes around once in a generation. The 4-cylinder turbo is the engine of choice because the V6 isn't that much more powerful.

Cons: Due to the narrow side windows, outward visibility is limited. The convertible roof features a conventional cloth design in this era of retractable hardtop designs. The smooth and refined ride may not be stimulating enough for performance-oriented drivers.

Nissan 370Z

Rating	Must try
Price	Coupe: $40,000-$53,000 Convertible: $51,000
Engine	3.7L V6 with 332hp
Standard safety features include	Front, side and curtain airbags, ABS, traction and stability control
Average fuel consumption	N/A
Fuel rating	11.6L/100km (24mpg) city 7.7L/100km (37mpg) hwy
Warranty	3-year/60,000 km
Initial quality score	4/5
Dependability score	5/5

Pros: Introduced in 2009, the 370Z replaces the successful 350Z sports coupe and convertible. Built to beat the best coupes in the world at a price nobody can touch, the 370Z is a relative bargain in the sports car realm. The potent 332hp V6 engine is a giant—able to take on anything Germany has to offer. Complete with a 7-speed automatic, the 370Z is very fast and nimble. The interior has been significantly updated, removing the hard plastics that were all too prevalent in older models. With a long list of standard features, updated exterior styling and more power, the 370Z is positioned to be a class leader.

Cons: The back seat is really only for show as it would be hard pressed to carry even children. The convertible is a soft-top design, which is fine, but many cars in this class have moved to retractable hardtop designs. Even though this is a wonderful refinement of the Z-car legend, the market for sports cars is rather small; many buyers can find similar power, refinement and even handling in a sedan.

VW Eos

Rating	TOP PICK
Price	$36,000-$46,000
Engine	2.0L turbo 4-cylinder with 200hp
Standard safety features include	Front and side airbags, ABS, traction and stability control
Average fuel consumption	1700L/year
Warranty	4-year/80,000 km
Initial quality score	3.5/5
Dependability score	2/5

Pros: If you are in the market for a European retractable hardtop and don't want to splash out for a BMW or Mercedes, then this is the best option. The Eos is based on the solid Jetta/Golf platform and has a spunky turbo 4-cylinder engine, providing good performance and great fuel mileage. Styling is good and the interior has plenty of room in the back seat for children. The roof provides an all-weather option for buyers who want a cozy car in the winter and a convertible in the summer.

Cons: As is the case with all retractable hardtops, the trunk is very small when the roof is down. Some drivers might find the Eos a bit slow off the line until the turbo kicks in. If you don't care about the retractable hardtop, then the BMW 1 Series is a great alternative.

CONVERTIBLES OVER $55,000

BMW 6 Series

Rating	Worth consideration
Price	Coupe: $95,000-$121,000 Convertible: $105,000-$131,000
Engines	4.8L V8 with 360hp 5.0L V10 with 500hp
Standard safety features include	Front, side, knee and curtain airbags, ABS, traction and stability control
Average fuel consumption	4.8L V8, 2250L/year 5.0L V10, 3003L/year
Warranty	4-year/80,000 km
Initial quality score	N/A
Dependability score	N/A

Pros: The 6 Series is an ultra-stylish coupe or convertible featuring either a powerful V8 or potent V10 engine. The large dimensions of this car make it feel like a touring car, capable of putting the miles away with ease. Buying a 6 Series isn't just about driving a very capable car; it is also about making a statement about the driver's fashion-forward style.

Cons: Just like the 5 Series, this car also has a stark almost utility-like interior. The iDrive computer interface system takes a great deal of time to learn, plus other manufacturers in this class offer much better and more intuitive systems.

BMW Z4

Rating	Must try
Price	$54,000-$62,000
Engines	3.0L 6-cylinder with 255hp 3.0L turbo 6-cylinder with 300hp
Standard safety features include	Front and side airbags, ABS, traction and stability control
Average fuel consumption	3.0L engine, 1864L/year 3.0L turbo, 1862L/year
Warranty	4-year/80,000 km
Initial quality score	N/A
Dependability score	N/A

Pros: Wow! What a sexy-looking car. The latest model was introduced in 2009 and it features a new retractable hardtop, sleeker styling and an updated interior. All of this comes together to make the Z4 a much better car than the older model. The powerful engines and low-to-the-ground design provides an exhilarating experience with the top up or down. This has to be one of the most elegant, yet sporty looking, cars on the road.

Cons: In my opinion the original Z4 was ugly and I have to ask—why did it take so long to make these wonderful improvements?

Infiniti G

Rating	Must try
Price	$57,000-$61,000
Engines	3.7L V6 with 325hp
	3.7L V6 with 328hp
	3.7L V6 with 330hp
Standard safety features include	Front, side and curtain airbags, ABS, stability and traction control
Average fuel consumption	3.7L V6, 1971L/year
	3.7L AWD, 2000L/year
Warranty	4-year/100,000 km
Initial quality score	5/5
Dependability score	4/5

Pros: The G sedan, coupe and convertible have taken the established premium compact class by storm. The leader in this class is the BMW 3 Series, but the Infiniti products are almost as good for a lot less money. The powerful 3.7L engine is spectacular, the handling is sublime, especially in AWD trim, and the interior is nicely finished. The computer interface is easy to use, plus the interior materials are all first rate. Infiniti cars have been receiving better and better quality scores, so a G sedan is a good choice.

Cons: The only problem with the G is the lack of room for taller and heavier people. Headroom is limited for drivers over six feet, and some people will find the width of the driver cockpit too narrow for comfort. If the G were a tad bigger, it would easily win this class.

Mercedes SLK-Class

Rating	Worth consideration
Price	$57,000-$85,000
Engines	3.0L V6 with 228hp
	3.5L V6 with 300hp
	5.5L V8 with 355hp
Standard safety features include	Front, side and curtain airbags, ABS, traction and stability control
Average fuel consumption	3.0L V6, 2000L/year
	3.5L V6, 2100L/year
	5.5L V8, 2440L/year
Warranty	4-year/80,000 km
Initial quality score	3.5/5
Dependability score	5/5

Pros: The SLK was one of the first modern roadsters to include a retractable hardtop, and it makes an SLK an all-weather car. Improvements have been made over the years to improve handling and performance, and now the SLK is worthy of most cars in this class. The optional V8 engine makes this car a monster in straight-line acceleration. The interior is tight for big people, but for those that fit, it is a fun roadster to own. The solid quality score is reassuring.

Cons: Buyers who want a pure performance roadster will be better served buying a Porsche Boxster. The new BMW Z4 might have an edge on the SLK in the styling department. Trunk space is very small when the roof is down and interior space is limited for bigger people.

Mercedes SL-Class

Rating	Worth consideration
Price	$125,000-$238,000
Engines	5.5L V8 with 382hp
	6.2L V8 with 518hp
	5.5L turbo V12 with 510hp
	6.2L turbo V12 with 603hp
Standard safety features include	Front, side and curtain airbags, ABS, traction and stability control
Average fuel consumption	5.5L V8, 2580L/year
	6.2L V8, 2920L/year
	5.5L V12, 3060L/year
	6.0L V12, 3040L/year
Warranty	4-year/80,000 km
Initial quality score	N/A
Dependability score	N/A

Pros: The SL-Class has been a staple in the Mercedes lineup for decades, making it a roadster that many buyers aspire to own. The retractable hardtop makes it an all-weather car for comfy driving in cold weather and easy roof-down driving in the summer. The refinement of the interior, first-class materials and stunning styling make the SL a head turner. The high-performance versions are wickedly quick and very expensive. This really is a prestige car.

Cons: As with any high-end car, depreciation is very rapid, so buying one of these cars used makes a great deal of sense, but only if it is still under warranty. As with any retractable hardtop, the trunk is tiny when the roof is down.

Porsche Boxster/Boxster S

Rating	TOP PICK
Price	$58,000-$71,000
Engines	2.6L 6-cylinder with 255hp
	3.4L 6-cylinder with 310hp
Standard safety features include	Front, side and head airbags, ABS, traction and stability control
Average fuel consumption	2.9L engine, 1900L/year
	3.4L engine, 1900L/year
Warranty	4-year/80,000 km
Initial quality score	N/A
Dependability score	N/A

Pros: The Boxster or the Boxster S is the Top Pick in this class for several reasons. First, you get a Porsche through and through. This might be a less-expensive Porsche, but it still has all the characteristics of the more expensive models. Second, the Boxster is equipped with two trunks, one under the bonnet and another in the back. Third, the Boxster can easily be used as a daily commuting vehicle because it is so easy to drive. Fourth, it's a convertible! Handling is unparallel at this price point and the more powerful "S" model is the choice for driving enthusiasts. Even though the Boxster does not have an individual quality score, Porsche as a brand has ranked right at the very top over the past several years.

Cons: The only problem with the Boxster is that many Porsche owners or potential owners believe that the only car to own is the 911. The roof is a conventional ragtop and not a retractable hardtop but this also frees up storage room. The Boxster might not have the status of the 911, but it is a very satisfying car to drive every day.

Porsche Carrera/911

Rating	Must try
Price	Coupe: $95,000-$235,000 Convertible: $108,000-$174,000
Engines	3.6L 6-cylinder with 345hp 3.8L 6-cylinder with 385hp 3.6L turbo 6-cylinder with 480hp 3.8L 6-cylinder with 435hp 3.6L turbo 6-cylinder with 530hp
Standard safety features include	Front, side and curtain airbags, ABS, traction and stability control
Average fuel consumption	3.6L engine, 1940L/year 3.8L engine, 1900L/year 3.6L turbo, 2220L/year 3.6L GT2, 2320L/year
Warranty	4-year/80,000 km warranty
Initial quality score	5/5
Dependability score	3/5

Pros: The 911 is one of the most recognized and sought-after cars on the road, and it has been for over 40 years. What makes the 911 unique is that it can be driven daily to work or flogged at the racetrack, and it does both with ease. These cars are very well built; in fact, it has a perfect quality score, and Porsche as a brand has been on top of quality studies for years. The performance and handling are second to none, and the 911 has built a very loyal following among driving enthusiasts around the world. This is a perfect car for a driver who wants a sports car but needs to drive it every day.

Cons: These cars are very expensive and they are subject to the same laws of depreciation, so they make an excellent used car. Expect to spend a lot of extra money on every single option, as most features cost extra.

COUPES UNDER $35,000

Chevy Camaro

Rating	Worth consideration
Price	$27,000-$41,000
Engines	3.6L V6 with 340hp
	6.2L V8 with 400hp
	6.2L V8 with 426hp
Standard safety features include	Front, side and curtain airbags, ABS, stability and traction control
Average fuel consumption	N/A
Warranty	3-year/60,000 km
Initial quality score	N/A
Dependability score	N/A

Pros: The all-new Camaro is helping to bring back the muscle-car era of the late 1960s with stunning retro styling. Based on the same rear-wheel-drive platform as the defunct Pontiac G8, this new car rides nothing like the muscle cars of old; in fact, the Camaro is a very civilized car to drive. The 3.6L V6 is more than enough engine for the average driver; the V8 will be purchased by true muscle-car enthusiasts. The Camaro is very well priced.

Cons: Outward visibility is limited due to the retro shape of the body. Finding a comfortable driving position can prove to be tricky, and so the Camaro is not the most comfortable car to take on a long trip. The interior is well appointed, but the materials used could be of better quality.

Dodge Challenger

Rating	Must try
Price	$26,000-$46,000
Engines	3.5L V6 250hp
	5.7L V8 with 372hp
	6.1L V8 with 425hp
Standard safety features include	Front, side and curtain airbags, available ABS, stability and traction control
Average fuel consumption	3.5L V6, 2071L/year
	5.7L V8, 2192L/year
	6.1L V8, 2544L/year
Warranty	3-year/60,000 km
Initial quality score	N/A
Dependability score	N/A

Pros: The Challenger is a fully modern muscle car, evoking the image of the late 60s "pony" car era. It is beautifully styled, sitting on large wheels and looking tough. It is built on the same platform as the Chrysler 300 sedan and benefits from the same solid road manners and sophisticated suspension. The base model offers all the looks with a sensible engine; the V8-powered cars truly bring back the muscle-car theme. The Challenger is a very easy car to drive and enjoy, due to the comfortable seats and smooth suspension.

Cons: The interior is functional but not enough attention was paid to the selection of materials and finish. The large dimensions of the Challenger make it a touring car and not a sports car.

Hyundai Tiburon

Rating	Genesis coupe is a better choice
Price	$19,000-$29,000
Engines	2.0L 4-cylinder with 138hp
	2.7L V6 with 172hp
Standard safety features include	Front airbags. Optional: ABS, side and curtain airbags.
Average fuel consumption	N/A
Fuel rating	2.0L engine, 10.2L/100km (27mpg) city
	7.1L/100km (39mpg) hwy
	2.7L engine, 12.2L/100km (23mpg) city
	8.1L/100km (35mpg) hwy
Warranty	5-year/100,000 km
Initial quality score	N/A
Dependability score	N/A

Pros: With companies like Toyota getting out of the inexpensive coupe market, there have been few choices for buyers looking for a small, stylish coupe to fill their needs. The Tiburon is a great-looking car with plenty of power when equipped with the V6 engine. Handling is first rate and the ride is smooth and quiet. The price is as attractive as the car.

Cons: Be forewarned, the Tiburon is only for small people. Tall and hefty people need not apply. The roofline is very low, the legroom is cramped and the back seat is of little use. Nice car but interior room is limiting.

Hyundai Genesis

Rating	TOP PICK
Price	$25,000-$37,000
Engines	2.0L 4-cylinder turbo with 210hp 3.8L V6 with 290hp
Standard safety features include	Front, side and curtain airbags, ABS, traction and stability control
Average fuel consumption	3.8L V6, 1902L/year
Warranty	5-year/100,000 km
Initial quality score	5/5
Dependability score	N/A

Pros: The Hyundai Genesis sedan took the auto industry by storm when it was introduced in 2009, winning several awards. The large rear-wheel-drive sedan has excellent driving dynamics for a luxury car with a spirited 3.8L engine and potent 4.8LV8. The price of the Genesis is what makes this vehicle a real winner, offering the same level of refinement that is typically found in cars costing twice as much. Beautiful car and at a price many people can handle. The coupe has the same name but is actually a very different car, putting emphasis on performance and not luxury. The Genesis scored top marks in the 2009 JD Power and Associates quality study in its very first year!

Cons: The only knock against the Genesis is that many people will not try it because it is a Hyundai, which is a shame because they are missing out on one of the true value cars on the market.

Ford Mustang

See review above at page 267.

Mitsubishi Eclipse

See review above at page 270.

VW Beetle

See review above at page 270.

COUPES $35,000-$55,000

Mazda RX-8

Rating	Only rotary for a reason
Price	$38,000-$44,000
Engine	1.3L rotary engine with 212hp
Standard safety features include	Front, side and curtain airbags, ABS with optional traction and stability control
Average fuel consumption	2236L/year
Warranty	3-year/80,000 km
Initial quality score	N/A
Dependability score	N/A

Pros: The RX-8 is a unique car due to the fact it is the only production car to utilize a rotary engine. Instead of pistons pushing up and down, the rotary engine has one triangular-shaped rotor that spins. The advantage is that a rotary engine has a very flat torque curve and is capable of high RPMs. The RX-8 is also unique because it is a four-door sports car, yet looks like a coupe, making it a more functional alternative to a regular sports car. Handling is very good and the four-door design detracts nothing from the sports car feel.

Cons: The 1.3L engine can be very thirsty on fuel and requires constant attention to oil consumption. The rotary engine does provide flat torque, but the drone of the engine and limited power can leave the driver wanting more. The RX-8 might be the only rotary powered car for a reason.

Audi TT

See review above at page 271.

Infiniti G

See review above at page 274.

Nissan 370Z

See review at page 271.

COUPES OVER $55,000

Audi R8

Rating	Must try
Price	$141,000 (price for the R8 V10 was not available at the time of printing)
Engines	4.2L V8 with 420hp 5.2L V10 with 525hp
Standard safety features include	Front, side and curtain airbags, ABS, traction and stability control
Average fuel consumption	2860L/year
Warranty	4-year/80,000 km
Initial quality score	N/A
Dependability score	N/A

Pros: The R8 was one of the most exciting cars introduced in the last several years. With stunning good looks, a powerful engine, refined and spacious interior and a price that beats any other exotic car on the road, the R8 is a relative bargain. The sound from the engine is intoxicating and the handling is as good as any in this class. In fact, the R8 is very easy to drive fast.

Cons: The sequential automatic transmission is rather sloppy, making for dramatic shifts instead of precise and quick transitions. The manual is the way to go for the best performance. Some drivers might find the smooth and refined ride a bit too easy, maybe opting for a car with more feedback like the Porsche GT3.

Nissan GT-R

Rating	Must try
Price	$99,000
Engine	3.8L turbo-charged V6 with 485hp
Standard safety features include	Front, side and curtain airbags, ABS, traction and stability control
Average fuel consumption	2298L/year
Warranty	3-year/60,000 km
Initial quality score	N/A
Dependability score	N/A

Pros: The GT-R is a purpose-built go-fast machine that took the world by storm in 2009. It was developed to take on the established high-powered, high-priced German sports cars and beat them in the performance arena and kill them on the price front. The GT-R is able to run with cars more than twice the price and do it with relative ease. The GT-R is very easy to drive fast, the engine is silky smooth and the AWD system keeps the GT-R firmly planted on the road. The host of electronic gadgets and driving aids are cutting edge and will appeal to young drivers. This is a wickedly fast car that will change the face of the super-cars class for a long time to come.

Cons: The GT-R is a long and wide car, making it feel much bigger than the Porsche 911. The smooth AWD system and powerful engine are so refined that the driving experience can be a little dull, even at high speed. There is no manual transmission offered, which also makes the driving experience slightly disconnected. Yes, the GT-R is a very fast car and it is able to do many things well for a fraction of the price but might be too big and easy to drive for some.

Porsche Cayman/Cayman S

Rating	Must try
Price	$58,000-$71,000
Engines	2.6L 6-cylinder with 265hp
	3.4L 6-cylinder with 320hp
Standard safety features include	Front, side and head airbags, ABS, traction and stability control
Average fuel consumption	2.9L engine, 1900L/year
	3.4L engine, 1900L/year
Warranty	4-year/80,000 km
Initial quality score	N/A
Dependability score	N/A

Pros: The Cayman is based on the Boxster, but instead of a convertible it has a fixed roof, providing a less expensive coupe option than splashing out for a 911. There is plenty of storage under the bonnet and in the large hatch, making the Cayman a very useful daily driver. The handling is superb, due to the mid-engine design and Porsche suspension design. The Cayman is a very satisfying car to drive in the city or at high speeds, even on the racetrack. The interior features a high level of fit and finish and the Porsche brand has been at the very top of quality scores over the last few years.

Cons: The only problem with the Cayman is that many Porsche owners or potential owners believe that the only car to own is the 911. The Cayman might not have the status of the 911, but it is a very satisfying car to drive every day.

Porsche Carrera/911

Rating	TOP PICK
Price	Coupe: $95,000-$235,000 Convertible: $108,000-$174,000
Engines	3.6L 6-cylinder with 345hp 3.8L 6-cylinder with 385hp 3.6L turbo 6-cylinder with 480hp 3.8L 6-cylinder with 435hp 3.6L turbo 6-cylinder with 530hp
Standard safety features include	Front, side and curtain airbags, ABS, traction and stability control
Average fuel consumption	3.6L engine, 1940L/year 3.8L engine, 1900L/year 3.6L turbo, 2220L/year 3.6L GT2, 2320L/year
Warranty	4-year/80,000 km warranty
Initial quality score	5/5
Dependability score	3/5

Pros: The 911 is one of the most recognized and sought-after cars on the road, and it has been for over 40 years. What makes the 911 unique is that it can be driven daily to work or flogged at the racetrack, and it does both with ease. These cars are very well built; in fact, it has a perfect quality score, and Porsche as a brand has been on top of quality studies for years. The performance and handling are second to none, and the 911 has built a very loyal following among driving enthusiasts around the world. This is a perfect car for a driver who wants a sports car but needs to drive it every day.

Cons: These cars are very expensive and they are subject to the same laws of depreciation, so they make an excellent used car. Expect to spend a lot of extra money on every single option, as most features cost extra.

BMW 6 Series

See review above at page 273.

Minivan Category

Chrysler Town & Country/Dodge Grand Caravan

Rating	Must try
Price	$22,000-$38,000
Engines	3.3L V6 with 175hp
	4.0L V6 with 251hp
Standard safety features include	Front, side and curtain air bags, ABS, stability and traction control
Average fuel consumption	3.3L V6, 2100L/year
	4.0L V6, 2054L/year
Warranty	3-year/60,000 km
Initial quality score	2.5/5
Dependability score	3/5

Pros: Many van buyers overlook the Town & Country/Grand Caravan products in favour of the more expensive Japanese products, which is a shame. Chrysler has been at the minivan game a long time and the innovative features that are available in these products are fantastic. "Stow-n-Go" seats are a perfect example of Chrysler innovation. These vans are the smoothest and quietest vans on the road and the available 4.0L engine and 6-speed automatic make it a very comfortable van to drive. With an amazing starting price, owning a van makes a lot of sense for larger families. Buyers who have not tried these products before will be surprised at how good they are.

Cons: The dash is very simple and has a bit too much hard plastic. The 3.3L engine only has a 4-speed automatic, which really lets this van down. If you can afford the larger engine, go for it. Resale value is always a concern when buying a domestic van.

Honda Odyssey

Rating	Must try
Price	$31,000-$50,000
Engine	3.5L V6 with 244hp
Standard safety features include	Front, side and curtain airbags, ABS, stability and traction control
Average fuel consumption	2228L/year
Warranty	5-year/100,000 km
Initial quality score	2/5
Dependability score	3/5

Pros: The versatile Honda Odyssey has an almost cult-like following. This helps to provide a very strong resale market, making the Odyssey good value even though it is expensive when new. The interior offers plenty of room for all three rows of passengers and has many well-thought-out convenience features. The 3.5L V6 is a willing partner for all driving situations and the smooth ride provides a relaxing experience.

Cons: The dash has an overly complex array of buttons, especially on the top models. Speaking of top models, the Odyssey can become very expensive when equipped with all the toys. Unlike its archrival, the Toyota Sienna, the Odyssey is not offered in all-wheel drive. The Odyssey is very big and can be a handful to park without park assist, and it tends to be thirsty at the gas pump. Also try the Dodge Grand Caravan—it might surprise you.

Kia Sedona

Rating	Must try
Price	$27,000-$39,000
Engine	3.8L V6 with 250hp
Standard safety features include	Front, side and curtain airbags, ABS. Optional: traction and stability control.
Average fuel consumption	2244L/year
Warranty	5-year/100,000 km
Initial quality score	N/A
Dependability score	2.5/5

Pros: For buyers who are looking for a less expensive van than a Toyota Sienna or Honda Odyssey and don't want a Chrysler van (why, I don't know), the Kia Sedona offers a practical alternative. The V6 engine is the highlight of this van, making it quick off the line; it has lots of passing power and is quiet on the highway. The standard features are wonderful as is the long list of safety equipment. The higher-end models offer the most savings when compared to the other top-end products in this category. Now that Hyundai is no longer producing its van, Kia has the Korean van market to itself.

Cons: The second row of seats doesn't lock in the upright position, and some of the high-end electrical gadgets are not offered in the Sedona. Resale value is always a worry since many people believe that Kia doesn't make good products, when it actually is not the case.

Nissan Quest

Rating	Worth consideration
Price	$30,000-$45,000
Engine	3.5L V6 with 235hp
Standard safety features include	Front, side and curtain airbags, ABS, traction control. Optional: stability control.
Average fuel consumption	2175L/year
Warranty	3-year/60,000 km
Initial quality score	3.5/5
Dependability score	2/5

Pros: The Quest is the largest of the minivans (kind of an oxymoron). The large dimensions provide great seating for all passengers with good visibility, even for third-row passengers. The 3.5L V6 is a worthy engine and Nissan has engineered the Quest to have above-average handling in this class. The Quest is unique looking, which might appeal to some buyers who don't like the "soccer mom" image. For families who want to "spread out," the Quest is very comfortable.

Cons: The uniqueness of the Quest is also one of the major drawbacks. The dashboard design is quirky, making it overly complex and unusual to look at. The exterior styling might leave some buyers shaking their heads. A good van, but a bit too fashion-forward for some.

Toyota Sienna

Rating	TOP PICK
Price	$31,000-$51,000
Engine	3.5L V6 with 266hp
Standard safety features include	Front, side and curtain airbags, ABS, stability and traction control
Average fuel consumption	FWD, 2016L/year AWD, 2318L/year
Warranty	3-year/60,000 km
Initial quality score	3/5
Dependability score	3/5

Pros: Many consumers cross-shop the Sienna van with the Honda Odyssey van. Both are excellent products, but buyers should also try the Chrysler and Dodge vans. The Sienna made my Top Pick due to the availability of all-wheel drive and good resale value. If Chrysler had continued to produce an AWD van, it would be my Top Pick, it is that good. The Sienna, unlike the Odyssey, is an example of how to execute a good dashboard design without it being too complex. The Sienna is not too big either, making it easy to manoeuvre and park, although it is roomy enough for most families. The 3.5L V6 is powerful and can move fully packed Siennas with little effort.

Cons: The Sienna can be loaded up with all kinds of goodies, but the price will jump very quickly turning a basic family van into a luxury barge. The exterior styling is not as strong as many other vans in the market but who buys a van for looks? The V6 might be powerful, but it can be rough at idle and noisy under acceleration. If you want a quiet-running van, the Dodge is the best on the market.

VW Routan

Rating	Must try
Price	$28,000-$40,000
Engine	4.0L V6 with 253hp
Standard safety features include	Front, side and curtain airbags, ABS, traction and stability control
Average fuel consumption	2053L/year
Warranty	4-year/80,000 km
Initial quality score	N/A
Dependability score	N/A

Pros: I suggest you read the comments for the Dodge Grand Caravan, because the Routan is a re-badged Chrysler that is built in the same plant. Now, before you turn up your nose, consider that the Dodge product is one of the best on the road and the VW version is a real bargain compared to buying the original. It comes with a nicer interior, bigger standard engine, standard 6-speed automatic, sportier suspension and steering, and has all of this for less cost than a domestic. Try it—you might like it.

Cons: Buyers looking for a German-designed and -made van will be disappointed that this isn't really a VW, but a Dodge. Great van, but will VW buyers want it? I wish VW would bring in the European Touran compact van with the diesel engine.

Pickup Category

COMPACT PICKUPS

Ford Ranger / Mazda B-Series

Rating	TOP PICK
Price	$17,000-$26,000
Engines	2.3L 4-cylinder with 143hp 4.0L V6 with 207hp
Standard safety features include	Front airbags, ABS
Average fuel consumption	2.3L engine, 1764L/year 4.0L V6, 2347L/year 4.0L 4X4, 2536L/year
Warranty	3-year/60,000 km
Initial quality score	3.5/5
Dependability score	5/5

Pros: This really is the only option in the compact pickup segment, so it wins Top Pick by default. That being said, for buyers who want a basic truck, on the cheap, to do light-duty work, the Ranger has been doing that for years and years. The Ranger is sold under the Mazda name as the B Series.

Cons: The Ranger/B-Series is getting ancient; other than modest styling updates, it has been in consistent production for almost 15 years. It is small and cramped, the ride is basic and the interior is cheap looking, plus the 4.0L V6 is hard on fuel. The slightly larger compact/mid-size pickups are a better option for many because they feature newer designs and newer engine choices.

MID-SIZE PICKUPS

Chevy Colorado/ GMC Canyon

Rating	Worth consideration
Price	$23,000-$35,000
Engines	2.9L 4-cylinder with 185hp
	3.7L 5-cylinder with 242hp
	5.3L V8 with 300hp
Standard safety features include	Front and curtain airbags, ABS, traction and stability control
Average fuel consumption	2.9L engine, 2021L/year
	2.9L 4X4, 2085L/year
	3.7L engine, 2158L/year
	3.7L 4X4, 2198L/year
	5.3L V8, 2360L/year
	5.3L 4X4, 2582L/year
Warranty	3-year/60,000 km
Initial quality score	2/5
Dependability score	2/5

Pros: The Colorado is a small to mid-size pickup truck with a large range of engine choices and prices to suit most buyers. The 5-cylinder engine is unique because it uses only slightly more fuel than a 4-cylinder, but has much more power and torque. This is a good alternative to the very basic and smaller Ford Ranger.

Cons: The quality scores are not as good as the full-size Chevy trucks, and in this class the Toyota Tacoma is the clear winner due to higher resale value.

Dodge Dakota

Rating	Must try
Price	$22,000-$27,000
Engines	3.7L V6 210hp
	4.7L V8 with 302hp
Standard safety features include	Front airbags, ABS. Optional: side and curtain airbags.
Average fuel consumption	3.7L V6, 2356L/year
	3.7L 4X4, 2549L/year
	4.7L V8, 2688L/year
	4.7L 4X4, 3653L/year
Warranty	3-year/60,000 km
Initial quality score	5/5
Dependability score	2/5

Pros: The Dakota helped develop the mid-size pickup truck segment. The not too big, not too small dimension of this truck is the number one reason to give it a try. There is plenty of room inside when equipped with four doors, and the choice of 4X2 or 4X4, V6 or V8 engines makes it easy to find a Dakota to fit any budget. The bed is a useful size, making it a better choice than the Ford Sport Trac. The quality score is reassuring.

Cons: The seats are a bit hard and the interior trim looks cheap. This is a basic truck but it shouldn't look basic. The larger Dodge Ram shows what can be done right on the inside of a truck.

Ford Explorer Sport Trac

Rating	Not a pure pickup
Price	$31,000-$41,000
Engines	4.0L V6 with 210hp
	4.6L V8 with 292hp
Standard safety features include	Front, side and curtain airbags, ABS, traction and stability control
Average fuel consumption	4.0L V6, 2721L/year
	4.0L 4X4, 2772L/year
	4.6L V8, 2466L/year
	4.6L 4X4, 2641L/year
Warranty	3-year/60,000 km
Initial quality score	2/5
Dependability score	3.5/5 (2005 model)

Pros: The Explorer Sport Trac is a unique vehicle offering the interior of a conventional mid-size SUV with the bed of a pickup truck. Built on the pickup truck-based Explorer SUV, the owners of these vehicles love the flexibility they offer for on-road comfort, off-road capability and cargo capacity. The small bed is perfect for light-duty work, and this vehicle offers an alternative to the very basic Ford Ranger.

Cons: Even though the Sport Trac falls between the Ranger and F-150 pickup, it really isn't a mid-size unit. The bed is rather small and the vehicle is sold in one configuration, making a true mid-size truck like the Tacoma or Dodge Dakota a better choice for work duties. The Honda Ridgeline is a much more sophisticated vehicle to drive.

Honda Ridgeline

Rating	Worth consideration
Price	$35,000-$43,000
Engine	3.5L V6 with 250hp
Standard safety features include	Front, side and curtain airbags, ABS, stability and traction control
Average fuel consumption	2433L/year
Warranty	5-year/100,000 km
Initial quality score	4/5
Dependability score	4/5

Pros: The Ridgeline is unique because it is not built on a separate truck chassis like all other pickups. It features a unibody design like a cross-over. This delivers a smoother ride than most trucks; it is lighter and is targeted at a buyer who wants a light-duty vehicle. The AWD system provides most of the power to the front wheels for better fuel economy, and due to the rear suspension design Honda was able to include a lockable and watertight trunk in the bed. The interior offers a lot of room for front and rear passengers, plus a funky design. I like to call the Ridgeline the "white collar pickup" for weekend, light-duty work. This is a good alternative to a compact pickup.

Cons: The Pilot is out of its depth when compared to full-sized truck-based pickups. It isn't going to find its way to too many construction sites or farm fields. The bed is limited in size and the choice of engines is limited to one.

Nissan Frontier

Rating	Worth consideration
Price	$23,000-$38,000
Engines	2.5L 4-cylinder with 152hp 4.0L V6 with 261hp
Standard safety features include	Front airbags, ABS. Optional: traction and stability control.
Average fuel consumption	4-cylinder 4X2, 2929L/year V6 4X2, 2385L/year V6 4X4, 2423L/year
Warranty	3-year/60,000 km
Initial quality score	4/5
Dependability score	2/5

Pros: The Frontier bridges two classes: the compact and mid-size pickup truck, leaning more toward the mid-size class due to the standard King Cab and Optional Crew Cab designs. With two capable engines and useful design, the Frontier is a worthy competitor to others in this class.

Cons: Unfortunately the 2.5L 4-cylinder engine is only offered on the very base model, so most Frontiers come with the large and thirsty 4.0L V6. The lack of standard safety features is an issue not only for the Frontier, but most pickup trucks. Should pickup truck owners not be protected in the event of an accident? The Top Pick Toyota Tacoma does a better job of providing standard safety features.

Suzuki Equator

Rating	Why?
Price	$34,000
Engine	4.0L V6 with 261hp
Standard safety features include	Front, side and curtain airbags, and ABS
Average fuel consumption	2268L/year
Warranty	3-year/60,000 km
Initial quality score	N/A
Dependability score	N/A

Pros: The Equator is another joint venture, this time not with General Motors, but Nissan. This truck is essentially a re-badged Nissan Frontier pickup truck and is sold as a 4-door Crew Cab 4X4.

Cons: Since the Suzuki version is only sold in one high-end trim level, it will limit the number of buyers. No 4X2, no 4-cylinder, no King Cab. The fact that this is a Nissan Truck makes me wonder why anyone would buy this and not just buy the Frontier. I bet this truck will be history in a few short years.

Toyota Tacoma

Rating	TOP PICK
Price	$21,000-$38,000
Engines	2.7L 4-cylinder with 159hp
	4.0L V6 with 236hp
Standard safety features include	Front, side and curtain airbags, ABS, stability and traction control
Average fuel consumption	4-cylinder 2X4,1857L/year
	4-cylinder 4X4, 2139L/year
	V6 2X4,2394L/year
	V6 4X4, 2558L/year
Warranty	3-year/60,000 km
Initial quality score	4.5/5
Dependability score	3/5

Pros: The Tacoma is the Top Pick in the mid-size pickup truck category due to its versatile configurations, excellent quality scores and high resale value. Whether it is a basic 4-cylinder manual transmission unit or a top V6 equipped with four doors, the Tacoma does most things well. As more and more buyers of full-size trucks are reconsidering their requirements, due to fuel costs, the Tacoma fills this market very well.

Cons: Even though the Tacoma is a mid-size pickup truck, the Double Cab versions are long, making them feel cumbersome in tight situations. The 4-cylinder offers good fuel consumption, but the large V6 can get thirsty. For buyers looking for a basic yet powerful truck, the larger Tundra base models might be worth a look.

FULL-SIZE PICKUPS

Chevy Avalanche

Rating	Worth consideration
Price	$41,000-$56,000
Engine	5.3L V8 with 310hp
Standard safety features include	Front and curtain airbags, ABS, traction and stability control
Average fuel consumption	2552L/year
Warranty	3-year/60,000 km
Initial quality score	4.5/5
Dependability score	3/5

Pros: Is the Avalanche a pickup truck with a short bed or a full-size SUV with a bed attached? Well, it fits in both categories and that is one of the things that make this vehicle appealing. The interior is very roomy and comfortable, like a full-size SUV but the five-foot bed makes it perfect for owners who need occasional hauling capacity. The on-road manners are excellent, adding to the already comfortable feel. The Avalanche has been awarded strong quality scores.

Cons: There is only one large V8 engine offered, which might turn some buyers toward the thriftier Honda Ridgeline.

Chevy Silverado 1500/GMC Sierra

Rating	Must try
Price	$24,000-$46,000
Engines	4.3L V6 with 195hp
	4.8L V8 with 295hp
	5.3L V8 with 315hp
	6.0L V8 with 375hp
	6.2L V8 with 403hp
Standard safety features include	Front and curtain airbags, ABS, traction and stability control
Average fuel consumption	4.3L V6, 2451L/year
	4.3L 4X4, 2656L/year
	4.8L V8, 2571L/year
	4.8L 4X4, 2693L/year
	5.3L V8, 2504L/year
	5.3L 4X4, 2544L/year
	6.0L V8, 2570L/year
	6.0L 4X4, 2654L/year
	6.2L 4X4, 2919L/year
Warranty	3-year/60,000 km
Initial quality score	4/5
Dependability score	3/5

Pros: With an extensive list of engine options, plus bed and cabin configurations, there is a Silverado for everyone. The Silverado is wonderfully comfortable on the inside with a wraparound dash that makes it easy to use the interior function. (Toyota should take note.) The ride is very comfortable and the Silverado feels stable on the road, especially with stability and traction control. The 4X4 system can be operated manually or set to an advanced setting for an on-demand type system. This is a very well-thought-out vehicle that has good quality scores and a huge fan base.

Cons: The pickup truck market never sits still for long, and with the introduction of the Toyota Tundra and all-new Ford F-150 the Silverado needs a few tweaks to make it truly competitive. The base 4-speed automatic is overdue to be replaced with a 6-speed unit in the full line (most Silverados come with a 6-speed) and the innovative side and rear stepladders on the F-150 are genius. Still a great truck, though.

Dodge Ram 1500

Rating	Must try
Price	$19,000-$30,000
Engines	3.7L V6 with 210hp
	4.7L V8 with 310hp
	5.7L V8 with 390hp
Standard safety features include	Front and curtain airbags, ABS, stability and traction control
Average fuel consumption	3.7L V6, 2528L/year
	4.7L V8, 2688L/year
	4.7L 4X4, 2852L/year
	5.7L V8, 2612L/year
	5.7L 4X4, 2754L/year
Warranty	3-year/60,000 km
Initial quality score	2.5/5
Dependability score	2/5

Pros: The Ram was totally redone for the 2009 model year, putting more emphasis on interior finish, ride comfort and unique storage ideas. The Ram is at the top of the class for cabin comfort and appointments; it also wins for on-road comfort and quietness. Ram buyers are attracted to its rugged styling and the complete line of engine choices. Ford has dropped the base V6 engine, so now Dodge has a slight advantage in the entry level for buyers of basic trucks. The long list of features and complete safety items makes it a compelling package.

Cons: The Ram is a good truck, but the quality scores could be better, especially in light of the strong competition in this segment. There is no 6-speed automatic offered.

Ford F-150

Rating	TOP PICK
Price	$24,000-$43,000
Engines	4.6L V8 with 292hp
	5.4L V8 with 320hp
Standard safety features include	Front, side and curtain airbags, ABS, traction and stability control
Average fuel consumption	4.6L V8, 2466L/year
	4.6L 4X4, 2688L/year
	5.4L V8, 2606L/year
	5.4L 4X4, 2744L/year
Warranty	3-year/60,000 km
Initial quality score	4.5/5
Dependability score	4/5

Pros: The F-150 has been the best-selling vehicle in North America for decades, and the latest version is the best one yet. With a long list of standard safety features, unique convenience features like the side and tailgate step along with a first-rate cabin, the F-150 is the Top Pick in this class. Because the F-150 and larger Super Duty versions can be equipped with an amazing list of cab, bed and engine choices, there is an F-150 for every occasion. The inclusion of a 6-speed on most of the F-150s makes it a more fuel-efficient truck than before. Look for a new V6 turbo-charged model called "Ecoboost" for buyers who want even better efficiency.

Cons: The F-150 is a remarkable truck, but for some buyers it is too big. Ford should consider bringing in a mid-size truck, maybe the F-100 they had years ago. The Toyota Tundra is a very good choice also but due to the lack of bed, cab and engine options it misses out.

Nissan Titan

Rating	Worth consideration
Price	$32,000-$51,000
Engine	5.6L V8 with 317hp
Standard safety features include	Front airbags, ABS. Optional: traction and stability control
Average fuel consumption	V6 4X2, 2872L/year V6 4X4, 3016L/year
Warranty	3-year/60,000 km
Initial quality score	3/5
Dependability score	2/5

Pros: The Titan is slightly smaller than the majority of full-size pickup trucks, giving it an advantage for buyers who are looking for something just a tad smaller. The interior is the standout on the Titan, providing very comfortable seating, well-thought-out design and a roomy cabin in King Cab and Crew Cab configurations. The 5.6L V8 and slick 5-speed automatic make it a solid performer for a large number of potential buyers. The Titan is easy to like, easy to drive and easier to manoeuvre due to its slightly more compact design.

Cons: On the flip side, for buyers who require a real workhorse, the Titan can come up short. There is only one engine available and no diesel offered. The lack of 6-speed automatic puts it out of step with the Ford F-150 and Toyota Tundra. The lack of standard safety equipment is a major oversight. Good truck but out-classed by solid contenders.

Toyota Tundra

Rating	Must try
Price	$25,000-$53,000
Engines	4.6L V8 with 310hp
	5.7L V8 with 381hp
Standard safety features include	Front, side, knee and curtain airbags, ABS, stability and traction control
Average fuel consumption	4.6L V8, N/A
	5.7L 2X4,2653L/year
	5.7L 4X4, 2879L/year
Warranty	3-year/60,000 km
Initial quality score	N/A
Dependability score	3.5/5

Pros: Toyota has finally come to market with a full-size pickup truck worthy of competition for the domestic vehicles. It has the size, capacity and powerful engines that help it to compete, day in and day out. The 5.7L V8, matched to the slick 6-speed automatic, makes this big truck very powerful, even quick, and the introduction of an all-new 4.6L V8 offers almost as much power but it is the thriftiest full-size truck on the road. The interior has plenty of room for passengers and the towing and cargo capacities rival the best.

Cons: Toyota is new to the full-size pickup truck game and its lack of experience shows in some areas. The dash is simple to use but many of the controls are too far away from the driver, especially the radio and navigation system. The front seats sit too high and might be a tight fit for big, tall drivers. The two engines offered are as solid as one could hope for, but there is no diesel option and buyers looking at domestic trucks have more engine choices. The Tundra is a great truck, but GM, Ford and Chrysler have been at this game a long, long time and it shows.

Hybrid Category

Chevy Tahoe / GMC Yukon / Cadillac Escalade hybrid SUVs

Rating	Must try
Price	$67,000-$94,000
Engine	6.0L V8 plus electric motor equals 332hp
Standard safety features include	Front and curtain airbags, ABS, traction and stability control
Average fuel consumption	6.0L engine, 1906L/year 6.0L 4X4, 2037L/year
Warranty	Tahoe and Yukon, 3-year/60,000 km Escalade, 4-year/80,000km 8-year/160,000km on hybrid systems
Initial quality score	N/A
Dependability score	N/A

Pros: The Tahoe, Yukon and Escalade hybrids operate on the 2-mode system that was co-developed with BMW, Mercedes and Chrysler. The advantage to this system is that the vehicle runs on battery power at low speeds, and at higher speeds half of the eight cylinders shut down as power is delivered through the electric motor. This system is as smooth and seamless as any on the market and it makes these full-size SUVs even smoother and quieter than they already were. The fuel mileage improvements are on par with a V6 engine, yet all of these trucks are still capable of towing.

Cons: The best fuel consumption results are achieved when the driver is most attentive to the operation of the hybrid system. When driven normally, these expensive vehicles get good mileage, but not great mileage. Maybe a smaller lighter vehicle is a better choice, like a V6 full-size crossover. Did I mention expensive?

Chevy Silverado / GMC Sierra hybrid pickups

Rating	Must try
Price	$47,000
Engine	6.0L V8 plus electric motor equals 332hp
Standard safety features include	Front and curtain airbags, ABS, traction and stability control
Average fuel consumption	1906L/year
Warranty	3-year/60,000 km 8-year/160,000km on hybrid systems
Initial quality score	N/A
Dependability score	N/A

Pros: The Silverado and Sierra operate on the 2-mode system that was co-developed with BMW, Mercedes and Chrysler. The advantage to this system is that the vehicle runs on battery power at low speeds, and at higher speeds half of the eight cylinders shut down as power is delivered through the electric motor. This system is as smooth and seamless as any on the market and it makes these full-size pickups even smoother and quieter than they already were. The fuel mileage improvements are on par with a V6 engine, yet all of these trucks are still capable of towing.

Cons: The best fuel consumption results are achieved when the driver is most attentive to the operation of the hybrid system. When driven normally, these expensive vehicles get good mileage but not great mileage. Maybe a smaller lighter vehicle is a better choice, like a V6 mid-size pickup.

Ford Fusion hybrid

Rating	Must try
Price	$32,000
Engine	2.5L 4-cylinder plus electric motor equals 156hp
Standard safety features include	Front, side and curtain airbags, ABS, stability and traction control
Average fuel consumption	N/A
Fuel rating	4.6L/100km (61mpg) city and 5.4L/100km (52mpg) hwy
Warranty	3-year/60,000 km 8-year/160,000km on hybrid system
Initial quality score	N/A
Dependability score	N/A

Pros: The Ford Fusion hybrid is a marvel of engineering and sophistication, making it second only to the 2010 Prius as the Top Pick in the hybrid class. The Prius gets slightly better mileage or the Fusion hybrid would be the Top Pick. The hybrid system is seamless, making driving this car a no-sacrifice alternative to a conventional car. The digital dash cluster behind the steering wheel is one of the most inventive on the market, making it easy to read, plus it also aids the driver in getting the best mileage.

Cons: The poor image that North American cars have is a drawback to resale values. Maybe as people come to learn that the Fusion is a well-made car, the values will improve.

Honda Civic hybrid

Rating	Worth consideration
Price	Sedan: $27,000
Engine	1.3L 4-cylinder plus electric assist equals 93hp
Standard safety features include	Front, side and curtain airbags, ABS, traction and stability control
Average fuel consumption	902L/year
Warranty	5-year/100,000 km
Initial quality score	4.5/5
Dependability score	3/5

Pros: The Civic Hybrid is visually the same as the regular sedan except for the unique wheel design. This gives owners the pleasure of driving a hybrid without giving up the attractiveness of the Civic. Honda's Motor Assist Technology delivers the closest experience to driving a regular gasoline car because the engine is always turning over—there is no switching back and forth to just the electric motor. The only time the Civic Hybrid shows itself is when the car comes to a complete stop; the engine switches off and then restarts. Easy to drive, easy to like and good on gas.

Cons: Since Honda has introduced the new, cheaper Insight Hybrid 4-door hatchback, the appeal of the Civic Hybrid will be narrower. The Insight has a more useful design, it is cheaper and gets better fuel economy, plus it has some unique and innovative electronic features. If you drive in stop-and-go traffic, the gasoline engine stopping and restarting can get annoying. This is one area where the Toyota Prius is a superior vehicle.

Honda Insight

Rating	Must try
Price	$23,900 -$27,500
Engine	1.3L 4-cylinder plus electric assist equals 93hp
Standard safety features include	Front, side and curtain airbags, ABS, traction and stability control
Average fuel consumption	N/A
Fuel rating	4.8L/100km (58mpg) city 4.5L/100km (62mpg) hwy
Warranty	5-year/100,000 km
Initial quality score	N/A
Dependability score	N/A

Pros: The second-generation Insight has been totally redesigned for 2010 and now has the advantage of being the cheapest hybrid on the market. It is now a 4-door hatchback, featuring a very usable design giving room for four passengers and plenty of cargo space. The Insight has not enjoyed the same sales success as the Prius, but this new model is a much better car than the original. The gasoline engine is always turning over, even on just electric power, simulating a regular gasoline car, making the Insight easy to adapt to. The on-board computer interface prompts the driver to drive with a light foot and it works letting the driver easily get close to, or actually achieve, the posted fuel ratings.

Cons: When equipped with the navigation/radio device, the placement is too far away from the driver. Handling is above average, but under hard acceleration the small 1.3-litre engine is over-stressed. The auto stop and re-start feature can be annoying in heavy stop-and-go driving.

Lexus GS hybrid

Rating	Must try
Price	$63,000
Engine	3.5L V6 with electric motor equals 339hp
Standard safety features include	Front, side, knee and curtain airbags, ABS, stability and traction control
Average fuel consumption	N/A
Fuel rating	8.7L/100km (32mpg) city 7.8L/100km (36mpg) hwy
Warranty	4-year/80,000 km 8-year/160,000km on hybrid system
Initial quality score	5/5
Dependability score	3/5

Pros: For buyers who want a luxurious sedan but also want to make less of an impact on the environment, the GS450h is an option. The already smooth driving dynamics of the gasoline version are amplified with the use of the Lexus hybrid system that provides an even more relaxed driving experience.

Cons: The idea of buying an expensive luxury hybrid puzzles me. If a potential buyer really wants to make less of an impact on the environment, then they can buy a smaller, lighter, more fuel-efficient car. The Mercedes E Class with the Blue TEC diesel engine is even more fuel efficient and has a more dynamic driving experience, but it is about $5000 more expensive.

Lexus LS hybrid

Rating	Must try
Price	$120,000
Engine	5.0L V8 with electric motor equals 438hp
Standard safety features include	Front, side, knee and curtain airbags, ABS, stability and traction control
Average fuel consumption	1985L/year
Warranty	4-year/80,000 km 8-year/160,000km on hybrid system
Initial quality score	5/5
Dependability score	5/5

Pros: The LS600hL should be considered an ultra-luxury car and not just a hybrid version of the regular LS. The hybrid system makes an already smooth car even more so, providing limousine-like refinement. Since this car is only offered in the long wheelbase configuration, the back seat has extra legroom and the seats can be reclined, making the LS600hL an option for buyers who have a personal driver. (Not me.)

Cons: Most drivers will never get a chance to drive one of these fab cars!

Lexus HS

Rating	Must try
Price	N/A at time of printing
Engine	2.4L 4-cylinder with electric motor equals 187hp
Standard safety features include	Front, side, knee and curtain airbags, ABS, stability and traction control
Average fuel consumption	N/A
Warranty	4-year/80,000 km 8-year/160,000km on hybrid system
Initial quality score	N/A
Dependability score	N/A

Pros: The HS250h is based on the Prius. It offers buyers who might have considered a Prius, but would have rather had a more luxurious car, the option to own the first Lexus model that is sold only as a hybrid. Mileage will be less than what the Prius delivers due to the larger 4-cylinder engine.

Cons: Full model information was not available at time of printing.

Lexus RX hybrid

Rating	Must try
Price	$59,000
Engine	5.0L V8 with electric motor equals 295hp
Standard safety features include	Front, side, knee and curtain airbags, ABS, stability and traction control
Average fuel consumption	N/A
Fuel rating	6.6L/100km (42mpg) city 7.2L/100km (39mpg) hwy
Warranty	4-year/80,000 km 8-year/160,000km on hybrid system
Initial quality score	5/5
Dependability score	5/5

Pros: As with all Lexus hybrids, the addition of the hybrid system makes their already smooth vehicles even more luxurious. The quiet and smooth ride is perfect for buyers who want a luxury mid-size SUV, but also want to limit their impact on the environment.

Cons: Yes, the hybrid is smooth and can deliver good mileage, but the driving dynamics of the vehicle suffer. The RX hybrid is not the most inspiring vehicle to drive unless fuel savings inspire you. Once again, if you want to make less of an impact on the environment, then a smaller, lighter vehicle can achieve the same results.

Nissan Altima hybrid

Rating	Must try
Price	$33,000
Engine	2.5L 4-cylinder plus electric motor equals with 198hp
Standard safety features include	Front, side and curtain airbags, ABS, traction and stability control
Average fuel consumption	1158L/year
Warranty	3-year/60,000 km 8-year/160,000km on hybrid system
Initial quality score	5/5
Dependability score	3/5

Pros: The Altima Hybrid is very well equipped and comes with a full line of standard safety features. The Altima hybrid has not been widely promoted by Nissan, but is worthy of consideration because there are so few hybrids on the market—you should try them all. Nissan's hybrid system is borrowed from the Toyota Camry hybrid, but the Altima has a more sporty feel.

Cons: The biggest problem with the Altima hybrid is that it is more expensive than the direct competition. Also try the Ford Fusion, Toyota Camry and Toyota Prius hybrids.

Toyota Camry Hybrid

Rating	Must try
Price	$31,000-$36,000
Engine	2.4L 4-cylinder with electric motor equals 187hp
Standard safety features include	Front, side, curtain and knee airbags, ABS, traction and stability control
Average fuel consumption	1140L/year
Warranty	3-year/60,000 km
Initial quality score	5/5
Dependability score	5/5

Pros: The Camry Hybrid is a wonderful option for buyers already in the market for a well-designed mid-size sedan. The higher starting price versus the conventional 4-cylinder might put some buyers off, but there are many standard features included in the hybrid that cost more on the regular car. The hybrid system is as smooth and seamless as you will find and when driving in full electric mode makes the already smooth Camry that much smoother.

Cons: The basic 4-cylinder Camry is already an efficient car, so those looking for the lowest overall cost might be better served with the regular sedan. The smooth hybrid drive might not be for everyone because it makes an already laid-back sedan even more so. The Prius hatchback is a good choice for hybrid buyers who require their car to be a more versatile, multi-purpose machine.

Toyota Prius

Rating	TOP PICK
Price	$28,000-$33,000
Engine	1.8L 4-cylinder with electric motor equals 134hp
Standard safety features include	Front, side, knee and curtain airbags, ABS, stability and traction control
Average fuel consumption	N/A
Fuel rating	3.7L/100km city (76 mpg) and 4.0 L/100km hwy (71 mpg)
Warranty	5-year/100,000 km 8-year/160,000 km on hybrid system
Initial quality score	4.5/5
Dependability score	5/5

Pros: The 2010 Prius marks the third generation of this iconic fuel-saving car. New for 2010 includes a lower starting price, better fuel consumption, larger dimensions, added safety equipment and improved ride. Exterior styling is stronger than the last model, plus the interior has been updated to provide a more upscale design. The interior is roomy and the relaxed drive makes for a comfortable commuter car. The Prius and its futuristic technology have proven to be very reliable. Buys of older models are some of the most outspoken advocates for the Prius. The Prius is the Top Pick for overall return on investment and best design, futures and value in the hybrid marketplace.

Cons: An almost $28,000 Prius might not be the best choice for buyers who are only concentrating on the bottom line, because there are plenty of less expensive compact and subcompact cars that offer almost as much versatility and are a lot less expensive to buy. For example, the Corolla can be purchased for roughly $10,000 less and it has fuel ratings that put most cars to shame. The Prius drive is very relaxed and some might find it too laid back.

Toyota Highlander Hybrid

Rating	Must try
Price	$43,000-$55,000
Engine	3.3L V6 plus electric motor equals 270hp
Standard safety features include	Front, side, knee and curtain airbags, ABS, stability and traction control
Average fuel consumption	1534L/year
Warranty	3-year/60,000 km 8-year/160,000km on hybrid system
Initial quality score	4/5
Dependability score	5/5

Pros: The hybrid version of the Highlander takes an already smooth and relaxing vehicle to new levels of refinement and luxury. If you are in the market for an ultra-smooth and quiet SUV, the Highlander will not disappoint.

Cons: The Highlander hybrid is more about making a statement than saving money. If you are in the market for a fuel-efficient vehicle and want to save money, there are plenty of cheaper 4-cylinder vehicles that can help to keep costs down. Spending over $40,000 to get a more fuel-efficient hybrid SUV is overkill when buyers could opt for a three-row 4-cylinder RAV4 or 4-cylinder Venza and keep all the money they save for gasoline. If you want to save money and have a smaller impact on the environment, buy a smaller, lighter vehicle! The Highlander hybrid is an alternative to buying a high-end gasoline Highlander or other luxury SUV. Even though it is very smooth and relaxing to drive, some drivers will find it a bit dull.

Zack Spencer is a Canadian automotive journalist with over 25 years of broadcasting experience and nearly 20 years as an automotive journalist. He is host of the popular show *Driving Television*. Zack receives hundreds of e-mails and phone calls every month from people seeking car advice. For more information about Zack and cars, visit www.motormouth.ca and www.drivingtelevision.com.